British Women Short Story Writers

British Women Short Story Writers

The New Woman to Now

Edited by Emma Young
and James Bailey

EDINBURGH
University Press

© editorial matter and organisation Emma Young and James Bailey, 2015
© the chapters their several authors, 2015

Edinburgh University Press Ltd
The Tun – Holyrood Road
12(2f) Jackson's Entry
Edinburgh EH8 8PJ
www.euppublishing.com

Typeset in 10.5/13 Adobe Sabon by
Servis Filmsetting Ltd, Stockport, Cheshire,
and printed and bound in Great Britain by
CPI Group (UK) Ltd, Croydon CR0 4YY

A CIP record for this book is available from the British Library

ISBN 978 1 4744 0138 8 (hardback)
ISBN 978 1 4744 0139 5 (webready PDF)
ISBN 978 1 4744 0727 4 (epub)

The right of Emma Young and James Bailey to be identified as the editors of this work has been asserted in accordance with the Copyright, Designs and Patents Act 1988, and the Copyright and Related Rights Regulations 2003 (SI No. 2498).

Contents

Acknowledgements	vii
Foreword *Ali Smith*	viii
1. Introduction *Emma Young and James Bailey*	1
2. The Elusive Melody: Music and Trauma in New Woman Short Stories *Maura Dunst*	15
3. Beyond the Haunted House? Modernist Women's Ghost Stories and the Troubling of Modernity *Emma Liggins*	32
4. Potboilers or 'Glimpses' of Reality? The Cultural and the Material in the Modernist Short Story *Rebecca Bowler*	50
5. War and the Short Story: Elizabeth Bowen *Adam Piette*	66
6. 'Haunted, whether we like it or not': The Ghost Stories of Muriel Spark *James Bailey*	81
7. Disaggregative Character Identity and the Politics of Aesthetic In-betweenness in Angela Carter's Short Narratives *Michelle Ryan-Sautour*	96
8. New Waves of Interest: Women's Short Story Writing in the Late Twentieth Century *Ailsa Cox*	114

9. Feminist F(r)iction: Short Stories and Postfeminist Politics
   at the Millennial Moment 133
   Emma Young
10. Class as Destiny in the Short Stories of Tessa Hadley 148
    Sue Vice
11. Address, Temporality and Misdelivery: The Postal Effects
    of Ali Smith's Short Stories 163
    Ben Davies
12. Housewives and Half-Stories: A Question of Genre and
    Gender in Microfiction 179
    Holly Howitt-Dring
13. Postscript: British Women's Short Story Writing 193
    Clare Hanson

Contributor Biographies 199

Index 202

Acknowledgements

The editors wish to thank all of the individual authors in this collection for their hard work and the engaging contributions they have made; it has made the project a particularly rewarding one. A sincere thanks is also due to Jackie Jones at Edinburgh University Press for her support, guidance and her much appreciated enthusiasm for this edited collection.

Foreword

A short story walked into a bar.
– Ouch. It was an iron bar.
Okay, start again.
A short story walked into a bar. The bar was called Ye Old Fighting Cocks. Outside it there was a sign saying the words above a picture of two chest-out cockerels. The sign had been painted by the chain who owned the pub to look like it was an old pubsign. It swung slightly in the wind, like it was supposed to.
The short story went up to the counter.
What single malts do you have? the short story said.
The barmaid looked apologetic.
Ah. I'm sorry, she said. We don't serve stories here.
You don't? the story said.
No, the barmaid said.
What about them, then? the short story said and nodded towards a group of inebriated-looking novels, some thick, some thin, carousing round a table covered in emptied glasses, the sides of the glasses laced with the realist foam of the beer they'd been drinking.
No. What I mean is. I'm not meant to serve shorts, the barmaid said.
Is this a joke? the short story said.
Well, that's the thing, isn't it, a traditional-looking novel said loud enough to be heard. Fish or fowl. You never quite know what they are.
The short story cleared its throat.
A single Talisker, please, it said.
I told you, the barmaid said, we don't –
But I can see all the whisky bottles lined up behind you, the short story said. A Talisker, please.
The novels had stopped their incredibly authentic-sounding background pub chat and were all leaning forward to hear.
Or women, the barmaid said.

What? the short story said.

We don't serve women in here, the barmaid said.

But I'm a story, the short story said. I don't have a gender.

I think you'll find, an academic-looking book with a 1980s cover piped up, that that's a pretty debatable premise, because if you go back to the beginnings of the English lang –

All the novels round it yawned and made bored-sounding noises.

No, see, the story said to the barmaid. Being a story. I don't have actual genitals. And neither do they.

It nodded towards the novels. This made several of the hardbacks stand up, shrugging off their covers.

Coming in here, sounding off, knowing fuck all about our lives, one said.

Not even two minutes long, another said.

Look, I don't want a fight. I just want a drink, that's all, the short story said. I won't stay longer than the time it takes to –

Yeah cause this is real life darlin', and you're not up to it, you just can't keep it up, a paperback in a tudor costume cover shouted.

Besides, everybody knows, a weighty literary-looking tome added. Hardly anybody buys you. You're far too short. You're far too disturbing. Difficult. Insubstantial. Quite unsettling. Deeply troubling. People prefer novels. All the publishers say so and they're never wrong. They're the ones who really understand readers.

That's not true, the short story said. Time and time again, statistics show that readers actually love –

Tell Shorty to try that wine bar up the street, an old broken-spined paperback called. Tell her there's no room in here for all that perfection of the moment no proper punctuation do anything you like with the form flash of detail essential distilled momentousness of the moment stuff here.

This made several of the novels restless and edgy.

I beg to diff – a novel with a Vanessa Bell painting on its cover began, polite, witty.

But the rest of what it said was drowned out by the shouts: Dialogue! Proper plot! Explication! Speech marks! Beginnings middles ends! Proper length! Reliably unreliable narrators! Oeuvre! Right way! Wrong way! Themes! Likeable! Memes! Flashbacks! Major work!

Glasses flew. Pages ripped. A riot ensued. A documentary crew arrived.

The short story sighed. Major work.

It made itself invisible. It slipped out the door as the camera crew shoved its way in.

Down the road from the pub, though, the story, nearly over, heard someone give a low whistle and turned.

It was the barmaid. She'd come out of the bar and was waving round the corner of it.

Quick, she said. I haven't long.

She waved something glassy and amber in the air. It caught the light.

There was a little space of green across from the back of the pub, the noise from which, still going on, sounded far away and long ago.

Kids played football. The sign stuck in the grass said NO BALL GAMES. NO DOGS. A dog was sniffing at the foot of it. The barmaid held out the whisky. She poured one for herself too.

She sat with the story for as long as the story lasted. While it did, the night came down. The moon was a white smile above streetlamps. There was that fine summer scent, one of the nearby gardens, jasmine.

Ali Smith
February 2015

Chapter 1

Introduction
Emma Young and James Bailey

In reflecting on the development and resurgences in short story criticism it is useful to borrow a metaphor most readily associated with feminism, that of the wave. According to this narrative, three key waves of interest in the short story exist, and they are denoted by significant bodies of literary criticism. This is how the story of the short story is told. However, throughout these three waves of critical discussion there still remains a paucity of scholarship that interrogates the literary tradition of British women's short story writing. With this in mind, *British Women Short Story Writers: The New Woman to Now* offers a collection of essays which, individually, scrutinise what this vibrant literary genre has offered to women writers since the turn of the nineteenth century. Collectively, these essays map a tradition of women's short story writing and illuminate the synergies and divergences, overlaps and disjoints in women's relationship with, and treatment of, the short story. By covering what has been referred to as the 'long twentieth century', this collection commences with the New Woman writer, traces the development of the modern short story through Literary Modernism, two world wars and the growth of the women's movement, before concluding with reflections on contemporary innovations in women's short story writing. As such, *British Women Short Story Writers* contributes yet another story to the larger discourse of the genre's history, development and purpose.

It is now commonplace, one might even say cliché, to commence any discussion of the short story by returning to the work of Edgar Allan Poe (1842). However, while Poe's review of Nathaniel Hawthorne's *Twice-Told Tales* was certainly at the forefront of the first wave of scholarly debate on the short story, his work was not an isolated entity. In this early period, Brander Matthews wrote 'The Philosophy of the Short-Story' (1901) and Robert Wilson Neal published *Short Stories in the Making* (1914). Following this emerges H. E. Bates's *The Modern*

Short Story (1941) and Seán Ó Faoláin's *The Short Story* (1948). All of these earlier pieces of criticism share a desire to define the short story and to answer the question, 'What makes a short story'? This wish to delimitate the properties and features of the short story continues in the second wave of scholarly criticism which is marked by a preoccupation with the aesthetics of the short story. As such, early short story criticism tends to focus on either defining the short story, tracing its origins and history, identifying the 'masters' of the genre or, finally, theorising some of the 'how' and 'why' questions (Brown 1). From the 1960s through to the 1980s critics including Nadine Gordimer (1968), Charles E. May (1976), Ian Reid (1977) and Mary Rohrberger (1979) all undertook taxonomical work on the short story. While critics pinpointed unity, tone, subject, character, lyricism, plot and time as important characteristics, as Suzanne Ferguson summarises, 'there is no single characteristic or cluster of characteristics that the critics agree absolutely distinguishes the short story from other fictions' (218). Perhaps most famously of all of the criticism to emerge in this period is Frank O'Connor's *The Lonely Voice* (1963), in which he argues that 'the short story has never had a hero' (18), and that there is always a sense in the short story 'of outlawed figures wandering about the fringes of society' (19). This thesis, that the short story is a form suited to representing the 'submerged population' (18), is furthered by Clare Hanson (1989) who, in her introduction to *Re-Reading the Short Story*, suggests that the genre 'has offered itself to losers and loners, exiles, women, blacks – writers who for one reason or another have not been part of the ruling "narrative" or epistemological/experiential framework of their society' (2). In forging a link between the aesthetics of the genre and its subsequent offering to women writers (amongst other marginalised social groups), Hanson's work also indicates a subtle shift occurring at this time in how scholars were approaching discussions of the genre.

The move from solely focusing on definitions and aesthetics to a broader consideration of these issues in tandem with wider socio-cultural and historical dynamics affecting the short story, generally speaking, summarises the key tendency of the third wave of interest in the genre. In the 1990s important studies including Dominic Head's *The Modernist Short Story: A Study in Theory and Practice* (1992), which examines the '*prevailing tendencies* rather than essential qualities' (2; original emphasis) of the short story in this period. In retrospect, Head's work can be seen as a watershed moment in the history of short story criticism in that he proposes an explicit 'connection between the generic capabilities of the short story which stems from a special kind of literary experience relevant to readers, as well as to writers' (1). In this study of the modernist short story, Head interweaves the aesthetic innovations in the genre with the socio-economic and cultural climate of Literary Modernism and establishes a precedent for subsequent short story scholarship. Equally, significant attention begins to be paid to gender in relation to the short story with Julie Brown's edited collection *American Women Short Story Writers* (1995) scoping out another important literary tradition. Finally, Charles E. May's *The New Short Story Theories* (1994; a revised edition of his earlier 1976 text) demarcates a turning point in the field and the updated title of this collection heralds the subsequent proliferation of 'new short story theories' in the twenty-first century.

This third wave of short story criticism originates in the 1990s; however it is with the new millennium that a plethora of studies emerge and a renewed sense of vibrancy envelops short story criticism. Key texts in this decade include Adrian Hunter's *The Cambridge Introduction to the Short Story in English* (2007), Andrew Maunder's encyclopaedic-style *A Companion to the British Short Story* (2007), Ailsa Cox's edited collection *The Short Story* (2008), Paul March-Russell's *The Short Story: An Introduction* (2009), *The British Short Story* by Emma Liggins, Andrew Maunder and Ruth Robbins (2010), and David Malcolm's *The British and Irish Short Story Handbook* (2012). Although these studies engage with women's short story writing, it is with the publication of Roxanne Harde's *Narratives of Community: Women's Short Story Sequences* (2007), Ellen Burton Harrington's *Scribbling Women and the Short Story Form: Approaches by American and British Women Writers* (2008) and Claire Drewery's *Modernist Short Fiction by Women: The Liminal in Katherine Mansfield, Dorothy Richardson, May Sinclair and Virginia Woolf* (2011) that greater attention begins to be paid to women's short story writing. Further, while studies of a female tradition remain preoccupied with American authors, as the previous list of titles suggests, in short story criticism more generally a welcome fascination takes hold with the British tradition.

A British Tradition

The seeds of new interest in the British short story were planted by Dean Baldwin's essay 'The Tardy Evolution of the British Short Story', published in *Studies in Short Fiction* in 1993. In this piece Baldwin suggests 'that the late appearance of the modern short story in Britain can best be understood as a question of literary economics', before outlining how 'the business of literary production, in combination with aesthetic and theoretical factors, retarded the evolution of the short story in Britain until late in the nineteenth century' (23). As well as providing a thorough explanation for this premise and proposing reasons for the burgeoning of the modern short story in the late nineteenth century, Baldwin's overview also encourages further critical debate on the modern British short story in the twenty-first century. By 2007, in *A Companion to the British Short Story*, Maunder quite rightly asserts that 'the acknowledgement of the short story's place in British literary history is one of the most striking developments of recent years' (v). The critical attention given to the British short story, especially in the last decade, is not an isolated phenomenon, but it is part of a wider cultural revival in which the short story is recognised as a mainstay of British fiction.

This revived interest has done much to assuage fears that the genre has become an 'Endangered Species', to quote the dismal prognosis offered by Debbie Taylor, the founder of the women's writing magazine *Mslexia*, in a 2003 article of the same name. For Taylor, the short story was languishing following the declining sales of established short story journals such as *Granta* and *Ambit* and the lack of a British 'equivalent to the *New Yorker*, *Harper's* or *Atlantic Monthly*', becoming 'a taste that is atrophied in the British reader' (11). At the turn of the millennium, Taylor was hardly alone in expressing such concerns. The 'Save Our Short Story' campaign, founded in 2002 by Margaret Wilkinson and supported publicly by prominent women writers such as Jackie Kay and Val McDermid, assessed the health of the genre by investigating British publishing, sales and library lending figures for short stories, and was later adopted by organisations including Booktrust and the Scottish Book Trust in the form of a successor campaign, 'Story'. Since then, the genre has enjoyed something of a return to popularity and critical standing, due in no small part to the launch of the annual short story festival, Small Wonder, in 2004, and the foundation of literary prizes including the BBC National Short Story Award (est. 2006), the Royal Society of Literature's V. S. Pritchett Memorial Prize (est. 1999) and the Sunday Times EFG Short Story Award (est. 2009). Women writers have achieved a notable degree of success in these prizes; presently, the V. S. Pritchett Memorial Prize has seven female winners including Carys Davies, Gabriela Blandy and Kate Clanchy, while the BBC National Short Story Award has been presented to British women writers such as Sarah Hall, Clare Wigfall, and most recently, Lionel Shriver. Women's work within the genre is celebrated and promoted more directly by single-sex prizes including the *Mslexia* Short Story Competition (est. 2009) and the Asham Award (est. 1995), with the latter publishing the stories of its winners and runners-up alongside those of well-known women writers in a regular anthology series.

The recent increase in creative writing courses in British universities, in which short stories are both studied and written, also marks a significant and positive development. Between the 2002–3 and 2011–12 academic years, enrolment figures for degrees relating to 'Imaginative Writing' (which encompasses prose, poetry and script-writing) rose from 2,745 students to 6,495, reaching a peak of 7,455 in 2010–11 (Munden 8). Such changes to the literary landscape have inspired a proliferation of new works by women writers working within the genre (an example being Holly Howitt-Dring, featured in the present collection, whose doctoral studies in creative writing have enabled her to specialise in creating innovative microfictions). The combination of critical theory and creative writing featured on many of these courses can also be seen to stimulate literary innovation and experimentation. As Lauri Ramey asserts, a stimulating critical/creative relationship on such courses will result in writers 'putting their critical knowledge to inventive uses' via 'techniques such as self-reflexivity, pastiche, parody, irony and other frame-breaking operations' (51), all of which have strong theoretical underpinnings. In her postscript to this collection, Clare Hanson compares the rise of such courses to the presence of community writing groups during the 1980s and 1990s; in both cases, critical and creative engagement with the genre is actively encouraged, and bold, inventive works by new writers are produced.

Given this collection's focus on British women writers, the inclusion of chapters on Katherine Mansfield (born in New Zealand in 1888) and Elizabeth Bowen (born in pre-Republic Ireland in 1899) requires some justification. While Mansfield grew up in a British colony, before moving to London in 1903 and publishing her fiction through British publishers, Bowen was an author of Anglo-Irish heritage, who moved to Kent as a child in 1907 and remained in England until 1952. Living and writing in Britain for much of their lives, both authors were actively engaged with British culture and its literary landscape. A discussion of British literature would be similarly lacking without reference to the dramatic political changes resulting in the devolution of political authority to Scotland in 1997. Such developments not only impact the historiography of the British short story, but can also be perceived as drivers of literary innovation. In his 2006 essay, 'Devolving the Scottish Novel', Cairns Craig examines the rise of both cultural and literary nationalism in Scotland, focusing specifically on the relationship between devolution and the formal and thematic concerns of the contemporary Scottish novel. For Craig, Scotland's efforts to establish its sovereignty are mirrored by the protection and celebration of a sense of national identity as expressed in its post-devolution fiction. If storytelling is central to the formation and ongoing substantiation of national identity, then the short story is an especially valuable literary vehicle for engaging with regional and national identities. This is evidenced by the vibrancy of contemporary Scottish short stories such as Jackie Kay's 'Grace and Rose' (2012), Ali Smith's haunting 'Scottish Love Songs' (2003) and A. L. Kennedy's 'As God Made Us' (2009), in which the individual's intimate (or even inextricable) relationship with Scotland and Scottish identity is a prominent theme. Thus, in focusing on a British tradition of women's short story writing this collection acknowledges the diverse and hybrid identities that must inform our understandings of 'Britishness'. At the same time, when considering extant critical studies and the contemporary global perspective on the short story, it is crucial to assert the significance and vitality of a distinctly British tradition.

A Female Tradition

While the short story has facilitated the fictional negotiation of regional identities, the genre has been equally valuable in offering a space for women writers to explore issues of identity, belonging and selfhood. O'Connor refers to the short story as a modern art form that has never had a hero. In actuality, it is a modern art form with a literary tradition that includes many heroines. Reflecting on the emergence of the modern short story, in one of the earliest pieces of short story criticism, Bates suggests that in the 1890s a strong feature of the short story was its masculinity. According to Bates, it had a 'culminating point' which leaves the reader 'stimulated but satisfied. In such a story femininity, passivity, introspection, the subtle and oblique will have little or no place' (105–6). The sexualised and phallocentric nature of Bates's observation is notable, as too is the gender binary system that underpins his discussion of the short story. It is interesting therefore that, in regard to the 1890s–1930s, Bates considers the work of Katherine Mansfield to be 'the most important influence on the English short story' (119). This isolated focus on Mansfield is echoed by Malcolm Bradbury when he suggests 'the great precursors [of the modern short story] were Chekhov, Henry James, Katherine Mansfield, James Joyce, and Sherwood Anderson', and that the genre was developed by 'Hemingway, Faulkner, Babel and Kafka' (11). Once again the tendency remains to prioritise male short story writing as *the* tradition, and in this critical context Mansfield adopts a quasi-male persona. Without diminishing the significance of Mansfield, there is a far richer tradition of women short story writers in this period (and beyond) than is readily recognised by these works.

The link between the rise of the short story in the late nineteenth century and the development in the periodical press is long established, but the implications of this for women writers should not be overlooked. *The Yellow Book*, a publication strongly associated with the literary avant-garde, emerged in 1894 and was central to the short story's growth. Lorraine Janzen Kooistra (2012) outlines how it 'refused to publish serialized fiction, a staple of contemporary periodicals', and as a consequence 'the magazine sponsored significant developments in the style and content of the modern short story' (4). Further, *The Yellow Book* did not place word count restrictions upon pieces, meaning '"New Women" authors, including George Egerton and Ella D'Arcy, were free to experiment' (ibid.). With Ella D'Arcy on the editorial board, *The Yellow Book* also provided a welcoming space for women writers of the period to publish, especially for those whose politically challenging work was not always well received. Feminist literary critic Elaine Showalter considers the appeal of the short story for nineteenth-century women writers in *Daughters of Decadence*: 'the short story offered flexibility and freedom from the traditional plots of the three-decker Victorian novel, plots which invariably ended in the heroine's marriage or her death' (viii–ix). The provision of alternative modes of narration complemented the New Woman writers' desire for a fresh perspective on issues of gender, sexuality and women's identity. As Hunter summarises, 'the rise of "plotless" psychological realism in the 1890s, then, was closely bound up with gender-political debate' (35). The testing of literary boundaries, via the short story, is entwined with the challenge to political and social boundaries that the New Woman writer and her feminist companions were battling with during this period. With the birth of the so-called modern short story, then, arises a distinct relationship between the aesthetics of the genre and the wider socio-cultural and political context.

Such literary innovation continues in the twentieth century, throughout the modernist period, and the genre offers an experimental space for women writers. As Virginia Woolf writes in a letter to David Garnett in 1917, the short story offers the potential of inventing 'a completely new form' (*Letters 2*, 167). At a time when social change was accelerating at a rapid pace, this ability to capture the world in a 'new form' was a pressing concern for many writers. While the New Woman writer was explicitly preoccupied with gender politics and women's suffrage, the modernist woman writer echoes many of these concerns but also focuses on social modernity, technological advancement, social class, the war and women's sexuality to a much greater extent. During this period the short story's aesthetic ability to foster tension, ambivalence and uncertainty became a significant factor in its popularity with women writers who were fascinated with representing identity in a new, non-restrictive and more realistic manner. At a time when women wanted to challenge cultural foundations, the short story, as the 'vanguard of experimental writing' (Hanson 1985: 172), was a preferential genre. After all, it is a particularly hospitable space to explore the modernist aesthetics of fragmentation, uncertainty and the heterogeneity of human experience. With Mansfield, Woolf, Dorothy Richardson, Edith Nesbit and May Sinclair, to name a few, producing short stories in this period, a notable body of writing emerges that furthers the innovations of the New Woman writer.

In her 1936 introduction to *The Faber Book of Modern Short Stories*, Elizabeth Bowen poignantly refers to the short story as 'a young art: as we now know it, it is the child of this century' (256). In a statement that reverberates with Woolf's earlier passion for the short story as a potentially 'new form', Bowen's remark illuminates the ways in which women writers directly engaged with the genre, and even celebrated its potential. Bowen continues, 'the short story as an art has come into being through a disposition to see life in a certain way' (ibid.), and she suggests it is characterised by 'its freedom from forced complexity, its possible lucidness' (262). The reflective nature of Bowen's assessment replicates the ways in which, during this period, women's short stories offered significant insight into the socio-political issues of the day. Just as World War I haunted the work of many modernist writers, the shadows of World War II are palpable on the pages of much mid-century writing. The social changes instigated by war altered women's lives dramatically, and these shifts are prominent features of much of their short fiction. In particular, women's relationship with domestic space and gender roles re-emerges in the mid-twentieth century, casting auspicious affinities with the earlier work of the New Woman. The shifting nature of women's role in society plays out in the open space of the short story, as women attempt to realise the complex nature of their everyday experiences.

Finally, as the women's movement developed and second-wave feminism became an increasingly pressing issue in the 1970s and 1980s, the short story experienced a further renewal. The fairy tale underwent a startling transformation as women writers explored the feminist potential provided by the act of (re)writing the genre. In this context the oral storytelling tradition of the short story is reinvented and the influence of feminism shapes both the form and content of short fiction. With acclaimed writers including Angela Carter, Fay Weldon and A. S. Byatt employing this medium, the contemporary fairy-tale narrative is a hybrid of the traditional and modern short story. In yet another moment of literary haunting, the influence of feminism on women's short story writing is particularly pronounced. However, while this aspect of women's short story writing is well discussed in academic studies, a lesser-known but equally interesting development in this period is the proliferation of the short story anthology. As with the fairy tale, at the heart of the anthology lies the act of revision: 'the act of looking back, of seeing with fresh eyes, of entering an old text from a new critical direction' (Rich 18). According to Adrienne Rich, revision is therefore 'an act of survival' (ibid.). By bringing together the works of a variety of writers (both past and present), the editor of an anthology is not only involved in a sisterly act of reclamation, but is carrying out an act of revision by placing the original work in a new light, editing a collection in a particular way, and therefore shaping how the reader receives the text.

The publication of a body of anthologies including *Tales I Tell My Mother: A Collection of Feminist Short Stories* (1978) edited by a collective of women (Zoë Fairbairns, Sara Maitland, Valerie Miner, Michèle Roberts and Michelene Wandor), *The Secret Self: A Century of Short Stories by Women* (1987) and *The Secret Self 2: Short Stories by Women* (1987) edited by Hermione Lee, *Daughters of Decadence: Women Writers of the Fin-de-Siècle* (1993) edited by Showalter, and Susan Hill's three edited collections *The Penguin Book of Modern Women's Short Stories* (1990), *The Penguin Book of Contemporary Women's Short Stories* (1995) and *The Second Penguin Book of Modern Women's Short Stories* (1997), highlight the preoccupation with women's short story writing across these decades. The political climate of second-wave feminism, in which women's consciousness-raising, sisterhood, collectivism and the reclamation of neglected voices was rife, resonates with the anthology, and marks it out as a relevant literary medium for the publication of women's narratives. Consequently, the short story genre is shown to contain further potential for women writers and becomes an especially relevant literary vehicle in the context of second-wave feminism. While the magazine has been an important publishing outlet for women writers across the twentieth century, from suffrage journals and *The Yellow Book* through to *Cosmopolitan* and *Mslexia*, the anthology has offered another vital publishing space. At the dawn of the twenty-first century, questions about the feasibility and financial viability of publishing short stories are transposed onto a digital context, and the rise of new technologies provokes uncertainty about the possible opportunities and threats to women's short story writing.

From this broad overview of British women's short story writing it is apparent that the genre has undoubtedly appealed to women across recent centuries. There is a certain freedom inherent in the aesthetic qualities of the short story, as the author Nadine Gordimer describes it, 'certainly the short story always has been more flexible and open to experiment than the novel' (459), and this characteristic is one factor in the genre's appeal. In 'Gender and Genre' Mary Eagleton proffers some connections between the short story and women writers, which includes the link between domestic production, time, and the ease in which women can therefore produce short stories (62). Equally, Eagleton notes the association of the one-to-one nature of the genre, its intimacy, and the focus on a single incident; but she warns that such a reduction risks marginalising both women and the genre to a 'lesser' status. In a similar vein, Lee suggests that there is 'no value in suggesting that women writers are better suited to the short story form than men' (x), instead we should consider 'the particular qualities of women's stories' (ibid.). In developing these earlier approaches, the essays in this collection trace some of the ongoing tendencies of women's short story writing; they ask questions about the relationship between the genre's formal features and the wider social context, and the contributors all illuminate the vibrant innovations of a body of writers across the long twentieth century. Throughout, the readings in this collection return to certain characteristics of the genre including the politics of time, the significance of the short story's ending, episodic nature and narrative brevity, the open and ambiguous nature of the form, the implications of the short story collection, the relationship between the text and reader, and the treatment of character and voice. By interrogating the intricacies of the short story's enduring popularity with women writers, these essays provide an overview of one particular cultural tradition of short story writing and interrogate a wide range of issues from the economic constraints and benefits of short story publishing through to the potential liberation and subversive social critique facilitated by the genre.

Mapping British Women's Short Story Writing

Opening the collection, in 'The Elusive Melody,' Maura Dunst studies the intersection of music and trauma in the short stories of George Egerton to examine the gender politics of artistic creation in the New Woman short story. In stories including 'Pan' (1897) and the tripartite 'Under Northern Sky' (1893), Dunst observes, music offers comfort and security to women suffering the effects of past traumas, while also carrying a haunting reminder of the incidents themselves. Continuing this fascination with living a haunted existence, Emma Liggins investigates the ways in which modernist women writers such as E. Nesbit and May Sinclair confront the 'shock of the new' with tales of the uncanny set 'Beyond the Haunted House' of the Victorian ghost story. By depicting ghosts who dwell in 'unspectral settings' ranging from suburban villas to motor cars, Liggins identifies how stories including Nesbit's 'The Violet Car' (1909) reflect contemporary anxieties concerning technology, modernity and suburbia. The relationship between the short story and modernist aesthetic forms is extended by Rebecca Bowler's chapter, which investigates the economic and cultural conditions in which short stories were produced by women writers in the early twentieth century. Bowler identifies how Dorothy Richardson, May Sinclair and Katherine Mansfield were confronted with opposing ideas of the short story's function: that it should be a 'pot-boiler', produced quickly in order to make money, and should present a significant 'moment' which was concise, coherent and self-contained. As Bowler argues, these writers' attempts to negotiate between what was expected of them and what they expected of themselves came to shape the modernist short story, as it is now known.

Adam Piette's chapter on Elizabeth Bowen moves the focus of analysis from the centrality of modernist aesthetics to a consideration of World War II. For Piette, the modernist short story's characteristic 'obliqueness, jump-cut suddenness and inconclusiveness' made it the ideal medium for representing the 'psychological intensities and broken temporalities' of wartime in Bowen's fiction, such as her ghost story 'The Demon Lover' (1945). The chapter culminates in an examination of Bowen's wartime short story as a hybrid form, comprised of modernist and Victorian influences, yet situated (and written) within an uncanny, unsettled present war temporality. Unsettled narratives and uncanny tales are also central to James Bailey's chapter on the early short fictions of Muriel Spark, which concern hauntings enacted by, and upon, female characters and explore the intertwining themes of spectrality, gender and narrative agency. Bailey discusses how the ghost story enabled Spark to experiment with textual self-consciousness in 'Harper and Wilton' (1953) and 'The Portobello Road' (1958), before examining the author's concern with the ghostly 'absent presence' of women within patriarchal society in 'The Girl I Left Behind Me' (1957) and 'Bang-Bang You're Dead' (1961). Issues of character are the focus of Michelle Ryan-Sautour's study of the revisionist and speculative tales of Angela Carter. Analysing the unstable, multifaceted nature of characters in some of Carter's lesser-known short fictions, including 'Reflections' (1987) and 'Elegy for a Freelance' (1985), Ryan-Sautour considers the relationship between the author's experimental short story forms and her complex treatment of character identity. Carter's methods of characterisation, she argues, play upon the reader's suspension of disbelief to generate 'a complex interplay of illusion and ideas'.

Focusing on the period between 1987 (in which Bradbury celebrated a 'new wave of interest in short fictional forms') and the launch of the English and Scottish Arts Council's 'Save Our Short Story' campaign in 2002, Ailsa Cox's chapter examines the availability of publishing outlets for short stories written by women. Providing a detailed discussion of the significant roles of anthologies, small press publications and writers' workshops, Cox explores how this marginalised genre was sustained during a markedly challenging period and the implications of these issues for women. The 1990s, a decade of opposing feminist discourses, provides the contextual backdrop to Emma Young's chapter, 'Feminist F(r)iction'. Young examines stories from the respective turn-of-the-millennium collections of feminist authors Helen Simpson and Michèle Roberts, *Hey Yeah Right Get a Life* (2000) and *Playing Sardines* (2001), as texts which utilise the short story to offer reflexive critiques on such discourses, from the tensions between second- and third-wave feminism in Roberts's stories to issues of parenthood and individual agency in Simpson's. In reflecting and engaging with such debates, Young argues, the short story serves as a vital literary medium for feminist writers.

Issues of social class provide the focus of Sue Vice's chapter on the short stories of Tessa Hadley, published in the collections *Sunstroke* (2007) and *Married Love* (2012). Examining the relationship between domestic and subjective interiors in the author's work, Vice draws upon the Bakhtinian concept of polyphony to explore the various, conflicting views that Hadley's characters have of one another, which she finds to be rooted in a modernist ambivalence of third-person narration. Developing the consideration of contemporary writers, Ben Davies offers a study of temporality and address in the stories of Ali Smith. The brevity of Smith's stories, Davies suggests, as well as their use of the second person pronoun, produce a 'fictional postal effect' by gesturing self-consciously towards a mode of reading unique to the short story: one in which the end is always in sight and the reader and the narrator are held within a fleeting yet forceful engagement. Holly Howitt-Dring's 'Housewives and Half-Stories', the final chapter in the collection, focuses on contemporary British female writers of microfiction, and examines the use of the genre's formal features to narrate tales of domesticity and motherhood. A practitioner as well as a reader of microfiction, Howitt-Dring reflects upon her own writing's engagement with matters of 'motherhood, relationships, control, domination and loss' in stories including 'Dinner Time' and 'Flesh and Blood' (2008).

While the content of this chapter echoes many of the themes discussed elsewhere in the collection, it also gestures toward the innovative future of the short story genre in just one of its many guises.

Finally, in a postscript to the collection, Clare Hanson reflects upon the contribution made by these essays to future studies of British women's short story writing. Hanson notes the prominence of themes concerning 'the uncanny, the spectral and the spiritual' that runs throughout the collection as a whole, and relates this to the short story's characteristic concern with mortality, the afterlife and memory. Indeed, from the chilling tales of Egerton in which music often sinisterly haunts the protagonist's life through to the haunted houses that feature in the modernist short stories of many women writers, the essays in this collection highlight the significance of this motif across the decades. Equally, the reoccurrence of political issues such as social class and feminism, and the testing of generic boundaries through microfiction in contemporary women's short stories emphasise a commonality in women's writing that transcends temporal allegiance. After all, these were all issues and concerns of the New Woman and modernist short story writer too. As such, *British Women Short Story Writers* offers another narrative of literary haunting by illuminating the synergies and overlaps between women's short story writing from the New Woman to now.

Works Cited

Baldwin, Dean (1993), 'The Tardy Evolution of the British Short Story', *Studies in Short Fiction*, 30:1, pp. 1–10.
Bates, H. E. (1972), *The Modern Short Story: A Critical Survey* [1941], London: Michael Joseph.
Bowen, Elizabeth (1945), 'The Short Story in England', *Britain To-Day*, 109, pp. 11–16.
Bowen, Elizabeth (1994), 'The Faber Book of Modern Short Stories', *The New Short Story Theories*, ed. Charles E. May, Athens, OH: Ohio University Press, pp. 256–62.
Bradbury, Malcolm (1988), 'Introduction' [1987], *The Penguin Book of Modern British Short Stories*, ed. Bradbury, London: Penguin, pp. 11–14.
Brown, Julie (2000), 'Introduction' [1995], *American Women Short Story Writers: A Collection of Critical Essays*, ed. Brown, New York: Garland Publishing, pp. xv–xxx.
Craig, Cairns (2006), 'Devolving the Scottish Novel', *A Concise Companion to Contemporary British Fiction*, ed. James F. English, Malden, MA: Blackwell, pp. 121–40.
Eagleton, Mary (1989), 'Gender and Genre', *Re-Reading the Short Story*, ed. Clare Hanson, Houndmills: MacMillan, pp. 55–68.
Ferguson, Suzanne C. (1994), 'Defining the Short Story: Impressionism and

Form', *The New Short Story Theories*, ed. Charles E. May, Athens, OH: Ohio University Press, pp. 218–30.

Gordimer, Nadine (1968), 'The International Symposium on the Short Story: South Africa', *The Kenyon Review,* 30:4, pp. 457–63.

Hanson, Clare (1989), 'Introduction,' *Re-Reading the Short Story*, ed. Hanson, Houndmills: Macmillan, pp. 1–9.

Hanson, Clare (1985), *Short Stories and Short Fictions, 1880–1980*, Houndmills: Macmillan.

Head, Dominic (1994), *The Modernist Short Story: A Study in Theory and Practice* [1992], Cambridge: Cambridge University Press.

Hunter, Adrian (2007), *The Cambridge Introduction to the Short Story in English*, Cambridge: Cambridge University Press.

Kooistra, Lorraine Janzen and Dennis Denisoff (2012), 'Introduction to the Yellow Nineties', *The Yellow Nineties Online*, ed. Dennis Denisoff and Lorraine Janzen Kooistra. Ryerson University, Web. 11 December 2013. <http://www.1890s.ca/HTML.aspx?s=Intro_Y90s.html>.

Lee, Hermione (1995), 'Introduction', *The Secret Self: A Century of Short Stories by Women* [1987], ed. Lee, Weidenfeld: Phoenix Giants.

Liggins, Emma, Andrew Maunder, and Ruth Robbins (2010), *The British Short Story*, Basingstoke; New York: Palgrave Macmillan.

Maunder, Andrew (2007), *A Companion to the British Short Story*, New York: Facts on File.

Munden, Paul (2013), *Beyond the Benchmark: Creative Writing in Higher Education*, York: The Higher Education Academy, Web. <https://www.heacademy.ac.uk/sites/default/files/resources/HEA_Beyond_the_Benchmark.pdf> [Last accessed 2 October 2014]

O'Connor, Frank (1963), *The Lonely Voice*, London: Macmillan.

Ramey, Lauri (2007), 'Creative Writing and Critical Theory', *The Handbook of Creative Writing*, ed. Steven Earnshaw, Edinburgh: Edinburgh University Press, pp. 42–53.

Rich, Adrienne (1972), 'When We Dead Awaken: Writing as Re-Vision', *College English*, 34:2, pp. 18–30.

Showalter, Elaine (1993), 'Introduction', *Daughters of Decadence: Women Writers of the Fin-de-Siècle*, London: Virago, pp. vii–xx.

Taylor, Debbie (2003), 'Endangered Species', *Mslexia*, 16, pp. 9–13.

Woolf, Virginia (1978), *The Letters of Virginia Woolf, Volume 2: 1912–22*, ed. Nigel Nicolson and Joanne Trautmann, Orlando: Mariner.

Chapter 2

The Elusive Melody: Music and Trauma in New Woman Short Stories
Maura Dunst

New Woman fiction, the cultural arm of the late nineteenth-century political phenomenon known as the New Woman, swept across *fin-de-siècle* Britain; triple-decker novels like Sarah Grand's *The Heavenly Twins* (1893) weighed down the bookshelves of curious readers in Britain and beyond. But it was not just the controversial novels that made waves amongst their readership: New Woman writers were experimenting with the short story, manipulating its form and making it their own. One of the most striking areas of experimentation is the use of music in the texts, an intriguing move stylistically and a choice that came loaded with centuries of gender politics attached. This chapter will address both the style innovations and the political statements involved in composing music in short stories, with particular focus on the relationship(s) between music, gender and trauma in the short stories of George Egerton. While other New Woman writers used trauma and music in fascinating ways,[1] Egerton's approach was unique and unusual – not least because it came from the pen of a woman who declared herself apolitical, came from financial insolvency, and was of Irish and Welsh descent, and yet is firmly associated with the New Woman, a strongly political, middle-class, mostly English movement.[2]

Egerton's perspective provides an exciting way of looking at the *fin-de-siècle* short story. In her collections, music accompanies women during painful or traumatic situations: the music of the earth eases a woman through childbirth; a violin provides a soundtrack to a young woman's suicide; the music of a hurdy-gurdy alerts a girl to the upsetting presence of a cruelly treated disabled boy, and the same song finds her again in adulthood as she is blackmailed into becoming a mistress. But music also provides protection: a young family keeps ghosts at bay through piano playing; a Norwegian woman sings to calm a raging, drunken and abusive husband. Egerton's collections include musical notation in the text, an unusual and innovative move, and are named using musical terms – *Keynotes* (1893), *Disc*(h)*ords* (1894), *Symphonies* (1897), *Fantasias* (1898) – as though she was creating her own opus. Elsewhere, I have called this compositional convergence of music and literature 'melopoetic composition', a thread which I will continue here.[3] Between the exploration of women's suffering, the inclusion of music, and the influence of Norwegian thinkers and short story writers like Amalie Skram, Henrik Ibsen and Knut Hamsun, Egerton changed the trajectory of the British short story; her anonymous narrators, non-chronological narrative progressions, and deep exploration of women's interiority made Egerton's work stand out, though her notoriety was short-lived and her contributions to the twentieth-century short story form and to modernism often are left unacknowledged.

The New Woman Writer

The following cautionary 'prediction' appeared in *Punch*'s 6 October 1894 issue: 'A Safe Prediction: That the New Woman of this decade will be the Old Maid of the next' (165). This hypothesis sought to frighten New Women by suggesting that no man would marry them. However, the writer of the prediction seems to have missed the point; or rather, he or she unintentionally highlighted the very gender issues the New Woman spoke out against. Indeed, despite being largely forgotten for the first two-thirds of the twentieth century, the New Woman was on the tip of *fin-de-siècle* Britain's tongue. She parked her bicycle – which she rode unchaperoned – and sauntered into the public sphere, sans corset, smoking a cigarette and demanding equal consideration under the law and unlimited access to education. She spoke at political rallies; she campaigned for women's suffrage; she wore fabulous hats and rational dress. She promoted women's freedom in all areas, which smacked of sexual deviance. To some, she was a beacon of hope for the future, but to others, perhaps to most, she was a terrifying and grotesque vision of hell to pay if women with 'views' were left unchecked. Whether the New Woman was viewed as a saviour or a succubus, at the end of the nineteenth century she was, according to Ann Heilmann (2000), 'a vibrant metaphor of transition' which 'stood at once for the degeneration of society and for that society's moral regeneration' (1). Illustrating the difficulty in offering a single definition of a plural concept, Heilmann continues,

> Who or what was the New Woman? A literary construct, a press fabrication and discursive marker of rebellion, or a 'real' woman? A writer, social reformer, or feminist activist? A middle-class daughter eager to study for a

career, a married woman chafing against legal inequality, a woman-loving spinster, a reluctant mother, a sexual libertarian? (ibid.)

This plurality shows the New Woman was not one figure, or one set of ideals, but like a Rorschach test, she manifested differently for each individual viewer.

The New Woman was not just viewable at political scenes and in the periodical press – indeed, she was perhaps most visible on the pages of popular books. It is clear that the New Woman had a 'complex interrelationship and productive engagement with contemporary culture and literature' (Heilmann 2005: 33), particularly with regard to her literary labours. Springing from the head of the New Woman, like a literary Athena, came the artistic facet of the political movement: New Woman fiction hit the scene in the 1880s and quickly gained purchase, becoming so popular that in the 1890s *Punch* was no longer just lampooning the New Woman generally, but honing in on literary household names like Madame Sarah Grand, Mona Caird and George Egerton. New Woman writers took advantage of the 'close alliance between literature and social reform' (Heilmann 2004: 1), and their work became a popular part of Victorian culture, with over 100 novels written between 1883 and 1900 that were about the New Woman (Heilmann 2000: 1), not to mention short stories, poems, articles, essays and plays. New Woman fiction was 'characterized by the representation of strong heroines who rebel against the limitations placed on their lives and demand the same education and economic opportunities as men enjoy' (Nelson 2000: xii), thus aligning the literary New Woman with her political counterpart. New Woman fiction became so popular that, according to Sally Ledger, 'the figure of the New Woman was utterly central to the literary culture of the *fin de siècle* years' (1997: 1).

Writing mere decades after a census declared unmarried women were 'surplus', suddenly the New Woman seemed instrumental to the advancement (or regression) of British society.[4] However, it is worth noting that the New Woman was 'essentially middle-class'; working-class women:

> led lives so totally remote from the cosy domesticity and shining feminine ideal against which the New Woman was reacting that this kind of revolt could do nothing for them ... the problems of working-class women were entirely different from those of the middle classes, and received very little attention from writers on the New Woman. (Cunningham 1978: 11)

It is also worth noting the New Woman's new spin on female sexuality in Victorian Britain: 'It is clear that the New Woman is regarded as a highly sexual being, all the more dangerous since she cannot be dismissed as a prostitute or a fallen woman' (ibid. 14). However, in spite of the progress the New Woman seemed to be making during her heyday, she was, according to Gail Cunningham, ultimately unsuccessful; Cunningham sees the New Woman as a failed attempt to move women forward at the *fin de siècle*, and calls the 'apparent liberation of the New Woman . . . fragile and ephemeral' (ibid. 156). Patricia Stubbs, in turn, dismisses Grand as 'not good enough' as a writer to turn her material 'into an important challenge to the literary tradition' (1979: 120).

However, in 1990 Ann Ardis's *New Women, New Novels: Feminism and Early Modernism* further explored New Woman writing, positing it as a precursor to, or an early form of, modernism, a position which was supported by Lyn Pykett's *The 'Improper Feminine': The Women's Sensation Novel and New Woman Writing* in 1992. The critical attention of the 1990s began to challenge the initial findings of New Woman scholars: in the Introduction to *Reading Fin de Siècle Fictions,* published in 1996, Pykett writes that the previous critical work tended

> to see the New Woman largely as a subject for fiction (rather than as a writing subject), and to read the women's writing of the 1880s and 1890s mainly as a preparation for (what [critics] see as) the more accomplished literary achievements of male writers. The perspectives on the New Woman writing offered by Stubbs, Cunningham, and Showalter are, to a great extent, products of their time; all three books were written when feminist literary criticism and literary history were in an emergent state. (7)

Though I disagree with Stubbs' earlier statement, I will not argue the literary merits of Grand here; however, the covert (and sometimes overt) point of my work on Egerton is to expose the assumption regarding New Woman fiction that Pykett mentions above as patently false. Egerton was not merely a stepping stone for modernists like James Joyce; she manipulated the short story in ways other British writers had not, and she experimented with literature more daringly and successfully than any of her contemporaries. She was modernist before modernism existed.

While Sarah Grand and Mona Caird were continuing to write traditionally structured Victorian novels, albeit with political twists, alongside their more experimental short stories and political essays Egerton sent off collections of short stories bearing the intellectual and stylistic imprint of her time spent in Norway.[5] Egerton abandoned the (mostly) linear plots followed by Grand and Caird for non-linear narratives with unnamed characters in unspecified locations. The stories shouted about the topics Egerton's contemporaries calmly discussed: rape, abuse, blackmail, cruelty; the dark underbelly of unchecked patriarchy was brought to the surface in no uncertain terms. The female characters were thoughtful, curious, competent and sexual, often bastions of morality in contrast to the corrupt men who divert their courses; this Egerton shared with her New Woman literary sisters (despite declaring herself apolitical). But the presentation was worlds apart.

George Egerton

While Egerton engaged in many stylistic experiments in her short stories, one in particular will be focused on in this chapter: the inclusion of music. The world of Victorian music was a deeply sexist one in which middle-class women, regardless of talent, were expected and trained to be lovely private performers, while male musicians were sifted, and the wheat was separated and regarded as genius. Not only were women generally limited in their musical education, but musical genius and composition were widely considered almost exclusively male concepts. Sophie Fuller writes that while some well-known female musicians and composers made their mark on the Victorian music scene, the 'commonly-held belief that a great woman composer is an impossibility' persisted (2004: 27). Likewise, Alisa Clapp-Itnyre suggests that while 'music empowered women to achieve artistic ability, even fame, more often it was yet another form of social oppression' (2002: 36). The limitations on female musicians were particularly strict for the middle and upper classes, to which most of the New Woman heroines belong. According to Nancy Reich, 'the appearance of a woman on the concert stage could undermine the hard-won social status of her bourgeois family; consequently even the most gifted were expected to confine their musical activities to the home' (1995: 132). So, Egerton's melopoetic compositions served a double purpose artistically, venturing into two areas of creation that were considered the realm of men (indeed, some thought women biologically incapable of creativity): not only was she composing innovative literature, she was also composing music, and furthermore was combining the two into a new hybrid form of artistic expression.[6]

Egerton connected music with myriad emotional and physical experiences in her short stories: spiritual growth, physical protection, pain, pleasure, epiphanies, tragedies and various types of trauma, among others.[7] Egerton's collections are filled with traumatic incidents, from physical abuse to heartbreak to murder to self-harm, and music accompanies the characters throughout.[8] Indeed, as mentioned in the introduction, even the titles of the collections themselves imply a musical element, and because the collections deal primarily with traumatic incidents, the two concepts are almost inseparable. Music provides comfort and protection to traumatised women, but also serves as a reminder of past trauma; thus, women's emotions and music are deeply connected in Egerton's work.

This connection begins, appropriately, at the beginning of Egerton's first collection, *Keynotes*, with the story 'Under Northern Sky' which is divided into three parts. The first, 'How Marie Larsen Exorcised a Demon', tells the tale of a Norwegian estate terrorised by a tyrannical, violent and drunken master:

> There has been a mighty storm, it has been raging for two days. A storm in which the demon of drink has reigned like a sinister god in the big white house, and the frightened women have cowered away, driven before the hot blast of the breath upon which curses danced, and the blaze of ire in the lurid eyes of the master. Only the pale little mistress has stood unmoved through the whirlwind of his passion. (124)

The master is crazed, abusive and vulgar; he treats all other creatures terribly. He makes it clear that he satisfied his sexual urges regardless of his partner's consent, thinking briefly about 'one long ago' whom he 'might have spared . . . she pleaded hard against me' (127). But he does not, and his brief moment of reflection on his actions is shattered when he finishes the thought by declaring the woman and her subsequent child 'jabbering idiots both!' (ibid.). Nothing seems strong enough to counteract the master's horrific behaviour.

More powerful than the master's fury (and the social standing which makes him virtually untouchable), however, is Marie Larsen and her music. The servants have scattered, 'and the master of them all is sitting exhausted in his big chair, and Marie Larsen and he are doing battle' (132). In this scene:

> She knits away and commences in Norwegian a sing-song recitative like the drowsy buzz of a fly on a pane. 'Yesterday we had a bazaar, a bazaar in the school-house, a bazaar for the poor black heathens in Africa. For the poor black heathens lost in the darkness of unbelief, and ignorant of the saving of the Lamb – oh, it was blessed work!' A savage roar from him, but she goes on unheeding with her narrative. (135)

Marie's 'sing-song recitative' manages to tame the master and mitigate the trauma suffered by his wife, employees and animals. The master fights back: 'She dodges a glass adroitly, and raises her voice to drown his shriek of what the merry devil she means' (136), but Marie is not discouraged, and 'she starts a key higher, for he is purple with fury and exertion' (137). The musical language here – 'sing-song' and 'a key higher' – shows the reader that it is not simply Marie's language which is counteracting the master's behaviour, but the music behind it. Egerton continues to use musical terminology: 'His vocabulary is exhausted, and he is inventing the weirdest oaths, hurling them forth, a deep accompaniment to her shriller sermon, with its sanctimonious sing-song tune and unctuous phrasing; for she is, perhaps unwittingly, mimicking the kapelan to life' (138). And as Marie wins that night's battle, she has music on her side:

> As a mother will change her lullaby into a quick hushoo, and pat mechanically with a drowsy nod as the child drops to sleep, so Marie puts her knitting tidily into her apron pocket, and folding her withered old hands, breaks into a hymn. He opens his eyes languidly, and protests feebly with a last damn, but Marie has exorcised the devil this time. (139)

For the time being, the residents of the estate are spared further physical, sexual and psychological trauma, as the source has been mollified through the use of music.

Part two of this story, 'A Shadow's Slant', is back at the same estate, where the master is now recovered, and where 'nature has ever a discordant note in its symphony' (140). The master and his wife listen to the music of a nearby gypsy family:

> Wild the music, wilder the dance, and he sits in his chair on the veranda the clean, clear air and the fresh breeze blowing in from the sea, stirring the white hairs in the curls at his temples, and listens and looks with no eye or ear for aught of its beauty – only a ribald jest as their petticoats rise, or their bosoms quiver in the fling of the dance . . . and she with a crimson shawl drawn round her spare shoulders, and a splash of colour in her thin cheeks holds one hand tightly pressed over her breast – to still what? What does the music rouse inside that frail frame, what parts her lips and causes her eyes to glisten and the thin nostrils to quiver? (147)

This is a telling moment for both the traumatiser and the traumatised. The former's true colours are shown: he does not care for the beauty of the music, or the dance, or even the girls; he only cares for the opportunity to make 'ribald jests' about the dancers' bodies. His wife, however, usually pale and wan, has a 'splash of colour' in her cheeks, and a look of rapture on her face. Egerton asks what effect the music has on her, but does not answer it for us (in true Egertonian fashion) and therefore leaves it to the reader to decide. It seems that the music provides a bright light in an otherwise grey existence; a moment of sensual pleasure, all the more exhilarating given her tendency to dull them in order to survive life with her husband. The scene continues with the master engaging with the gypsies as 'he throws silver lavishly to them and thrusts his hand with a coarse jest into the open bodice of the girl nearest him' (147). After the dance is over, the master and his wife head back to their house, where she falls asleep, but the healing power of music is not finished with her yet; down below:

> The Romany lass is humming a song, a song about love, and dance, and song; and the soul of the sleeping girl floats along at her side in a dream of freedom. She of the song looks up: 'Six moons will rise, then you will be free! (154)

It is as if the song weaves a web around the wife, and protects her.

The song's prediction also comes true. The wife's trauma is over, as foretold by the gypsy girl. In the third section, 'An Ebb Tide', the once great and powerful wave of the master subsides, and he is dying. The implication is that he has drunk himself to death, though, as per usual, the details are not given. It is revealed that he fathered a child with the estate's cowgirl; she seems to be the only resident mourning his death. The wife's internal monologue as the master is dying focuses on her lack of grief at his impending death, and also, perhaps now unsurprisingly, music:

> Things she has forgotten completely come vividly back to her. An old Maori man, who used to sell sweet potatoes, and quaint ring shells for napkin rings to the Pakeha lady in Tauranga Bay, floats before her inward vision as tangible as if he were next to her. And a soldier servant: she can hear his voice; he used to sing as he pipe clayed . . . Why did the stupid chorus come back to her now, what chink of brain did it lie in all these years? Oh what a brute she is and how callous! She ought to read prayers, or say things; in a few hours it will be too late to ever say a word more. She finds herself beating time with her foot to a jig tune, a bizarre accompaniment to the words 'too late.' She would give all she possesses to cry, yet she cannot; and so the day wears on. (170)

The knowledge that 'in a few hours it will be too late to ever say a word more' to her husband is exhilarating, and causes her to tap her foot to the melody of a jig; she wishes to feel sad, but cannot help but respond to the music in her head, which notates her internal emotions: she is, as the gypsy girl predicted, free.

After his death, as the wife waits to depart with his coffin, she is deep in thought and hums 'Lum tum, te tum, te tum . . . ! The dead march in Saul!' but stops herself when she remembers the superstition that every time a person hums this song, a soldier dies. 'Why should she kill a soldier? She used to like all soldiers, tum tum! . . . Is she going mad? How does one go mad?' (176). Her erratic thoughts continue, flitting uncontrollably like a bird that has just been released from a cage. Her mind wanders, but it's all variations on the theme of music. She even muses that 'he hated music', but 'the sea he loved! It seems to her that there is a cadence of pity in the eternal note of its quiet sadness' (178). The musical terminology continues in the penultimate paragraph, where the traumatised soul of the wife is comforted by the music of the world: 'And the night breeze sings sadly to the thrumming of unseen harps, and soothes her troubled spirit with tender whisperings that only the stricken in soul can catch in snatches from the spirit of nature' (184). Music has tamed the abuser, provided the accompaniment for his demise, and healed the abused.

This melding of music and trauma continues in *Discords*, published in 1894, a year after its predecessor. The collection begins with 'A Psychological Moment at Three Periods', which, like 'Under Northern Sky', is broken into three sections. What sets this story apart, however, is the inclusion of musical notation in the work: a G-minor chord, with G as its keynote, appearing above the text. In the treble clef there is an F sharp and a G sharp, making the chord extremely dissonant in this narrative.[9] The chord is loud, jarring, with three neighbouring semitones played at once (F#, G, and G#). The notation is the first thing you read, placed above the text; for those who can read music, the combination of text and imagined sound initiates the story with a synesthetic moment, which is part of the fabric of the composition. It seems that Egerton's theme of emotional, physical and/or sexual trauma will continue. The first section of the story, 'The Child', sets a scene of dreary darkness; the child in question grapples with there being 'so much pain in the world! It's everywhere!' (13). This sets the stage for the second section, 'The Girl', where the mood shifts; 'yellow sunshine' floods 'an autumn world, gold-brown leaves fall' (16). The world is aglow. The girl goes to a Kermesse, or carnival, in a nearby village and the music begins. 'The hurdy-gurdy in the pagoda strikes up a polka, well known through Holland and South Africa as "Polly Witfoet," and with many preliminary creaks and strains the round-about starts in a giddy circle' (23). Everyone around the girl is carefree, but her

> keen eyes note that at one point in the round the breeze blows aside the trappings of the pagoda; she peeps idly in, but each time after that her eyes seek it with a look of shrinking fascination. Her thin nostrils quiver, and her pupils dilate, and an indignant flush dyes her face in a beautiful way as she gazes – why? (24)

The girl's traumatic experience begins (with musical accompaniment, of course):

> An idiot lad is turning the handle of the hurdy-gurdy; he is fastened by a leathern strap round his middle to the pole in the centre of the tent. His head

is abnormally large; the heavy eyelids lie half folded on the prominent eyeballs, so that only the whites show; his damp hair clings to his temples and about his outstanding ears, his mouth gapes, and his long tongue lolls from side to side, the saliva forming little bubbles as the great head wags heavily as he grinds, – indeed, every part of his stunted, sweat-dripping body sways mechanically to the lively air of white-footed Polly. 'Polly Witfoet, Polly Witfoet, lallallallallala!' (24)

The girl is horrified; the light-hearted music which the 'lad' churns out stands in grotesque contrast to the reality of his awful existence. Saddened, the girl continues to look for the 'lad': 'Each time she looks, the heavy lids seem to droop more, the tongue to loll longer, the face to wax paler. Save for the strap, the scarcely human form would topple over with weariness. A whip is leaning up against the framework' (24). She watches 'with ever-growing indignation and disgust swelling her breast, causing her to clench her thin hands' (ibid.). None of the other children see the traumatising sight. 'I alone see' (25), she muses. As the polka grinds on, she can't escape from the trauma, causing her to abandon the village and run to the countryside, where she has an existential crisis: '"God, I tell you, you needn't have made him!" ... She throws herself breathlessly down at the foot of a great tree and bursts into tears, not sorrowful tears, but heaving, rebellious sobs against the All-father for His ordering of things here below' (26). In the countryside, crying, she hears 'the refrain of the common tune' being carried by the breeze (27). In this case, the music does not bring her comfort, but rather reminds her of the horror she witnessed.

Section three of the story, 'The Woman', jumps in time and place; a young woman and a wealthy, married man are in London, where he is trying to convince her to become his mistress. He offers to buy her anything she needs, but she wants no part. They continue to verbally spar, until he reveals his 'trump card' (35):

> He takes out a letter; it is a little soiled. She is very white, and scarcely draws her breath. Once she looks at him, and her eyes are kindled with a deadly hate. He points to the name of the receiver and to the signature. He holds it so that she can read it, opens it. There is a soiled, crumpled receipt in acknowledgement of money pinned inside. She reads with whitening face. A hurdy-gurdy outside the railings is grinding out: 'Polly Witfoet, Polly Witfoet, lallallallallala!' She starts, knitting her brows in vain endeavor to find what the tune brings back to her. (36)

In another moment of emotional trauma, the hurdy-gurdy's song finds her; though she can't remember what it reminds her of, the reader knows that the song has accompanied an earlier realisation about cruelty in the world. The music follows her, haunts her, reminds her of past trauma. The man considers his options:

> Is it worth it all? Shall he let her off? Be bested by a woman? and this particular woman, whose love or liking he cannot gain, and whose affection he fancies he craves for more than that of any one he has ever known? No, he'll be hanged if he will. Kismet! It is written. And the hurdy-gurdy grinds on White-footed Polly's polka. (37)

The story continues some time later, and the reader understands that the woman was indeed blackmailed into becoming the man's mistress. Now, they are 'miserable' (42). She looks out over the Paris night, considering her misery and the life she is living. The pain of reality is great, causing an episode of self-harm: 'She meets her teeth in her arm; it is a sort of relief to counteract the agony of her soul by a pang of physical pain' (ibid.). Her emotional trauma is so great that the woman hurts herself physically in order to ease her psychic pain. There is no music present in this scene or the moments that follow, but its absence is telling, and in many ways is as noisy as its presence: the music causes trauma, and when the story ends and she is freed from her bonds, there is silence.

The intermingling of pleasure and pain and their subsequent intersections with music continue throughout the collection, but music is restored to a positive force in 'Her Share'. In this story, music again becomes something healing, something intrinsic to the soul. The narrator says she 'had a song in my own heart so wondrously new and strange that I was jealous of every disturbing note' (73). She muses, 'all that summer there was a thrumming on an unknown chord in my innermost being, a wonderful by-song in my heart that I alone heard. Intense joy has its element of pain' (82). Like the wife in 'Under Northern Sky', this woman experiences an inner song that causes a reaction so intense it is difficult to tell whether it is pleasure or pain, or both. Her lover, a workman, sings to her: 'The words he sang were foreign, but the melody spoke passionately, warmly, caressingly, with a chord of despair that turned my heart to water, and touched the most secret fibres of my being, hurting me with love' (83). Again, music and pain are related, almost inseparable; the song hurts her with love.

In 'Pan', published in *Symphonies* in 1897, music again accompanies pain, only this time it is distinctly physical as well as emotional.[10] A girl, Tienette, exhibits the same inner melody as her predecessors, which causes the same combination of pleasure and pain:

> She had been troubled of late; her senses had quivered and tickled strangely; the notes of a melody that had played upon the lute strings of her soul all through the months, that had danced gladly by since the first voluptuous

stirrings of the southern spring, awoke in her and made her heart sick; it had vibrated in between the regenerative cry of the earth in her, and around her, until she seemed to listen for it with her very blood, as if every vein were an ear, conveying it with a clutching throb to her heart, causing a sickening weakness in every limb. (225)

She listens for the music of her soul, which causes 'a sickening weakness' – music is slightly sinister. She is enchanted by the old fiddler's music, which she thinks surely 'must have held witchery in its cadence' (226), as she finds herself hearing it everywhere. Indeed, 'ever since the cadence of his music had sung in her; she heard it in the sea, and in the trees when she gathered firewood in the forest, in the wind as it rushed through the valleys. All these months past it had weakened her' (227). The music both enchants and drains her, and she finds herself defenceless against the advances of an aggressive young man who pursues her. 'She shuddered when she thought of him, for he made her afraid, and the fatal melody vibrating in her had robbed her of force to resist his power' (228). The language here is fascinating – 'the fatal melody' robs Tienette of the ability to fight him off. Suddenly, she finds herself alone with him, and 'the witch melody . . . seemed to be struck into rougher chords by the man at her side' (230). The melody shifts and she is unable to control it.

The fatal melody accompanies her rape. Tienette exits the scene shaken, hurt and traumatised, hating both her attacker and the music which she feels left her in a weakened state. To make matters worse, she is pregnant, and the hated-but-loved music has abandoned her. 'Her gait was heavier than in summer; the magic music had been silent in her soul; never once has she heard the witch-white melody that proved her ruin since the day when it had made her bend as wax in the grasp of [the young man]' (236). Because of the music, as Tienette sees it, she is pregnant, and because of the pregnancy, she agrees to marry the young man, despite his cruelty and her loathing. But on their wedding night, she runs away from the party to the cliffs, where she is followed by the old fiddler; he goes after her because 'the look your eyes gave me to-day has haunted me like the melody I hear in the wind sometimes' (254). The music is back. The old fiddler asks why she married her then-husband, and she responds, 'because your music got into my soul, and melted me like wax in hot weather, so that I was soft to run into any mould, and – he came at the right moment' (ibid.). She then requests that he play a particular song of his own creation, and hands him his violin. As he plays:

> The girl drew softly away, until she stood silhouetted against the sky on a ledge where the cliff sank steepest. The melody crept in silver notes between

the skirl of the blast, now clear in the lull, now lost in the storm, rising louder and louder through a frenzy of passion and yearning to a cry of triumph; and as the last note died away the player opened his eyes as from a dream, and the wind kissed away all trace in the sand upon the ledge of the little feet of Tienette the golden-haired – but Pan still lives. (256)

The music serves as a sort of funeral dirge, and Tienette jumps to her death. Pan, the survivor and the story's namesake, seems a fitting figure: god of the rustic, the rural, associated with music and sexual powers, he has a hand in all elements of Tienette's story. Her emotional and physical trauma is deeply linked to music, the presence of which plays a significant role in the most traumatic moments of her life and, ultimately, her death.

Egerton's fourth and final installation of her music series, *Fantasias*, uses music to ease trauma rather than inspire it. In 'The Star-Worshipper', a woman with an abusive husband seeks out music to ease her pain:

> Her life would have been unbearable but that sometimes, as she lay with her ear close to the heart of Mother Earth, the myriad heath-bells – violet, pink, and purple – rang gayly or sadly in measure as the winds touched them, and played melodies that caused her to forget – forget even the girdle cakes to bake and the linen to bleach, and so got her many a beating. (14)

While there is a mischievous element to the music, overall it is presented as a comfort that makes the woman's life bearable. It accompanies her in childbirth, and the baby's character is described using musical language. As she goes into labour, it is as though the whole world plays a symphony for her:

> One night, when the reeds were swaying their slim green bodies to the rhythm of their old-world melody, and the river rippled and whispered to the flowers on its banks, and the white eggs of the night birds gleamed as sign-posts for the mother birds, out moth-faring in the gloom, and the night crooned lullabies, and the music of the spheres above stole down and mingled with the bass voice of the earth below, she gave birth to a little lad. Perhaps his birth hour and place determined his temperament, struck the dual note in his nature, – the symphony of the heavens warring ever with the trull song of the clay; the elusive melody of the moonbeam music, the cool softness of the dew, with the passionate strength of the winds. (5)

Here, the physical trauma of childbirth is mitigated by the music of the earth, with its 'old-world melody'. Indeed, the pain of labour is left unmentioned, and in its place comes a description of the orchestra of sounds that accompany the birth, including the 'dual note' of music in the baby's own soul. Similarly, in 'The Elusive Melody', music is used to protect a family from ghosts. A young girl with no prior knowledge of music sits down at a piano left in the haunted house; there she experiences some sort of synaesthesia in which 'numbers came dancing through her brains, – numbers that added up, and subtracted, and divided in a wonderful way, with a strange blending of colours. Following the impulse they gave her, she played a quaint melody with a dance measure in it', and this protects them from the ghosts (37). Eventually, the family no longer need protection from the ghosts, and the girl's musical gift leaves her; momentarily, music has served to block the trauma of ghostly haunting.

A discussion of George Egerton's experimentation with short story form at the end of the nineteenth century is as fruitful as it is underexamined. Egerton plays with narrative and style, examining women's interiority in ways that had not happened previously, using creative writing styles that were innovative and new. Much of her work is semi-autobiographical, if not entirely so, and much of the trauma which hovers over almost every page of her short stories can be linked directly to her own life, or the lives of those around her. Her life story is a dramatic tale of love and loss; she suffered at the hands of brutish men and saw the world with a shrewd eye. Her extant biographical material, some of which was gathered into Terence de Vere White's *A Leaf from the Yellow Book* (1958), provides ample understanding of Egerton's own personal trauma. What remains less clear is her connection to music, and yet it is present throughout her writing, and she displays a working knowledge of not only written music but musical terminology. Perhaps Egerton herself experienced the same emotional, internal connection to music that she gave to so many of her characters; while very few of her letters and diaries have been published, a letter to her then-publisher John Lane, signed, 'Yours in a most minor key', suggests a similarity between life and art (De Vere White 37). Regardless, the presence of music in Egerton's work is a fascinating area of inquiry, and its links to trauma provide a useful approach to a discussion of Egerton's short story style.

Egerton is best known as one of the New Woman writers, which is certainly deserved in some ways, but undeserved in others; she eschewed the overtly political statements made by other New Woman writers, and did not fit the middle-class English mould in which the New Woman was formed. From a working-class family of Irish and Welsh descent, Egerton could hardly have been more different from her wealthy English counterparts. Indeed, though her heyday was an exhilarating high, her fame was quickly eclipsed and she died alone and forgotten, in poverty. In comparing Egerton to James Joyce, Gerd Bjørhovde writes, 'both may be said to have made important contributions to the development of the modern short story, but whereas one of them remains one of the most-studied and most-admired writers in the world, the other is more or less forgotten today' (2012: 93). Egerton's neglect is undeserved, and her influence on British literature has been largely unrecognised. But if you trace back from modernist short story 'innovators', you might just find that their melodies are variations on the theme of Egerton.

Notes

1. Sarah Grand's short stories include 'Mamma's Music Lessons', where music is used to heal emotional wounds caused by traditional educational methods. In New Woman novels, music and trauma are also deeply linked: Grand's novel *The Beth Book* presents music as a healing art, and the main character is beaten by her mother while playing piano; *The Heavenly Twins* presents Angelica's violin playing as spiritually nurturing, but also causes a domino effect which results in the death of her beloved Tenor; Hadria, the protagonist of Mona Caird's *Daughters of Danaus*, experiences both hurt and healing through her musicianship.
2. The writers most commonly associated with New Woman Fiction include Sarah Grand, George Egerton, Mona Caird, Ella D'Arcy, Olive Schreiner, Annie Sophie Cory, Ella Hepworth Dixon and, to a lesser extent, George Gissing, Grant Allen and Thomas Hardy.
3. For a detailed outline of this theory, please see: Dunst, Maura (2014), 'Reading Music, Composing Literature: Melopoetic Composition in George Egerton's *Keynotes* and *Discords*', *Nineteenth-Century Gender Studies* 10.3, 18–42.
4. Women's societal value outside the home, or lack thereof, was made clear in the 1851 census, which 'revealed that there were 400,000 "surplus" women. Without a husband women had no one to keep them or to enable them to reproduce legitimate children; unmarried women were thus surplus to social/reproductive requirements' (Richardson and Willis 4).
5. For more on Egerton's connections with Norwegian literature, see the work of Gerd Bjørhovde.
6. See Boumelha and Weliver, among others, for a discussion of treatment of women artists in the Victorian periodical press.
7. Egerton's experiments with music in literature are discussed in detail in the manuscript version of my doctoral research, *Such Genius as Hers: Music in New Woman Fiction*, which is under preparation for submission.
8. My thanks to Alexandra Messem of Southampton University who completed her PhD research on trauma in New Woman fiction. Her insightful observations about trauma, and our discussions about the topic, which led to my own understanding of trauma in Egerton's work.
9. The inclusion of musical notation is one of the most interesting melopoetic elements of New Woman fiction for me, and I discuss this particular element of Egerton's work in greater detail in both my monograph and my article on melopoetic composition.

10. It is worth noting that by this time Egerton's fame was waning; the Wilde trials had caused her publisher, John Lane, to tighten up the reins editorially, and she no longer had the same freedom she had exercised in her first two collections. *Symphonies* thus contains a shift in tone and content; *Fantasias* even more so. Thus, the best examples of Egerton's work are contained in the earlier collections. There must have been a lengthy discussion with Lane, as well as extensive manuscript revisions, but the details of these are buried in library archives which have never been fully mined.

Works Cited

Ardis, Ann (1990), *New Women, New Novels: Feminism and Early Modernism*, New Brunswick, NJ: Rutgers University Press.

Bjørhovde, Gerd (2012), 'From "Discords" to "Dubliners": George Egerton, James Joyce, and Norway', *Nordic Irish Studies*, 11:1, 93–105.

Boumelha, Penny (1997), 'The Woman of Genius and the Woman of Grub Street: Figures of the Female Writer in British *Fin-de-Siècle* Fiction', *English Literature in Transition* 40, 164–80.

Clapp-Itnyre, Alisa (2002), *Angelic Airs, Subversive Songs: Music as Social Discourse in the Victorian Novel*, Athens, OH: Ohio University Press.

Cunningham, Gail (1978), *The New Woman and the Victorian Novel*, London: Macmillan Press.

De Vere White, Terence (1958), *A Leaf from The Yellow Book* [1894], London: The Richards Press.

Egerton, George (1894), *Discords*, London: John Lane.

Egerton, George (1898), *Fantasias*, London: John Lane.

Egerton, George (1893), *Keynotes*, London: John Lane.

Egerton, George (1897), *Symphonies*, London: John Lane.

Fuller, Sophie (2004), '"Cribbed, cabin'd, and confined": Female Musical Creativity in Victorian Fiction', *The Idea of Music in Victorian Fiction*, ed. Sophie Fuller and Nicky Losseff, Aldershot: Ashgate, pp. 27–56.

Heilmann, Ann (2000), *New Woman Fiction: Women Writing First-Wave Feminism*, Basingstoke: Palgrave Macmillan.

Heilmann, Ann (2005), 'The New Woman in the New Millennium: Recent Trends in Criticism of New Woman Fiction', *Literature Compass*, 3:1, 32–42.

Heilmann, Ann (2004), *New Woman Strategies: Sarah Grand, Olive Schreiner, Mona Caird*, Manchester: Manchester University Press.

Ledger, Sally (1997), *The New Woman: Fiction and Feminism at the Fin de Siècle*, Manchester: Manchester University Press.

Nelson, Carolyn Christensen (ed.) (2000), *A New Woman Reader: Fiction, Articles, and Drama of the 1890s*, Peterborough, Ontario: Broadview.

Pykett, Lyn (1992), *The 'Improper' Feminine: The Woman's Sensation Novel and New Woman Writing*, London: Routledge.

Pykett, Lyn (ed.) (1996), *Reading Fin de Siècle Fictions*, London: Longman.

Reich, Nancy B. (1995), 'Women as Musicians: A Question of Class', *Musicology and Difference: Gender And Sexuality in Music Scholarship*, ed. Ruth A. Solie, Berkeley: University of Los Angeles Press, pp. 125–48.

Richardson, Angelique and Chris Willis (2001), 'Introduction', *The New Woman in Fiction and Fact*, Basingstoke: Palgrave Macmillan.
'A Safe Prediction', *Punch* (6 October 1894): 165.
Stubbs, Patricia (1979), *Women and Fiction: Feminism and the Novel, 1880–1920*, Brighton: Harvester.
Weliver, Phyllis (2000), *Women Musicians in Victorian Fiction, 1860–1900*, Farnham: Ashgate.

Chapter 3

Beyond the Haunted House? Modernist Women's Ghost Stories and the Troubling of Modernity
Emma Liggins

Modernist women writers refashioned the haunted house setting of the Victorian ghost story in order to address the unsettling allure of the past and fears around an increasingly mechanised future. 'The past in the Gothic never quite stays dead', Diana Wallace claims, 'and is therefore never fully knowable. This is why Gothic fiction so often seems to demand psychoanalytic interpretations as a way of disinterring the repressed secrets of the past' (2013: 4). In the Victorian ghost story, the angry or jealous revenant prompts the revelation of the secrets of the past, putting what was unspeakable into discourse in order to stabilise family relations through inheritance and diffuse concerns about property and propriety. By the modernist period, the unknowability of the past is figured through the spectrality of empty, or strangely new, houses, indistinct shadows or spatial and temporal disruption in line with new formulations of the uncanny. Virginia Woolf's fragmented sketch 'A Haunted House', appearing in her first short story collection, *Monday or Tuesday* (1921), is typically modernist in its fashioning of its animated, 'pulsing' house in terms of emptiness, fragmentary memories, undisclosed secrets and psychic traces. Leaving a question mark over the gender of the dreamer and the identities of the 'ghostly couple' seeking 'buried treasure', it characteristically rejects the materialisation of the Victorian spectre, 'we hear no steps beside us; we see no lady spread her ghostly cloak' (Bradshaw 2008: 11). In a post-Freudian age, fascinated by what Woolf referred to as 'the dark places of psychology' (ibid. 11), ghosts were increasingly interpreted as hallucinations, or manifestations of psychic trauma. The flourishing of the Society for Psychical Research, established in 1882, fostered discussions about hallucinations, spiritualism, telepathy and communication with other realms, which remained a talking point well into the twentieth century.

In their discussion of Gothic modernisms, Andrew Smith and Jeff

Wallace contend that in modernist texts 'it is precisely in and through the confrontation with the idealised "new" that an effect of spectrality, of the Other which haunts progress and presence, is produced' (2001: 5). This chapter explores the strategies used by May Sinclair and E. Nesbit to confront the 'shock of the new' through spectralising suburban villas, motor cars, and scientific experimentation in their ghost stories. Often rewriting ghost-story conventions by employing liminal female narrators, such as servants, mediums and spinsters, these women writers explore gendered reactions to uncanny manifestations of modernity. Nesbit's fascination with technology and suburbia is in tension with the lure of the past as figured in the ancestral home; the desirability of motor cars and new houses without a history invites death and psychic disturbance, as well as eliding class distinctions. Going beyond well-worn psychoanalytic interpretations of Sinclair's work is revealing of the ways in which she deploys the dead wife narrative to comment on women's erotic desire, and exclusion within the domestic space. Her location of female experiences of adultery in a futuristic supernatural realm, where haunting may be mechanised, is a response to 'shocking' changes in female sexuality. Explaining the haunting of new houses in terms of concerns around suburbia, the dangers of female sexual liberation, technological advances, and scientific experimentation emphasises the alienation and dislocation shadowing modernist progress, and underlines the evolving ghost story's fascination with 'the interstices between past tradition and an imagined future' (Drewery 2011: 84).

Ghost Stories, Liminality and the Past

Recent accounts of both nineteenth- and twentieth-century ghost stories have emphasised the links between the ghostly, invisibility and liminality, part of a broader critical discussion which has established the short story's association with the marginalised. According to Andrew Smith, this liminality 'compromises models of a coherent, self-conscious and self-present, conception of identity ... the spectre thus makes visible the invisible contradictions that are represented as ghostly political possibilities which are silenced or made absent by the dominant culture' (Smith 2010: 2). Liminality has formal and thematic ramifications for modernist women's short fiction, expressing both generic possibilities and 'a range of threshold states ... [such as]: mourning, the literal or metaphorical journey, the uncanny, and the transient moment' (Drewery 3). If what is liminal lies outside our expectations of the coherent self, then the ghostly in short fiction not only represents what is taboo or marginalised in the dominant culture, but also underpins formal elements of the genre, such as disruptions of space and time. Women's uncanny stories, Wallace argues, 'use the Female Gothic to push at the boundaries of the traditional ghost story, and vice versa ... work[ing] on the ambiguous edge between the explained/unexplained supernatural' (2006: 58). Claire Drewery's claim that an embracing of liminality in short fiction can be used to 'negotiate its embodiment of an ominous threat of exclusion with a realm of creative and potentially subversive possibility' (13), is particularly pertinent to the relish for the unexplained supernatural in women's ghost stories, as the ambiguity of the endings, and the 'threshold states' occupied by liminal female narrators, can enable more liberating accounts of female social and sexual identity than in realist fiction.

Taxonomies of the modernist short story, with its brevity, fragmented nature and open-endedness (Richardson 2000: xlvi), have focused particularly on time and setting. If the experimental modernist short story 'capture[s] the episodic nature of twentieth-century experience', as Dominic Head has claimed (1992: 1–2), the disruptions in space and time in the ghost-story format exceed the usual conventions of an episode as an isolated moment. The settings of modernist short fiction, according to Drewery, are more likely to be 'in-between spaces' such as hotels and gardens, rather than family homes, or 'spaces ... occupied only on a transitory basis' such as railway carriages (3). A new interest in setting can be seen to coalesce with the modernist fixation on the transient moment: in her 1949 preface to *Encounters*, her first short story collection (1923), Elizabeth Bowen prioritises setting over character, claiming to have been inspired by 'susceptibility to places, particular moments, objects, and seasons of the year', singling out her admiration for 'the emptiness of an empty house' (Lee 1986: 122). Modernist ghost stories are sometimes devoid of dialogue, privileging the haunted house or the desolate landscape as a site of dislocation. Reinforcing the significance of time to the ghost story, Luke Thurston concurs, 'the moment of the ghost is thus presented ... as quintessentially non-empirical, a haunting interval excluded by definition from the ordinary temporal, representable ontology of worldly facts' (2012: 166). These haunting intervals are presented in an 'ironically disenchanted, "modern" style' (ibid. 1–2), evident in narrators' metafictional framing of ghost narratives with an appeal to 'sceptical modern rationalists' (ibid. 2).

The evolution of supernatural fiction and the characteristics of the 'spook of today' were addressed in the 1910s and 1920s, when the popularity of the ghost story was signalled by the appearance of the first anthologies. As editor of a series of such anthologies, Cynthia Asquith showcased the work of up-and-coming writers, like Clemence Dane, Mary Webb and Elizabeth Bowen, alongside more familiar names like D. H. Lawrence, Arthur Machen and Walter de la Mare. Asquith's *The Ghost Book: 16 New Stories of the Uncanny* (1926) flaunted its Freudian credentials by opening with May Sinclair's 'The Villa Désirée' and included Dane's story 'Spinsters' Rest', which attacked the repression of the maternal instinct by rewarding the modern over-worked spinster with a motherless child after a year's service to a fairy-tale old woman. Dorothy Scarborough's engaging introduction to *Famous Modern Ghost Stories* (1921) gestures both to the comic potential of 'the humorous ghost' and the terrors of scientifically based spectrality in the machine age: 'Whereas in the past a ghost had to stalk or glide to his haunts, now he limousines or airplanes ... in fact, his infernal efficiency and knowledge of science constitute the worst terror of the current specter' (10, 7). Tracking the differences between Gothic and modern ghosts in her full-length study *The Supernatural in Modern English Fiction* (1917), Scarborough focuses on the variety of modern, 'subjective ghosts', who might remain invisible or flaunt their corporeality and are just as likely to appear in broad daylight as in the small hours. Highlighting the shift in the supernatural narrative 'away from the physical towards the psychic' (Bleiler 2006: 125), she reinforces that the 'compressed' form of the short story, with its omissions and temporal disruptions, had the 'proper economy of thrills' (1917: 82) for narrativising the supernatural. In her review of this text, Woolf concurred that modern hauntings needed to be read in relation to the unknowability of the psyche, 'our sense of our own ghostliness has much quickened' (quoted in Drewery 82). The 'unspectral settings' frequented by modern ghosts, according to Scarborough, are not Gothic graveyards and the subterranean vaults of ancestral homes but 'the most prosaic places' (1917: 105) such as cheap lodging houses, hall bedrooms, and bungalows, or forms of public transport. Self-conscious references to the trappings of the traditional Victorian ghost story, indicative of the modernist trend for 'mock gothic' (Thurston 116), are often balanced against these disconcertingly unspectral settings, in order to figure the clash between old and new in an age of rapid modernisation.

The over-emphasis on the Freudian uncanny and the familiar/unfamiliar distinction in readings of the modernist ghost story has perhaps diverted our attention away from alternative readings of spectrality centred on issues around modernity, nostalgia and the shock of the new. The advent of World War I, new forms of housing, and the growth in mass communications and media, amidst fears around the mass destructiveness of modern technology, all impacted on conceptualisations of time, space and history, which could be reconfigured in the experimental short story form. Our re-readings of modernist culture through a discourse of spectrality (Smith 8) need to acknowledge the significance of history and memory in a transitional age; the ghost story, in particular, could jump between time periods and distort memories in order to trouble the boundary between past and future. Vernon Lee, whose supernatural collection *Hauntings* (1890) looked back with longing to Renaissance art and the decadence of eighteenth-century Italy, was one of the first to articulate the necessity of locating the modernity/history anxiety in the ghost-story form, famously proclaiming in her 1889 preface that a modern audience should take its ghosts 'from the more or less remote Past' (Maxwell and Pulham 2006: 39). Lee's 1897 essay, 'In the praise of old houses' explained the 'rapture' of the past in terms of both its deceits and its imaginative possibilities, 'the past is the unreal and the yet visible'. The old house, and its history, is endlessly charming in its unreality, as opposed to the emptiness of the future, 'filled only with the cast shadows of ourselves and our various machineries' (Madden 2006). The loss of history equated with the modern is at odds with the lure of the past: Elizabeth Bowen's self-confessed 'infatuation' with the new villas, 'unhistorical gimcrack little bubbles of illusion', she felt to be irreconcilable with her 'history-fed passion for the mighty, immortal and grandiose' (Lee 1986: 280).

The strangely unhistorical nature of the new house, often contrasted with the grandiosity of the ancestral mansion, underpins the ways in which modernist short fiction mediates questions of territory, memory and alienation. In Nesbit's 'The House of Silence' (*Windsor's Magazine*, 1906), an escaping thief, hiding in a deserted, old house, with its mouldering tapestries and empty rooms, goes through a portal into a previous time zone, into 'some other house' (227) richly furnished with 'the spoils which long centuries had yielded to the grasp of a noble family' (228). His 'rapture in the strange, sudden revelation of this concentrated splendour' (ibid.) is punished when he, 'like a rat in a trap' (230), cannot find his way out of a damp, vaulted passage with his stolen treasure. In an essay on memory and the illusions of the past, Bowen writes of the 'disturbing appeal' of the '"near" past', 'just over the frontier of living memory' (Lee 1986: 57), and the temptations of nostalgia in an age of mechanical reproduction, 'the aching, bald uniformity of our urban surroundings' (59). Reflecting the post-war culture of enforced domesticity, her uncanny stories, such as 'The New House', 'Coming Home', 'The Last Night in the Old Home' and 'Attractive Modern Homes', rework the Victorian trope of the home as site of Gothic terror by rendering the clash between old and new uncanny. The 'other life' offered by the haunted house 'with its mnemic archive', according to Thurston (167), can compensate for the alienation, restless dissatisfaction and triviality endured by the modernist protagonist, yet new houses sometimes produce alienation, either because memories link to hysteria or sometimes because their lack of memories renders them uncanny, unreal. Decaying town houses fallen into disrepair and new suburban environments with their 'unearthly' electric light and 'air of pasteboard unreality' (53) in Bowen's stories 'offer refuge from nothingness', argues Maud Ellmann, but 'often turn out to be mausoleums' (2003: 12). Attractive modern homes display gadgetry, bric-a-brac and stylish furniture, but are also often mouldy, damp and visually unsettling. In 'The New House' in *Encounters* (1923) parvenu Herbert and his sister have triumphantly moved into an old country house, where 'every echo from the tiles and naked boards derided and denied the memory of that small brick villa ... where their mother's wedded life had begun and ended; that villa now empty and denuded, whose furniture looked so meagre in this spaciousness and height' (55). The movement from a new house to an old, candle-lit one is, however, 'disordered' and disorientating. The flickering candle flames give Herbert 'the creeps, this groping through an echoing, deserted house with a ghost-ridden, lackadaisical woman', with a 'suspicion that the house was sneering at him' (56). The spoils of the unreal past cannot be so easily appropriated for a modern age. Looking nostalgically over the threshold into another time, or crossing portals into other time zones, were distinctive features of modernist women's ghost stories, which betrayed an uneasiness that urbanisation, technological advances and new houses had not diminished women's feelings of alienation and marginality.

Science, Motors and Machinery in the Stories of E. Nesbit

After publishing her first supernatural collection *Grim Tales* (1893), Edith Nesbit contributed ghost stories and poems to publications such as *The Yellow Book*, *Windsor Magazine* and the *Saturday Evening Post,* as well as to the new illustrated, fashionable magazines established in the 1890s such as *Black and White* and *The Strand*. Her later collection *Fear* (1909) has been virtually ignored by critics, perhaps because of its uses of humour and its mock-Gothic capitalisation on sensationalist subjects such as drug abuse, scientific experimentation and advertising. In Nesbit's stories 'delicious' ghostly happenings are often narrated to entertain disbelieving groups of frivolous guests at country houses or transient inhabitants of hotels, in order to confront the uncertainty of their social positions, or the fragility of their masculinities. In the darkly comic 'No 17' (1910), the commercial-traveller narrator is only saved from slitting his throat like the previous occupants of hotel room number 17, terrified by a vision of a ghost in the mirror while shaving, because he is using one of the new safety razors. Telling ghost stories and accepting a dare to sleep in the supposedly haunted pavilion ends badly for an eligible bachelor tricked by his friend and strangled by a man-eating creeper in 'The Pavilion' (1915). The plain, 'overlooked' Amelia who foresaw the danger is then left without a husband, as her struggle to prevent the death by entering the pavilion late at night is gossiped about as a fateful 'indiscretion', 'the sort of thing that stamps a girl' (99). Nesbit's liminal female narrators are usually more receptive to, if damaged by, the uncanny. Comparatively, the men openly scoff at, but later suffer more from, unexplained ghostly encounters, their feminised hysteria or mysterious deaths puncturing their bravado.

Signalling her engagement with the interface between the supernatural and modernity, Nesbit's *Strand* stories are positioned alongside articles on polar expeditions, technology and science, as well as coloured art deco-inspired fashion plates. Her story 'The Haunted House' (1910) appeared after an illustrated article on 'Motor-Cars: Yesterday and To-day'. *Strand* stories were often accompanied with rather lurid sensationalist illustrations of characters cowering in terror, or shrieking at the discovery of dead bodies; Graham Simmons' illustrations for 'The Haunted House' show a gagged character staring at a 'horrible' white-shrouded form rising from a coffin, though typically this is not a ghost at all but only the servant dressed up in order to rescue the engineer Desmond from an evil scientist. The advertised request to have 'phenomena investigated' at a 'Haunted House' is then a cover-up for some sinister transfusions, rather like those ordered by the female vampire fearful of ageing in Mary Elizabeth Braddon's *Strand* story, 'Good Lady Ducayne' (1896). The violence of the self-confessed vampire owner of 'The Haunted House', who drugs his visitors and servants in order to transfuse their blood for his own experiments in immortality, is less supernatural than a product of the thirst for scientific discovery and class superiority. 'The Three Drugs' is a futuristic tale of a mad Frankenstein-like figure who believes he has found the secrets of immortality by experimenting on hapless young men lured into his deathly house, through a door left ajar in a deserted street. The narrator Roger recoils from the knowledge that the horrible smell in 'the room of death' next to his is that of the embalmed bodies of those who have died under the doctor's experiments. The desire for scientific breakthrough evident in the doctor's menacing boasts that he will create 'the superman', 'splendid superhuman life' (53) with his three drugs, reveal the haunted house to be a disguised laboratory controlled by vampiric scientists, rather than the traditional ancestral home troubled by revenants from past generations, developing the ghost story's horrified fascination with the future of science.[1]

The perils of public transport, explored in nineteenth-century stories in the form of railway accidents, or phantom coaches, acquire a modernist edge through an examination of the spectrality of machinery. A chilling indictment of contemporary advances in the technology of transport, 'The Violet Car' from the 1909 collection *Fear* shows a couple haunted by the phantom of a 'mysteriously horrible motor' (73), which killed their young daughter, with the scene of haunting shifted to the quiet country roads which surround a neglected farm. Noiseless and empty, the driverless car, with its polluting smell, appears to be a hallucination, 'an imaginary motor', until it is seen in the final paragraphs by the disbelieving nurse narrator, who, like the deranged father, crushes herself into the hedge, 'as I should have done to leave room for the passage of a real car' (74). The 'hidden horror' (73) of the violet car is not that it is 'splashed with [the] daughter's blood' (72) as the nurse imagines, but its speed and its silence. Later in the story, when the father is knocked down by the car, 'there is no mark on him, no blood', as well as 'no tyre marks' (74), a contrast to the hit-and-run victims and roads marked by 'real motors' which also haunt the story. In modernist fiction, argues Andrew Thacker, 'the speeding motion of the motorcar offers a significant image for comprehending the connections between the new spaces and spatial experiences of modernity' (Thacker 2003: 62), at a time when motor car accidents were perceived as 'disruptions ... to established patterns of life', feeding 'anxieties about the changing composition of the English class structure' (ibid. 64–6). The phantom car, with its 'motor-devil' (72) driver carelessly indifferent to the next generation, signals the threat of nouveau riche families pushing out the unprotected inhabitants of 'unprosperous' farms like the Eldridges', with its 'solid mid-Victorian comfort' (66). The real car owned by the driver's widow, in which the nurse gratefully rides from the station, is almost alive, 'it moved like magic – or like the dream of a train' (64), 'pulsating, as though it were out of breath' (65), with its bright lights obscuring the countryside it threatens. The 'homely' father's excessive fear set against the modern nurse's unwilling admiration for motoring, despite its horrors, registers an ambivalence over modernity, and the shock of the new. The 'novelty' of motoring, with its modern 'whirring of machinery' (ibid.), is both glamorous and fatal, the empty, phantom car anticipating a dystopian future when fearful machines may be out of the control of their owners.

Nesbit's 'The Shadow', about something which 'wasn't exactly a ghost' (173), is explicitly directed at those bored with traditional stories of phantom coaches and horribly strange beds, though its metafictionality is deployed to complicate, rather than mock, issues of class and sexual rivalry. First appearing in the fashionable, avant-garde journal *Black and White* in 1905, its title echoes Braddon's story, 'The Shadow in the Corner' (1871) about a wronged servant whose suicidal body haunts her master's house, and draws on Braddon's depiction of the Victorian servant as automaton. Narrated to a group of young women by a usually silent, older housekeeper, a 'model of decorum and decently done duties' (170), it is framed by the words of the niece staying in her aunt's 'big country house'. Margaret Eastwich's story of her friend Mabel's death, which she tells to 'pay' for the cocoa she is sharing as a 'guest' in the girls' bedroom after a Christmas dance, questions the invisibility of servants. It prompts the female narrator to admire this 'new voice' of a woman she had previously dismissed and feared; the housekeeper's silence 'had taught us to treat her as a machine; and as other than a machine we never dreamed of treating her' (170). The malevolent shadow which kills Mabel, who is newly married to a man Margaret had loved herself, is glimpsed on the stairs and in dark passages and corridors, and, more unnervingly, at any hour of the day and night. Visible in the in-between spaces occupied by domestic staff and, in one scene, as Margaret heats milk for the pregnant Mabel after the servants have retired, the 'something about the house, that one could just not hear and not see' (176) vindicates the steps of the 'comforting' but liminal servants who silently bolster class privilege. It may also figure the 'curse' of the predatory, sexual rival: when Margaret turns round, it 'drooped and melted into my shadow' (174), and her ominous position on the threshold of Mabel's room after her daughter is born prefigures her friend's death. Her comment about the second wife's mourning of the husband's death, 'something black crouched then between him and me' (177), also signals her misplaced, secret desire.

The shadow is also produced by the unsettling newness of the nervous couple's 'gloomy' house in the London suburbs:

> there were streets and streets of new villa-houses growing up round old brick mansions standing in their own grounds . . . I imagined my cab going through a dark, winding shrubbery, and drawing up in front of one of these sedate, old, square houses. Instead, we drew up in front of a large, smart villa, with iron railings, gay encaustic tiles leading from the iron gate to the

stained-glass-panelled door and for shrubbery only a few stunted cypresses and aucubas in the tiny front garden. (172–3)

When Margaret pronounces the house 'homelike – only a little too new' (173), the unnamed husband replies, 'We're the first people who've ever lived in it. If it were an old house ... I should think it was haunted' (ibid.). The 'too new' house without a past, lit by modern gaslights, becomes uncanny. Even though 'the gas was full on in the kitchen', the husband agrees 'all the horror of the house' (175) comes out of the open cupboard at the end of a dark corridor, used to store empty boxes, as if the dazzling light of modernity cannot blot out the darkness and emptiness which shadows it, 'the future ... seemed then so much brighter than the past' (176). In modernist fiction, moving house, often compulsively, emphasises 'how modernity disrupts a stable sense of place' (Thacker 55), linking to concerns about shifting class identities, the rural/urban divide and the cultural ramifications of the new suburbs. Scarborough linked the modern revenant's appropriation of space to changes in modern housing:

> the spirit that haunts a locality rather than one room or house has a more malignant power than the more restricted ghost and this adds a new element of supernaturalism to modern fiction. But as houses are so much less permanent now than formerly, ghosts would be at a terrible disadvantage if they had to be evicted every time a building was torn down. (1917: 106)

This lack of permanence in the haunted house, and the rise of purpose-built forms of housing raise questions about history, community and identity, which are figured through the clash between old and new architectural styles. The new house as a space resonating death recalls Nesbit's earlier story 'The Mystery of the Semi-Detached', in which the male narrator foresees the gruesome murder of a young woman in the bedroom of the 'desirable' semi-detached residence his fiancée's family intend to purchase. The over-emphasised 'desirability' of new properties not only conceals but also invites an unexplained violence, which may signify the dangers lurking beneath the glossy, suburban facade.

Positioned on the threshold between visibility and invisibility, like the vampire who can only wreak evil after being invited in, the shadowy servant seems to hold the key to understanding 'The Shadow', as the violence of the past infects the present of the listening girls. The death of Mabel's daughter, the weakest of the group of girls who has fainted after the dancing, occurs after the shadow seen (or produced?) by the distraught Margaret approaches her sleeping form. Ostensibly explained in terms of heart disease inherited from the mother, the niece's conclusion that Mabel's daughter may have 'inherited something from her father' (178), referring to the dead woman's look of fear, may suggest that it is the husband's malevolence, or his fear of his jilted lover, which constitutes the 'unseen' explanation. The husband's words to the wronged Margaret, as he welcomes her across the threshold, 'forgive the past' (173) refer to a possible jilting, but also to a dangerous denial of what has come before (the metafictional response of one of the listening girls, 'What past?' shows a flippant disregard of the class oppressions which haunt modernist progress). The alignment of the potentially sinister housekeeper narrator with movements into new houses, (she offers to 'superintend the moving of . . . furniture into the new house already chosen' [176] while Mabel recuperates, and is embraced in the 'new home' of the youngest listening girl) shows her forward-looking liminality, though she may also have been the one to bring the secrets of the past across the threshold. Like the nurse narrator of 'The Violet Car', and the giggling girls listening to the story, the servant seems to be both admiring and fearful of the new. Nesbit's knowing manipulation of the unexplained supernatural, signalled by the disclaimer that it is 'not an artistically rounded off ghost story' (169), leaves the reader guessing as to whose repressed memories have activated the hauntings which continue to threaten the descendants of the big country house.

May Sinclair, Dead Wives and Women's Uncanny Gifts

As a member of the Society for Psychical Research and closely involved with the development of psychoanalysis in Britain, May Sinclair was well placed to contribute to debates about psychology and the uncanny. Beginning to publish stories in the 1890s, her collections of supernatural tales *Uncanny Stories* (1923) and *The Intercessor and Other Tales* (1931) reflect her growing interest in mysticism, hallucinations, spiritualism and telepathy; reprinting narratives which were first placed in avant-garde, little magazines such as the *English Review* and *Criterion*, edited by T. S. Eliot. 'The Intercessor' (1911), with its self-conscious reworking of 'the child-ghost clamouring for entry' to an isolated moorland farmhouse (Drewery 73) in *Wuthering Heights*, has been much discussed in terms of its treatment of motherhood, possession and trauma. Rejecting the Gothic emphasis on history, Sinclair's stories sometimes border on science fiction, a developing genre from the *fin de siècle*, with their imaginings of a dystopian future or a terrifying afterlife. The disconcerting temporal disruptions of the story 'Where Their Fire is not

Quenched' figure the nightmarish scenario of a compulsive mistress, unable to escape from an affair grown stale, who must repeat her tawdry assignations after death. Despite acquiring 'a reputation for sanctity' built on her repression of the scenes of her transgression, 'Schnebler's and the Hotel Saint Pierre ceased to figure among prominent images of her past' (35), Harriet is doomed to go back through a portal into the 'ash-grey', 'degrading' hotel corridors. The idea of memory is tampered with as the disorientated Harriet loses all sense of time, 'the future may affect the past' (44). The chilling final scene shows the denial of her attempted retreat to the safety of childhood, a place 'without memory' (45), as she is forced back into the persona of mistress, negating the possibilities of repression.

The Jamesian story 'The Flaw in the Crystal' explores the psychic, healing powers of the witch-like Agatha Verrall and her 'extraordinary, intangible, immaterial tie' (59) with two married men, Rodney Lanyon and the 'incurable' Harding Powell, both of whom are in thrall to, and threatened by, her 'power, the uncanny, unaccountable Gift' (60). This telepathic gift, according to Thurston, 'saves her from the sordid realities of ordinary sexual relations', yet leaves her 'vulnerable to psychical invasion' (2012: 103). While Rodney's Friday visits to Agatha's remote village are an 'escape' from his nervous wife, their 'increased and undisturbed communion, made possible by her retirement to Sarratt End' (63) fixes her as a kept woman, who by telling her friend Milly of her 'secret' commits an 'unspeakable discretion' (64). Like many of Sinclair's other *Uncanny Stories*, 'The Flaw in the Crystal' uses the ghost-story format to examine the unspeakability of adultery, a less shocking secret than in the Victorian age, but still a risk for women, whatever their 'immeasurable, inexhaustible' (73) powers. The gift of curing Rodney, 'mak[ing] him do things' (61) can only be maintained by keeping herself 'clean from the desire that he should come; clean, above all, from the thought, the knowledge she now had, that she could make him come' (60). But if restraint is the 'secret and the essence of her gift' (ibid.), it is a restraint which she cannot maintain, as her longing for Rodney's 'invisible, bodily presence' (82), and her more complicated desire to cure Harding of his insanity and insomnia, work against the purity needed for her powers. Stranded on the 'borderland' between safety and danger, Sinclair's characters, like Milly whose features are 'worn fine by watchings and listening on the border, on the threshold' (67) and her husband trapped behind the drawn blinds, from where he drains Agatha's strength, chafe against their liminality. Pushing men and their wives back over the border between sanity and insanity serves to tip Agatha over 'the verge', transforming her telepathy into a kind of possession: 'Harding's insanity had leaked through to her' (98), forcing her to see the world through the eyes of 'a soul that denied the supernatural' (95). An understanding of the uncanny in terms of technology, as Thurston notes (105–6), marks the evolution of the form into the modern ghost story – Milly becomes 'a fanatical believer in the Power . . . she would, if she could, have stuck her fingers into what she called the machinery of the thing' (81) – but it is a machinery which makes amends for women's dependence on men. If this story 'constantly privileges the psychic over the physical', as Seed suggests (2001: 55), then Rodney's 'submission' in their final encounter allows Agatha to regain control in the psychic realm, denying the physical desire which interferes with the 'flawless' purity of women's uncanny gifts.

Refusing the perspective of male rationality conventional to the ghost story, Sinclair's narrators are often female outsiders such as spinsters and mistresses, who validate their own oddity or power through their uncanny capacity to see, hear or feel what others cannot. Bleiler's claim that her stories ultimately advocate a rejection of 'inappropriate love' (134) does not take account of her leanings towards greater sexual liberation for women. 'Nowadays even the spectral women are setting up to be feminists', observed Scarborough, 'and have privileges that would have caused the Gothic wraiths to swoon with horror' (1917: 104). In 'The Token', Helen Dunbar, with her 'uncanny gift' (51) tells the story of her beloved sister-in-law Cecily haunting her husband's library, a room he had ordered her out of during her terminal illness as it had hindered him in his work. In Donald's eyes, his wife has less value than a precious paperweight, nicknamed the Token, given to him by George Meredith; his immersion in his work means that he has to be haunted by a phantasm ostensibly seeking the 'certainty' of his love, but also as a reminder of the dangers of repressing, or failing to recognise, erotic desire. The haunting allows the spectral woman to occupy a space from which she was excluded, not as a form of vengeance but more to correct his refusal to remember and his degeneration into a morose 'creature of habit and routine' (50). What Julian Wolfreys has called 'the hauntological disturbance' (2002: 3) takes the form of a 'perfect and vivid' phantasm, appearing like 'flesh and blood' (51), who occupies 'her chair', having the modern capacity to go out 'like a light you switch off', like a supernatural form of electricity (evoking the over-determined choice between candles or electricity/gas light in the modern haunted house). Although Donald might try to 'shake off the oppression of the memory' (53) of his dead wife, to confine her to the realm of unspeakability, Helen is required to intercede for her: the spirit's 'desperate searching' (55) for the lost paperweight, and Helen's unlocking of the drawer where it was hidden and putting it in her brother's hand are their demands for a token of his unexpressed love. Smith reads Donald's smashing of the token as the breaking of a male 'attachment to material realities' in the 'evidence' offered of a 'benign spiritual domain' (2010: 88), though this does not pay enough attention to the relations between women in the story. The fact that Helen as intercessor can see the 'distressed' ghost is testimony to her own repressed desire for her 'darling', a desire which can only be expressed on the borderland between life and death. The ghost could be interpreted as 'subjective', a projection of Helen's repressed desire, dismissed by her brother as her 'hysterical fancy' (51) – in the final scene, she thinks, 'I couldn't see the phantasm now, but I could feel it, close, close, vibrating, palpitating, as I drove him' (56), as if it is an element of her own anger. The presence of the good housekeeper Helen in the library, sewing while her brother works, may highlight the inadequate domesticity of her sister-in-law, implying that the hidden desire is an incestuous one: the spinster sister, relishing 'her place' (51), happily replaces the exorcised dead wife in her brother's affections. The lack of resolution of Sinclair's stories, despite her 'forward looking' ghosts, may be a typically modernist retreat from history, as Smith attests (2010: 92), but it also crucially draws attention to these marginalised spectral women, whose outsider status is challenged by using their uncanny gifts to ensure male submission.

Sinclair's story collections provide more variations on the enduringly popular dead wife narrative, where the jealous ghost's interference to prevent a second marriage or 'to make life wretched for the interloper', according to Scarborough, was a potent way of representing 'the embodied evil of the past' (1917: 117, 108). When the 'lascivious' interloper Pauline, already once divorced, tries to replace her 'innocent' predecessor Rosamund in 'The Nature of the Evidence', the ghost of Marston's dead wife bars the door to the bedroom and stops him from kissing Pauline in the patriarchal library, where, unlike Cecily in 'The Token', Rosamund had had 'her place', sitting with him, 'keeping quiet in a corner with a book' (115). In the 'exquisitely furnished' Gothic bedroom, with its 'seventeenth-century walnut wood' and purple counterpane (116), Marston is unable to consummate the marriage, because the phantasm occupies 'his place' in the bed, smacking Pauline's face with her long rope of hair. Both women's bodies become conduits for the uncanny; Pauline puts her hands on 'a woman's body, soft and horrible; her fingers had sunk into the shallow breasts' (119), while the vision of her own nakedness beneath a transparent nightgown strikes her husband as 'the uncanny and unnatural thing' (120); his second wife writhes on the floor, 'like a worm, like a beast' (121). Marston's disgust that such a creature is taking 'advantage of her embodied state to beat down the heavenly, discarnate thing' (ibid.), before he follows the phantasm to the library for some bodiless communion, figures Sinclair's preoccupation with the 'evidence' about phantasms and hallucinatory desire (an earlier story of Nesbit's 'From the Dead' (1893) ends with the husband both terrified and aroused by the vision of his beloved dead wife in her grave-clothes approaching his bed). Women's struggle to establish their places in the male domain of the library, where their sexuality seems more acceptable than in the Gothic bedroom, shows how the haunting of specific rooms can be mapped onto clashes over territory and the gendering of domestic space.

'The Villa Désirée', which subverts this subgenre by substituting a grotesque phantasm of the new husband for the dead wife, ostensibly presents the Gothic bedroom as male territory, yet allows for a female challenge to male brutality. Anticipating Angela Carter's dark rewriting of Bluebeard in 'The Bloody Chamber' (1979), the dashingly romantic fiancé Louis who kisses Mildred's feet, showers her with roses and plans for her to wait for him in his Mediterranean villa is actually a brutal fiend, an embodiment of 'beastliness' who makes his first wife die of fright on their honeymoon. The villa on its topmost terrace above the olive trees seems like a dream of modern Continental luxury, but inside it is 'fragile and worn, all faded gray and old greenish gilt' with a 'faint powdery smell from the old floor', 'a little queer and – unlived in' (78). Recalling Ella D'Arcy's chilling *Yellow Book* story 'The Villa Lucienne' (1896), in which the 'incommunicable thrill' (Dalby 1992: 301) of entering an 'eerie, uncanny' (307) villa on the Riviera becomes a confrontation with an uncertain past, 'so vague, so remote' (308), for a group of female tourists, the clash between old and new in descriptions of the haunted house is a warning sign that its undisclosed history will threaten female autonomy and class privilege. D'Arcy's tourists, who retreat in panic, are denied access to parts of the estate by the servants, in the same way that they are denied access to what happened to the ghostly inhabitants glimpsed by an accompanying child. In Sinclair's villa of desire, the 'beastly' bedroom where the first wife died is 'like a great white tank filled with blond water' where the 'high, rather frightening' bed and white furniture seem to be 'quivering in the stillness, with the hot throb, throb of the light' (77). Her friend Martha's unexpected look of shame that Louis might contemplate sharing the bedroom before their marriage is used to align Mildred with modernity: 'She could understand her friend's fear of haunted houses, but not these provisions of impropriety' (80). However, her airy dismissal of the supernatural, 'her poor little ghost won't hurt me' (81) rings hollow when the ghost which threatens her in the bedroom is not that of the dead wife but of a monstrous Louis with its 'loathsome shapelessness' (84), its breasts and phallic brutality. Wallace has linked this troubling gender ambiguity to the uncanniness of the male genitals, which 'deny/erase female selfhood' (2004: 63), yet the 'something that gave up the secret of the room and made it frightful and obscene' (84) can also be read as the complacency of the male belief that the bedroom is his domain. The ending of the story, with Louis unable to wait to exert his rights over his fiancé, may seem to leave Mildred trapped by male desire, but it also hints at the interloper's possible triumph over her dead rival. It anticipates Bowen's *Encounters* story 'The Shadowy Third', in which the frightened, pregnant wife is oppressed by her new marital home, her actions superimposed on those of the unnamed dead wife, 'Her', who like the dead, perfect hostess in Daphne du Maurier's *Rebecca* (1938), mocks her from the shadows. Haunted villas in these stories are places where giving into female desire may invite the secret obscenity of male sexual control and the difficulties of exorcising the secrets of the past, or the 'shadowy third' of the sexual rival, expose the dangers of modern living, the decay behind the facade.

Disrupted temporal sequences, ghosts who never materialise, unspectral settings, and a troubled disjunction between past and future all characterise uncanny modernist short fiction by women, showing how notions of apparitionality have shifted from the Victorian period to reflect anxieties about modernity, suburbia and the frontiers of memory. Combining 'a conventional repertoire of gothic stylistic devices . . . with an arch, self-consciously "modern" irony' (Thurston 2), Nesbit's metafictional ghost narratives were particularly appealing to sceptical modern readers, their spectralising of technology and science signifying the 'hauntological disturbance' generated by the machine age and a tendency within modernism to fetishise the 'rapture' of the past. While both writers explore the female narrator's fears of the unsettlingly new villa with its unexplained history of violence, it is Sinclair who locates women's psychic terrors in male-dominated rooms such as the library and the bedroom, developing the dead wife narrative to figure female alienation in male territory. As David Punter argues, 'there will never be a moment when the "robust frame" of the new house, the house of the new, will be free from the impress of the ghosts of the past' (2001: 16). For Sinclair, however, the 'house of the new' may be haunted by outdated gender conventions and undisclosed secrets, but these remain in uneasy tension with the power achieved by women through their uncanny gifts, and the delineation of 'shocking' female sexualities enabled by the unexplained supernatural.

Note

1. Nesbit's ghost fiction in *The Strand* tended to be published under her married name of E. Bland, perhaps with the intention of signalling the Fabian allegiances associated with her husband's name, or distancing herself from the persona of children's author, though in other periodicals she signed her ghost stories as E. Nesbit.

Works Cited

Asquith, Cynthia (1926), *The Ghost Book: 16 New Stories of the Uncanny*, London: Hutchinson.
Bleiler, Richard (2006), 'May Sinclair's Supernatural Fiction', *May Sinclair: Moving Towards the Modern,* ed. Andrew Kunka and Michele K. Troy, Aldershot: Ashgate.
Bowen, Elizabeth (1983), *The Collected Stories of Elizabeth Bowen*, introduced by Angus Wilson, Harmondsworth: Penguin.
D'Arcy, Ella (1992), 'The Villa Lucienne', *The Virago Book of Victorian Ghost Stories,* ed. Richard Dalby, London: Virago, pp. 301–8.
Drewery, Claire (2011), *Modernist Short Fiction by Women: The Liminal in Katherine Mansfield, Dorothy Richardson, May Sinclair and Virginia Woolf*, Aldershot: Ashgate.
Ellmann, Maud (2003), *Elizabeth Bowen: The Shadow across the Page*, Edinburgh: Edinburgh University Press.
Head, Dominic (1992), *The Modernist Short Story*, Cambridge: Cambridge University Press.
Lee, Hermione (ed.) (1986), *The Mulberry Tree: Writings of Elizabeth Bowen*, London: Virago.
Lee, Vernon (2006), *Hauntings and other Fantastic Tales,* ed. Catherine Maxwell and Patricia Pulham, Peterborough, Ontario: Broadview.
Lee, Vernon (2006), 'In the praise of old houses' [1897], *Quotidiana,* ed. Patrick Madden. 27 October 2006. <http://essays.quotidiana.org/lee/praise_of_old_houses> [Last accessed 21 January 2015.]
Nesbit, E. (2006), *The Power of Darkness: Tales of Terror,* ed. David Stuart Davies, Ware: Wordsworth.
Punter, David (2000), 'Hungry Ghosts and Foreign Bodies', in Andrew Smith and Jeff Wallace (eds) (2001), *Gothic Modernisms,* Basingstoke: Palgrave, pp. 11–28.
Scarborough, Dorothy (1921), introduction to *Famous Modern Ghost Stories*, New York and London: Knickerbocker Press.
Scarborough, Dorothy (1917), *The Supernatural in Modern English Fiction*, New York and London: Knickerbocker Press.
Seed, David (2001), '"Psychical Cases": Transformations of the Supernatural in Virginia Woolf and May Sinclair' in Andrew Smith and Jeff Wallace (eds), *Gothic Modernisms*, Basingstoke: Palgrave, pp. 44–61.
Sinclair, May (2006), *Uncanny Stories*, ed. Paul March-Russell, Ware: Wordsworth.

Sinclair, May (1996), 'The Villa Désirée' in Richard Glyn Jones and A. Susan Williams (eds), *The Penguin Book of Erotic Stories by Women*, Harmondsworth: Penguin.
Smith, Andrew (2010), *The Ghost Story, 1850–1940*, Manchester: Manchester University Press.
Smith, Andrew and Jeff Wallace (eds) (2001), *Gothic Modernisms*, Basingstoke: Palgrave.
Thacker, Andrew (2003), *Moving Through Modernity: Space and Geography in Modernism*, Manchester: Manchester University Press.
Thurston, Luke (2012), *Literary Ghosts, From the Victorian to Modernism: The Haunting Interval*, London: Routledge.
Wallace, Diana (2013), *Female Gothic Histories: Gender, History and the Gothic*, Cardiff: University of Wales Press.
Wallace, Diana (2004), 'Uncanny Stories: The Ghost Story as Female Gothic', *Gothic Studies* 6:1, 57–68.
Wolfreys, Julian (2002), *Victorian Hauntings: Spectrality, Gothic, the Uncanny and Literature*, Basingstoke: Palgrave.
Woolf, Virginia (2001), *The Mark on the Wall and Other Short Fiction*, ed. David Bradshaw, Oxford: Oxford University Press.
Woolf, Virginia (2008), 'Modern Fiction' [1919], *Selected Essays*, ed. David Bradshaw, Oxford: Oxford University Press, pp. 6–12.

Chapter 4

Potboilers or 'Glimpses' of Reality? The Cultural and the Material in the Modernist Short Story
Rebecca Bowler

In a letter to Elizabeth Bowen in 1946, Spencer Curtis Brown writes that he is 'very much opposed' to Bowen's current practice of writing essays and short stories: 'Your standing with the public depends ultimately on your books, and the dispersal of time of small committments [sic] is I think, not only uneconomical financially, but a bad policy for you as a writer' (Hepburn 2008: 5). The concerns raised in this letter are typical of the period. Despite, or perhaps because of the rise of the 'little magazine', short stories were viewed as a popular and ephemeral product. It was the novels that a writer produced that would create and sustain their reputation and their standing in the literary marketplace. Curtis Brown also, in this letter, denies the advantages of short story publication: time and money. Dorothy Richardson, Katherine Mansfield and May Sinclair all struggled with a lack of time and money, and could not help internalising and struggling with the kind of views expressed by Curtis Brown above. Was the writing of short stories a profitable way of spending time? Would it bring in money? Would it help to develop the writer's craft, and would it enhance the writer's reputation? Ford Madox Ford, writing in 1911, admitted to a certain preoccupation with his literary reputation. Upon a close examination of his motives, he admits that he is 'writing all the while for posterity':

> In the old days there was a thing that was called a pot-boiler. This was an occasional piece of inferior work which you produced in order to keep yourself from starvation, whilst you meditated higher and quite unprofitable flights. Your mind was set upon immortality and from posterity you hoped to receive the ultimate crown. (191)

Dorothy Richardson uses the term 'pot-boiler' to refer to the 'translations & oddments' that she produced in order to keep herself and her husband from financial dire straits (Letter to Powys, 24 June 1934).

Her long novel *Pilgrimage*, for which she is now remembered, was the epitome of the 'higher and quite unprofitable' artistic and intellectual lifework. She made very little on each individual 'chapter-volume' of *Pilgrimage*, and her artist husband, Alan Odle, found it increasingly difficult to obtain commissions for his Beardsley-esque illustrations: certainly rarely 'enough to boil his side of the pot' for very long (Letter to P. B. Wadsworth, 25 July 1927).

On some levels, Richardson is using the term 'pot-boiler' in the same way as Ford: the need to continually produce potboilers does mean that she struggles to make time for her 'own work'. On the other hand, the 'pot-boiler' can buy time for that work.[1] However, Richardson also has an eye on her literary and intellectual reputation, far too much so to allow anything she thought was 'inferior' into general circulation. Most of her potboilers were large projects, such as book-length translations of French and German texts. They took a lot of time, and she was very exacting with them. When George G. Harrap, who published her translation of Karl von Schumacher's *The Du Barry* (1932), sent her a corrected set of proofs with all the historical present cut out, she was 'furious'. She writes at length about the incident to Bryher: 'Then, if you please, Harrap's reader had "improved" my text in some sixty places where he considered its meaning needed sharpening & simplifying ... Can you imagine my wrath? I rang Harrap up & withdrew my signature' (20 October 1931).[2] Richardson will not have anything of dubious quality attributed to her. She is far too careful about her reputation.

Richardson's articles, short stories and sketches were also written as much to establish her reputation as a serious writer as to make money. She has a kind of scorn for the type of writer that churns out short stories *just* to make money, but also a certain awe, as this is something that she herself cannot do. She writes to P. B. Wadsworth, in 1930:

> I would like to know, if indeed it is possible to know, what is the reaction upon the author ... of perpetually turning out the pattern magazine story. I meet a number of these in my brother-in-law's Argosy & am horrified, fascinated, by their perfection [*sic*]. In style, arrangement, informativeness, psychological accuracy, they are vastly superior to the genuine work of the live goodish to good short-story writer. Yet dead. Yet an immense commercial success: because, as is the case with machine-made versus real lace, only the expert can tell the difference. (23 September 1930)

Richardson is struggling here to explain her admiration for the kind of art she feels she should not admire. The 'pattern magazine story' is beautifully structured, and contains all sorts of truths of the factual and psychological kind, but are they as good as real literature? Are they, in fact, better? She does not seem to have come to a conclusion. On the one hand, they are 'vastly superior' to literary short stories, but on the other, they are not 'genuine', not alive.[3]

Richardson's early sketches for the *Saturday Review* were written, not as pattern pieces, but as experiments in putting life on the page. Miriam in *Pilgrimage* also writes these sketches, and in the fictionalised version, Richardson explains some of the difficulties she faced. The magazine's editor (in *Pilgrimage* this is *The Friday Review*), Mr Godge, 'warns me that there is not a living to be made from sketches like *Auction* "because they take too much thought." What does he mean by thought? Imagination? Not in the sense of *making up*' (*IV*: 613). Miriam's *Auction*, and Richardson's 'A Sussex Auction', are not made up: they are an attempt to transpose life onto the page.

Richardson, despite naming the piece 'A Sussex Auction', is not interested in the auction itself: she is interested in the background, the scenery, the bystanders, and the overall beauty of the scene:

> The passage of the clouds across the wide sky, the pageant of the afternoon-light, the flight of birds over the rolling meadow-land, the kindly grey downs in the distance are all unnoticed. Except perhaps by the girls who hover round the margin of the moving group. But they, too, are in bondage. Even those among them who are as yet detached enough to see and feel the beauty of the day, whose perceptions are as yet unentangled, undimmed, see only in proportion as the shadow of fate draws alluringly on. (755)

The action of the auction and the drama of acquisitiveness, is what creates the 'bondage' and entanglement which blocks the sight of beauty from the eyes of the farmers. The narrator sees this, however, and wishes to highlight its importance in the scene. Richardson does not want to write the narrative drama of buying and selling; she wants to pin down a glimpse of beauty.

The people around Richardson viewed her writing of sketches as an apprenticeship.[4] Richardson herself started to think in the same way. She was going to write a book. 'It would probably be a novel, since that was what the editors of the *Saturday Review* had been urging her to write. Jack [Beresford] thought she should attempt it. So did Wells' (Fromm 65).

May Sinclair did not begin as a novelist either. When she first began to write, in the 1880s, she wrote verse. It was obscure and unprofitable verse, based on her philosophical readings, and on Hindu mythology. However, as Sinclair's biographer Suzanne Raitt points out: 'with William, Joseph, and Reginald [her brothers] still alive – she was not yet her mother's sole financial support, and could just afford to write what she wanted' (31). This situation, however, did not last long. As one brother after another died, she found herself the only breadwinner of the family. She began to write short stories as well as verse, but had 'little luck' placing them (64). She then, like Richardson, turned to translation. In 1894 she translated Rodolf Sohm's *Grundriss* from German into English; in 1895 she managed to get her first short story, 'A Study from Life', published in *Black and White*, a weekly periodical; in 1896 she is revising translations again, and despairing. In Raitt's words, 'she knew she could not survive – physically or psychologically – as a translator. There was one thing left to try: a career as a novelist' (65). The potboilers, when she was treating them as such, were relatively unsuccessful, and it was the novels she wrote that were to make her 'relatively wealthy' (77).

Katherine Mansfield was never poor, certainly not by Richardson's standards, but she appears to have felt to need to *pretend* to be poor. In a letter to E. J. Brady, who published her first short pieces, she says 'I am poor – obscure – just eighteen years of age – with a rapacious appetite for everything and principles as light as my purse' (*Collected Letters* 27). As Jenny McDonnell puts it: 'Mansfield adopted a pose as a poverty-stricken "artist" who both invited and resisted the commodification of her work' (2). She tells the editor that she is obscure (read principled) and simultaneously that she is unprincipled. It is almost as if she is, after setting herself up as a high-minded artist, then inviting the editor to corrupt her and commercialise her art. The ambivalence displayed by the young Mansfield here is one that was to recur. The story of the publication of 'Je ne Parle Pas Français' (1920), for example, is one of compromise and of bitterness. The more frank references to prostitution and pimping in the story were considered by the publisher to be too salacious, and cuts were proposed. As Anthony Alpers tells it:

> In 1920, when she heard from Murry of the excisions that Constable were demanding, Katherine replied that she was furious with Michael Sadleir and would never agree: 'Shall I pick the eyes out of a story for £40? ... The *outline* would be all blurred. It must have those sharp lines.' She gave in next day, deciding that she had been 'undisciplined,' but she later changed her mind once more, and wished she hadn't cut one word: 'I was wrong – very wrong.' (273)

Mansfield cannot decide whether agreeing to the cuts will mutilate her work of art (and damage her artistic integrity), or whether objecting to the cuts makes her petty and 'undisciplined' and therefore unprofessional. The distinction is one between a conception of the artist as an uncompromising, higher soul, and of the artist as worldly and financially successful. Mansfield cannot decide which camp she would like to belong to. This is the same distinction Richardson made in her admiration and horror of the 'pattern magazine story', and it is the same ambivalence.

Significant Moments or Sustained Visions: The Short Story and the Novel

In his introduction to the first published edition of Mansfield's scrapbooks, John Middleton Murry says:

> Her power of presenting a complete situation, or conveying an entire atmosphere, in a transparently simple page or paragraph became remarkable, indeed . . . Katherine 'saw' and wrote, in flashes. Sometimes the flashes were relatively long, sometimes very short indeed. But of steady and equable composition there is no trace in her manuscripts, nor in my memory of her at work. When the full tide of inspiration came, she wrote till she dropped with fatigue – sometimes all through the night, in defiance of her illness. (vii)

Mansfield's *The Aloe* (first published 1930) was originally conceived as a longer work. In a letter to Murry at the time, Mansfield called it her 'first novel' (*Letter to John Middleton Murry* 26). As it developed, it was to become a kind of elegy to her dead brother, and, as Vincent O'Sullivan puts it, a kind of writing 'so that she both preserved a memory for herself, yet gave it radiance and solidity as a work of art' (13). It was to end with her brother's birth, an episode that was eventually narrated in the short story 'At the Bay'. The ambitious longer narrative, *The Aloe*, became the short story 'Prelude', and was published by the Woolfs, at the Hogarth Press.

After *The Aloe* became 'Prelude', Mansfield made an attempt to explain it to her friend the painter Dorothy Brett. It is, she tells Brett, a memory of her childhood:

> I always remember feeling that this little island has dipped back into the dark blue sea during the night only to rise again at beam of day, all hung with bright spangles and glittering drops – (When you ran over the dewy grass you positively felt that your feet tasted salt.) I tried to catch that moment – with something of its sparkle and its flavour. (*The Letters of Katherine Mansfield* 83–4)

She categorises the story as an attempt to 'catch' and preserve a 'moment': just the one beautiful impression. However, 'Prelude' is about much more than just one moment. It is about childhood, the desolation and joy of leaving a familiar place, class relations in middle-class New

Zealand, the yearnings and sexual repression of unmarried women and the boredom and emotional repression of married women. It is about the performance of life, the reality of life, and death. To call it a 'moment' is to diminish its scope.[5] Possibly Mansfield felt the need to categorise her short version of the story *as* a fragment, or a moment, because she knew that in its original conception it was a larger whole.

'Prelude' charts *several* significant moments in the lives of its characters. Kezia's enchantment on the dray ride in the dark is one of these. She is leaving behind her familiar world, and the darkness makes this uncanny event the more uncanny: she 'could not open her eyes wide enough' (Mansfield 84). Linda has an epiphanic moment when she realises that as well as loving her husband, she hates him: 'It had never been so plain to her as it was at this moment. There were all her feelings for him, sharp and defined, one as true as the other . . . How absurd life was' (115–16). Beryl's significant moment is when she realises (although she has realised it before) that she is always playing a part: 'Oh God, there she was, back again, playing the same old game':

> If she had been happy and leading her own life, her false life would cease to be. She saw the real Beryl – a shadow . . . a shadow. Faint and unsubstantial she shone. What was there of her except the radiance? And for what tiny moments she was really she. Beryl could remember every one of them. (119)

The two grown-up women have significant moments that are darkly revelatory. They are dissatisfied with their lives, and no sea scene with its 'bright spangles and glittering drops' will alleviate that (p. 83). 'At the Bay', however, with its beautiful scenic opening, 'the leaping, glittering sea', and 'the smell of leaves and wet black earth' comes much closer to Mansfield's post-publication explanation of the 'moment' she had wanted to catch (282–3). Beryl and Linda are still preoccupied with their repressions and secrets, but there are moments when their relationship with their surroundings becomes more than merely that of a character to its backdrop. Linda, for example, becomes one with the flowers and leaves of the manuka tree under which she is sitting: 'Linda felt so light; she felt like a leaf. Along came Life like a wind and she was seized and shaken; she had to go' (295). Beryl is excited, as Kezia was in 'Prelude', by the adventure of being awake at night-time, in a 'far more thrilling and exciting world than the daylight one' (311). In 'At the Bay', the revelations are not simply that life is absurd, false and meaningless. They are rather that life, if lived in symphony with a beautiful backdrop, can hold exciting and meaningful moments.

The revelatory moments experienced by characters in Sinclair's fictions are also ones in which the self and the background of the life, the surroundings of the character, become one. Agatha Verrall in 'The Flaw in the Crystal', for example, is unable to marry the man that she loves, and sublimates her feelings through a combination of nature-communion and transcendence of the body. Agatha has a gift: she can heal sick people with the power of her will. In order to work this power, however, she needs first to perform her evening walk up the hill, through the woods, 'calling her thoughts home to sleep', and then go to bed and calm herself until 'all fleshly contacts were diminished' (Sinclair 2006: 74). Because of her gift, she can see 'Reality' at will: 'the very substance of the visible world; live and subtle as flame; solid as crystal and as clean' (77). Moments like this one appear in many of Sinclair's works: *The Creators* (1910), when, for Jane, 'of a sudden the world she looked at became luminous and insubstantial and divinely still' (107); 'The Flaw in the Crystal' (1912) where Agatha experiences 'an exaltation of sense that was ecstasy; when every leaf and every blade of grass shone with a divine translucence' (95); Gwenda's epiphany in *The Three Sisters* (1914), where 'the visible world, passing into her inner life, took on its radiance and intensity' (339); and *The Dark Night* (1924), a 'novel in unrhymed verse', where the frustrated narrator, having gone into the garden to gather her thoughts, sees a vision of God: 'suddenly, in a flash, my garden changed / The wall and the hot flagged walk were gold, / The larkspurs became a blue light, burning, / The beech-tree a green fire, shining' (8).

In her repeated emphasis on the importance of this 'moment' of revelation (always presented as a moment of light: luminous, shining, radiant, and with burning flames), Sinclair is drawing on ideas she had propounded in her 1917 philosophical treatise, *A Defence of Idealism*. The 'God' that Elizabeth sees is actually 'Reality', as described in Sinclair's *Defence*:

> Our perceptions, like our passions, maintain themselves at higher and lower intensities. It is with such rapid flashes of the revolving disc, with such hurrying of the rhythm of time, with such heightening of psychic intensity that we discern Reality here and now.
>
> No reasoning allows or accounts for these moments. But lovers and poets and painters and musicians and mystics and heroes know them: moments when eternal Beauty is seized travelling through time; moments when things that we have seen all our lives without truly seeing them, the flowers in the garden, the trees in the field, the hawthorn on the hillside change to us in an instant of time, and show the secret and imperishable life they harbour; moments when the human creature we have known all our life without truly knowing it, reveals its incredible godhead. (379)

The emphasis in *A Defence of Idealism* is on the ordinariness of the background on which Reality is glimpsed. All of the heroines who experience this moment are outside; in gardens and in woods; and they are looking at the same natural world that they see every day when suddenly their perception changes. All of the heroines allow that moment to sustain them in their ordinary workaday lives, so that the moment of illumination is enough to sustain them in their sufferings.

However, 'The Flaw in the Crystal' is different. Agatha is not living an ordinary life, with the occasional flash of an expanded consciousness as the sole illuminating and sustaining moment. Rather, her life is *made up* of these significant moments. There is very little cooking and cleaning and reading (although she must also, living alone, be doing those things); instead there is magic and illumination and psychic voyaging. Sinclair in 1910, with obvious glee, described the stories that were later collected as *Uncanny Stories*, as 'all queer subjects; "spooky" ones some of them' (Boll 87). The short story allows her a freedom that the novel (even the 'novel in unrhymed verse') does not. She can take the idea of the significant moment, in which an expanded feminine consciousness glimpses 'Reality', and make it 'queer' and 'spooky'. She can create a world in which, as in 'The Flaw in the Crystal', there is 'a current of transcendent power' that certain people can tap into. Instead of the moment of illumination being random and unexpected, this transcendence can be 'controlled': 'you shut your eyes and ears, you closed up the sense of touch, you made everything dark around you and withdrew into your innermost self; . . . you tapped the Power, as it were, underground at any point you pleased' (73). The spooky story allows for a more fantastic version of Sinclair's philosophical Reality, and also allows her to give her heroines a certain power: to raise them up to the level of God.[6]

'The Finding of the Absolute' is another short story in which Sinclair's philosophical bent is given free, fantastical rein. The hero, Mr Spalding, is 'devoured by a hunger and thirst after metaphysical truth' (Sinclair 2006: 162). At the beginning of the story, we find him in his garden, trying to 'find peace' (as has worked for so many of Sinclair's heroines) and not managing it: his wife has left him for a young Imagist poet, and his belief in the Absolute has been shaken by this event (161). Cue a fast-forwarding of events, the death of his wife and lover, and the death of Mr Spalding himself. He finds himself in a kind of heaven, in which space and time are made by the Will, and 'a state of consciousness carries its own reality with it as such; and the time state or the space state is as real as any other' (171). He immediately goes to see Immanuel Kant, in Kant's own private space-time, in order to discuss this heaven. Kant tells him: 'you may imagine, Mr Spalding, that I was very gratified when I first came here to find everybody talking and thinking correctly about time and space' (170). The story ends with Mr Spalding's realisation of God; a much more direct vision than an epiphany in a flower garden:

> He saw the vast planes of time intersecting each other, like the planes of a sphere, wheeling, turning in and out of each other. He saw other space and time systems rising up, toppling, enclosing and enclosed. And as a tiny insect in the immense scene, his own life from birth to the present moment, together with the events of his heavenly life to come . . .
> He passed from God's immanent to his transcendent life, into the Absolute. For one moment he thought that this was death; the next his whole being swelled and went on swelling in an unspeakable, an unthinkable bliss. (175–6)

This is, as Claire Drewery notes, 'a fictional response' (77) to the question Sinclair asks in *A Defence of Idealism*: 'I want to know what, if anything, lies behind or at the bottom of multiplicity and change' (344). It is an attempt to come to a conclusion about something: part of the 'modernist aesthetic wrestle to rationalise and communicate experience' (Drewery 84). The short story form here allows for a literal vision of God, both like and unlike the visions of God that the heroines of Sinclair's novels experience. No other form is flexible enough for Sinclair to reach the logical and lyrical end of her belief in God-as-Absolute; no other form will allow the hero or heroine to *become* God.

In 1927, Richardson wrote to her friend the writer and journalist P. B. Wadsworth, complaining about 'every kind of botheration': issues with the publication of *Oberland*, articles to write for *Vanity Fair* and *Close Up* magazine, a further instalment of *Pilgrimage* to get started, and the perennial money troubles. She then tells of her plan for a 'pot-boiler' entitled 'My Six Months Solitude'. *My Six Months Solitude* was to be a book comprising 'Twelve articles on the six winter months I spent in Cornwall writing my first book in a "haunted" cottage' (Letter to P. B. Wadsworth, 25 July 1927). Richardson wrote her first book, *Pointed Roofs*, in a cottage belonging to the Beresfords in 1913. Jack Beresford and his wife had rented this cottage, near Padstow, for the whole year, and when they left in the autumn to return to London, they left Richardson there alone. Richardson's biographer, Gloria Fromm, writes that 'the months that followed took their place in her memory as one of those magical moments in time that can never be duplicated' (65). The 'moment' was clearly important enough to write about: the articles that Richardson planned never materialised, but she did write a short story about the stay, entitled 'Seen From Paradise'. If she wrote this story in order to make money, it didn't work: 'Seen From Paradise' was not published until Trudi Tate published her selection of Richardson's stories in 1989. Rather, she seems to have written the story because the time it charts is so significant that it needed to be expressed, and needed to be fictionalised.

The story begins towards the end of the stay, with a letter signalling the end of solitude and the return of Jim and Sylvia, whose cottage the narrator is staying in. The story is a retrospective account of the circumstances that led to the narrator's Cornish solitude ('when I went indoors with my plan, they were incredulous'), and the moment of blissful solitude achieved when the couple have left ('the all penetrating relief of knowing the world retreated to [an] immeasurable distance') (Tate 1989: 90–1). The bliss is interrupted by practicalities: she is not going to be able to sit and write in peace, as the milkman, village store delivery man, and the laundress will come by most days. She remembers Sylvia's 'daily palavering', but then also remembers, with relief, that Sylvia sometimes left messages and money in 'the blessedly roomy covered porch' (91). This 'realisation of my security' then brings a further and deeper moment of bliss. The narrator gains perspective. All of her friends are seen at once 'with a kind of affection I had never known before. Deep, inclusive' (ibid.). As the vision of the friends fades, the feeling of 'warmth' only increases, spreading 'across the world'. The realisation of solitude enables a 'blissful expansion of my own being'; a 'revelation of my new relationship to all the world' (92). This 'warmth', and 'new relationship' of the narrator to the planet is not explained. The narrator's attention is very quickly turned to the problem of whether, when Sylvia and Jim return, and in all the years afterwards, she will be able to keep hold of the sense of being thus attained that had meant that she could write: 'When once more I am in the midst of humanity, will that first morning's revelations fade away, or will they have given me the beginning of a new design for living?' (ibid.).

The moment of revelation, and the inspiration that it generates, was important to Richardson because it was the spark that created *Pilgrimage*. When Louise Theis asked her, in 1931, what her ideal conditions of work were, she responded with a reference to this winter in Cornwall, and also, indirectly, to the condition of expanded being discovered then. Conditions favourable to work, writes Richardson, should be:

> Ideally, everything that favours collaboration between the conscious & the unconscious.
> The best conditions in my experience are winter solitude & inaccessibility. I mean solitude. Servantless, visitorless, &, save for a single agent, tradesmanless. Such conditions fell to my lot just once. Deliberately to seek them might be fatal. (Letter to Louise Theis, 5 October 1931)

The collaboration between the conscious and the unconscious, then, is the moment of 'warmth' and blissful expanded being. The narrator of 'Seen From Paradise' worries that once the winter solitude is over, this collaboration will never again be possible, but eventually decides that it might just be attainable, because it comes from the inside. It is born of solitude but is not dependent on solitude. It is a 'Universal Ivory Tower':

> Ivory Tower, the innermost sanctuary, sole reservoir for the tide ceaselessly flowing from beyond the spheres. Once this centre is reached, one's world is transformed. Will it remain transformed? At a price. The price of keeping the reservoir always available. (92)

This is the same 'strange journey down to the centre of being' that Miriam experiences when she makes her first forays into writing in *Pilgrimage* (*IV*: 609), and the ability to keep the 'reservoir always available' is what makes a writer an artist. In *Quakers Past and Present*, Richardson expands on this condition:

> With most of us . . . the times of illumination are intermittent, fluctuating, imperfectly accountable, and uncontrollable. The 'artist' lives to a greater or lesser degree in a perpetual state of illumination, in perpetual communication with his larger self. (34)

'Seen From Paradise' needed to be written because it describes the first moment of artistic inspiration that Richardson felt. It lays out her ideas about the importance for an artist of keeping this inspiration always available, and that this is possible even in difficult domestic circumstances (or, as she phrases it in her letter to Theis, it is possible to retain this even with *constant* interruption 'without quite reaching despair' [Letter to Louise Theis, 5 October 1931]). It is a short story about the difficulty of writing longer stories, and its subject is born of its material conditions.

'A Room of One's Own'

Virginia Woolf's famous line, 'a woman must have money and a room of her own if she is to write fiction' has shaped feminist discourse about women, writing and domestic space in modernism (4). In Woolf's essay the webs of fiction, however ethereal and divine they may seem, are dependent on these prosaic conditions for their production. They are 'attached to grossly material things, like health and money and the houses we live in' (53–4).

When Sinclair eventually managed to acquire a room of her own in which to write, read and think, she protected it fiercely. In 1902, Sinclair's good friend Katherine Hinkson wrote to the novelist with a warning against solitude: 'I wish you were not such a lonely little person', she writes. 'Perhaps it is good for the work, but it is bad for the human creature' (Raitt 83). Sinclair was living, at the time, completely alone: 'in lodgings without a maid or companion' (84). However, she refused to feel sorry for herself. She replies to Hinkson: 'You must not pity me too much for living alone. I can bear it better than most women can, & I have a great many things to do that I like doing, & life isn't long enough to get them all in! And then I have my friends' (84). The tone of this letter is interesting: by all accounts Sinclair loved living alone, and was very protective of her solitude, and yet the tone here is one of a woman trying to make the best of a bad job. 'You must not pity me *too* much'; 'I can *bear it*' [my emphasis]. She is, however, clearly protecting her time. She has so many things to do that she likes doing: reading, studying and writing; and if she had to live with, and pay attention to, someone else, then life would certainly not be long enough. The story of Sinclair's finances is a cheering one; she grew more and more prosperous, and in 1907, bought her own flat in Kensington.

Mansfield's illness and her perpetual house moving give her very little time and space in which to write. *The Aloe*, begun in Paris, and continued in Bandol, with herself and Murry 'sat by the fire, writing together all day' was abandoned because of one of these moves, when Murry and Mansfield returned to Cornwall to live near the Lawrences (Tomalin 142). The story of Mansfield's writing life is a story of upheavals and uncertainty. She finds favourable conditions in which to write, and then something happens, and those conditions vanish. Richardson, as we have seen, never manages to recreate the ideal working conditions she found in her first winter in Cornwall. In fact, she is often very far from finding any kind of time or tranquillity in which to write anything. She complains, for example, to Wadsworth that 'for the last few years I have felt well-off on the days which find me with an hour or two free for writing. But that is not enough. It is too often a space of time that finds me too tired to make the effort needed to throw off preoccupations & gain tranquillity' (25 January 1926).

Both Mansfield and Richardson struggle to find the time and the 'tranquillity' needed to write longer pieces of fiction. Mansfield never carried off her projected *The Aloe* for this reason, and the gaps between Richardson's 'chapter-volumes' of *Pilgrimage* grew longer and longer. This lack of time informs the attitude of both writers to the short stories they were producing. Were they merely 'pot-boilers', inferior pieces of work produced for purely financial reasons? Or were they works of art in their own right? Both Mansfield and Richardson believed that their short stories were important as art, and as slices of life, but the material circumstances in which the stories were produced forced them both to ask the question. Engagement with the literary marketplace produced doubt as to both motives and quality. Sinclair, by contrast, did not have to ask the question. Her short stories could be both playful and experimental. The novels, which brought in the money, were subject to more rules and restrictions: she must contextualise her thoughts and create and sustain a viable plot. Sinclair's comparative freedom comes from her ability to shut herself away from the world and ignore the people who try to categorise her work. When Murry says of Mansfield that she saw in 'flashes', and must therefore write in flashes (vii), he displays no awareness of the ways in which Mansfield's working conditions must bear on her working practice. He defines her, as Mansfield defines herself in her letter to Dorothy Brett, as someone who is naturally and instinctively a short story writer because she cannot sustain her vision for long enough to write a longer work.

In the introduction to *The Modernist Short Story*, Head writes of a 'critical prejudice which favours the novel as the fictional norm' (5). This prejudice leads to the idea that the novel must narrate a life, and the short story, by contrast, must limit itself to the portrayal of 'moments'. However, as Head points out, such a view does not take into account the modernist novel's reliance on the portrayal of those very 'moments' that are seen as the province of the short story: 'the identification between novel and full-length life is clearly inadequate, especially in relation to the modernist novel' (ibid.). Richardson's *Pilgrimage* sets out to narrate a life, in the tradition of novelistic writing, but it does so by portraying significant moments and episodes in the life of the heroine: not those that the reader would necessarily judge to be significant, but those that the author feels have a 'typicality' and evocativeness that enable the reader to make inferences about the whole life. This device is, as Head identifies, traditionally associated not with the novel, but with the short story: 'the short form often implies the typicality of a specific episode, while narrative limitation demands oblique expression through image and symbol' (7). Sinclair's novels *Mary Olivier: A Life* (1919), and *The Life and Death of Harriett Frean* (1922) (the latter being the most compressed of all of Sinclair's longer narratives) both similarly rely on oblique expression, and the typicality of significant moments in order to express what it means to be living that particular life. Mansfield's short stories 'Prelude' and 'At the Bay' tell the story, not of one significant moment, but of many. She draws a picture of the lives of a whole family, with their separate preoccupations and interests, and neuroses. The distinction falls apart.

Richardson, Sinclair and Mansfield were all aware that the prevailing critical view of short stories was that they should present a 'moment'; a unified vision. The tension that arises in their stories is when they refuse to follow the path laid out for them. When J. D. Beresford, H. G. Wells, and the editor of the *Saturday Review* implied to Richardson that they viewed her short story writing as an apprenticeship that would give her the skills to write a novel, she went ahead and planted her significant moments one by one into a long sustained narrative of a life. When Mansfield realised that she had a reputation for seeing in flashes and glimpses, she consciously used this reputation as a way of shaping how readers would read her stories: the complex interlocking narratives of 'Prelude' become one single 'moment', immortalised in prose. When Sinclair began to realise and embrace modernism in the early twentieth century, she wrote short stories, like 'The Finding of the Absolute', in which time speeds up and slows down, visions of God become literal, and Bergson and Einstein are discussed with dead philosophers, as a kind of prelude to dealing with these modernist preoccupations in novel form. None of these writers saw the short story as an inferior form to the novel, but all three felt the pressure to treat the story (at least in public declarations) as a practice for the longer narrative works that they were writing (or felt they should be writing). The precarious domestic and financial situations all three writers struggled with at one time or another created this pressure, and this ambivalence. The short story must be simultaneously a potboiler, capable of bringing in money quickly, and of artistic merit in itself (because what, after all, is the point of getting a piece in a magazine with your name on it, if it is not going to act as an advert for the author-as-product?). It must be either a testing-ground for ideas, or a place where those ideas that will not fit into novel form can be played with: because some ideas, and some moments, are too important to go unexpressed.

Notes

1. 'I hope for a scrap of time for my own work before the next pot-boiler' Letter to S. S. Kotelianski, 31 March 1934. British Library, London.
2. The problems were eventually resolved, and *Du Barry* did appear with Richardson named as translator.
3. Richardson's use of the word 'alive' refers to the aesthetic aim she returns to in all her work: the need to adequately portray 'contemplated reality' (Richardson *Pilgrimage I*: 10).

4. In *Pilgrimage*, Hypo Wilson in his attempt to plan out Miriam's life for her, lists the things she should do and the order in which she should do them: 'Middles. You've masses of material for Middles. Criticism. You could do that on your head. Presently *novel*.' Miriam is irritated by his assumptions, and thinks 'And Hypo's emphasis suggested that the hideous, irritating, meaningless word *novel* represented the end and aim of a writer's existence' (*IV*: 239).
5. Dominic Head's book *The Modernist Short Story* is invaluable to an understanding of the critical heritage surrounding the significance of the 'moment' in modernist short stories. The moment is often taken as the organising principal of these stories, which as Head observes, implies 'a unity established through the back door'. This is problematic, as it ignores the 'cultivated disunity'; the 'gaps and conflicts' of the modernist short story (20). In Mansfield, Richardson and Sinclair, there is rarely only one 'moment' to create a symbolic unity. Rather there are many moments, often contradictory.
6. The closest Sinclair allows herself to this kind of mystical 'queer subject' in her novels is at the end of *Mary Olivier* (London: Virago, 1980). Mary experiments with magic, as Agatha does ('supposing you could "work" it for him' [367]), and her vision of God is also one in which she becomes 'God': 'She saw that the beauty of the tree was its real life, and that its real life was in her real self and that her real self was God' (373). However, the novel form does not allow for any expansion of this spookiness, and Mary is herself unsure about the nature of whatever she has grasped, right up to the very closing pages of the novel: 'Supposing there's nothing in it, nothing at all?' (379).

Works Cited

Alpers, Anthony (1980), *The Life of Katherine Mansfield*, Oxford: Oxford University Press.
Boll, Theophilus (1973), *Miss May Sinclair: Novelist*, Rutherford: Fairleigh Dickinson University Press.
Bowen, Elizabeth (2008), *People, Places, Things: Essays by Elizabeth Bowen*, ed. Allan Hepburn, Edinburgh: Edinburgh University Press.
Drewery, Claire (2011), *Modernist Short Fiction by Women: The Liminal in Katherine Mansfield, Dorothy Richardson, May Sinclair and Virginia Woolf*, Farnham: Ashgate.
Fromm, Gloria G. (1977), *Dorothy Richardson: A Biography*, Urbana: University of Illinois Press.
Head, Dominic (1992), *The Modernist Short Story: A Study in Theory and Practice*, Cambridge: Cambridge University Press.
Hueffer, Ford Madox (1911), *Ancient Lights and Certain New Reflections: Being the Memories of a Young Man*, London: Chapman and Hall.
McDonnell, Jenny (2010), *Katherine Mansfield and the Modernist Marketplace: At the Mercy of the Public*, London: Palgrave Macmillan.
Mansfield, Katherine (2002), *Selected Stories*, Oxford: Oxford University Press.

Mansfield, Katherine (1951), *Katherine Mansfield's Letters to John Middleton Murry*, ed. J. M. Murry, London: Constable.
Mansfield, Katherine (1930), *The Letters of Katherine Mansfield*, Vol. I, London: Constable.
Mansfield, Katherine (1984–2008), *The Collected Letters of Katherine Mansfield*, Vol. I, ed. Vincent O'Sullivan and Margaret Scott, Oxford: Clarendon Press.
Murry, John Middleton (1939), 'Introduction', *The Scrapbook of Katherine Mansfield*, London: Constable.
O'Sullivan, Vincent (1982), 'Introduction', *The Aloe, with Prelude* by Katherine Mansfield, Wellington: Port Nicholson Press.
Raitt, Suzanne (2000), *May Sinclair: A Modern Victorian*, Oxford: Oxford University Press.
Richardson, Dorothy (1989), 'A Sussex Auction', *The Saturday Review,* 13 June 1908.
Richardson, Dorothy (1989), *Journey to Paradise: Short Stories and Autobiographical Sketches*, ed. Trudi Tate, London: Virago.
Richardson, Dorothy (2002), *Pilgrimage I*, London: Virago Press.
Richardson, Dorothy (2002), *Pilgrimage II*, London: Virago Press.
Richardson, Dorothy (2002), *Pilgrimage III*, London: Virago Press.
Richardson, Dorothy (2002), *Pilgrimage IV*, London: Virago Press.
Richardson, Dorothy (1914), *The Quakers Past & Present*, London: Constable.
Sinclair, May (1917), *A Defence of Idealism: Some Questions & Conclusions*, London: Macmillan.
Sinclair, May (1910), *The Creators: A Comedy*, London: Hutchinson and Co.
Sinclair, May (1924), *The Dark Night*, London: Jonathan Cape.
Sinclair, May (1980), *Mary Olivier*, London: Virago.
Sinclair, May (1984), *The Three Sisters*, London: Virago.
Sinclair, May (2006), *Uncanny Stories*, Ware: Wordsworth Editions.
Tomalin, Claire (1988), *Katherine Mansfield: A Secret Life*, London: Penguin.
Woolf, Virginia (2000), *A Room of One's Own and Three Guineas*, Oxford: Oxford University Press.

Dorothy Richardson's unpublished letters are in various archives:
Letters to John Cowper Powys and Bryher, Dorothy Richardson Collection, Beinecke Rare Book and Manuscript Library.
Letters to P. B. Wadsworth, Berg Library, New York.
Letters to S. S. Kotelianski, British Library, London.
Letters to Louise Theis, Dorothy Richardson Collection, Harry Ransom Center, Austin, TX.

Chapter 5

War and the Short Story: Elizabeth Bowen

Adam Piette

Elizabeth Bowen's World War II short stories set up filiations between short story form and the violence being wreaked both materially on cities under blitz and psychologically by the estranging conditions of wartime. For Bowen there was a link between the anxieties caused by twentieth-century modernity and modernist short story form, its breaks, cuts, cryptic mental processes. The alliance between psychology and form went critical in wartime: World War II was modernity made extreme, revealing the war's fantastic theatricality, its furious fragmentations and lethal explosiveness, its spatio-temporal splits in mind and city between pre-war and wartime, the intense isolating of emotions under bombardment, unconscious motivations stirred by violence and fear of death. For Bowen, perhaps the short story could best capture the psychological intensities and broken temporalities of the war. The obliqueness, jump-cut suddenness and inconclusiveness of the modernist short story became absolutely the psychological case during the war, formally tracking the inexplicable, random acts of war's violence, staying true to the weird pastlessness and futurelessness of wartime anxieties. Bowen became increasingly concerned with the gendered point of view of the imagination undergoing bombardment and contemplating ruin. She turned her critical sense of the modernist short story into an exploration of specifically female forms of the death wish as urge for passionate destruction under patriarchy.

This chapter will have three sections: the first examines Bowen's theories of the short story, specifically how the isolated moment at its heart is subject to historical pressures generated by political modernity. In her 1936 introduction to *The Faber Book of Short Stories*, Bowen breaks the modernist short story down to its bare bones as, severally, concentrating on deep reflexes and immediate susceptibilities, and characterised by oblique narration and unlikely placing of emphasis. These features combine to strengthen the main thrust of the modernist short story, namely its zooming in on the psychological core of the event, its deliberate inconclusiveness, and its political conditioning. The second section will look at the short stories 'Sunday Afternoon' and 'Mysterious Kôr', and the manner in which Bowen dramatises Anglo-Irish dreaminess as characteristic of Irish wartime neutrality; and how the wartime Irish/Anglo-Irish imagination secretly revels in the wartime bombardment of London, the imperial centre, specifically in terms of gendered death wishes. The last section will close-read 'The Demon Lover' to explore the theme of the female death wish as the crux around which the feminist-modernist short story stages its inconclusiveness as wartime Gothic and apocalyptic endgame, and reads the Bowen wartime short story as characteristically a hybrid vehicle, a modernist 'taxi', within which are fused Victorian and modernist forms, Chekhovian and Maupassant-esque styles, eerie past and future time zones within present war temporality.

The Short Story: Disoriented Romanticism, War Nervousness, Political Compulsions

In her 1936 introduction to *The Faber Book of Short Stories*, Bowen speaks of the short story's 'poetic tautness and clarity', its dramatic 'use of action' and alliance with the cinema. Both the short story and cinema are free of tradition, self-conscious in form, and share the same 'immense matter' as principal focus of their representations, 'the disoriented romanticism of the age' (7). She lists the features of the modernist short story as she sees it: 'the new literature, whether written or visual, is an affair of reflexes, of immediate susceptibility, of associations not examined by reason: it does not attempt a synthesis'. The short stories are characterised by 'oblique narration, cutting (as in the cinema), the unlikely placing of emphasis, and use of symbolism (the telling use of the object both for its own sake and as an image)' (ibid. 7–8). This taxonomy can be developed as follows: the modernist story, for Bowen, specialises in abrupt emotion, mood and feeling as instances of the ways Romantic intensities of affect related to self, others and environments have lost bearings under the compulsions of twentieth-century modernity. It uses cinematic cutting techniques to render these intensities since this allows for swifter and less rational control over the occasions, encouraging capture of knots and flows of feeling. The modernist short story deliberately avoids narrative closure in order to maximise the mystery of the psychological complex as captured in time. Its emphasis on symbols, reflexes and telling objects is clearly influenced by the new psychology, and the combination of intense attention to detail with oblique narration is designed to create a dense texture faithful to the political and psychological complexity of the slice of mental space-time under observation.

The short story, Bowen argues, encourages narrative breaks and inconclusive endings:

> The art of the short story permits a break at what in the novel would be the crux of the plot: the short story, free from the *longueurs* of the novel is also exempt from the novel's conclusiveness — too often forced and false: it may thus more nearly than the novel approach aesthetic and moral truth. ('The Short Story' 15)

Cutting to the emotional crux of the plot and breaking the story off before loose ends are tied renders the moment of modernity in terms both of the psychological reflexes that ungovernably attach themselves to the detail and of the historical circumstances that have led to this specific moment; raw history without neat eschatological interpretation. The moment is both political and psychological since this is what Bowen means by 'disoriented romanticism': the romanticism there in the interrelation of world and mental affect; the mental state 'disoriented' by the political and cultural changes of modernity. The disorientation entails what she calls 'extraverted coldness' in the style; turmoil of affect linking up with a chillingly neutral observation in the representation. The Irish and Americans have dominated the short story in English, she suggests, because of the ways 'either sexual or political passion makes society unsafe'; the extraverted coldness is a symptom of American and Irish 'high nervous tension' generated by heightened political circumstance, akin to a state of nervous war readiness:

> The younger Irish writers have almost all carried arms; American civilization keeps the Americans, nervously, armed men: fact there overtops fantasy. There is a state of living in which events assault the imagination, stunning it: such a state of living enforces its own, now no longer unique, literature. ('The Short Story' 11)

This nationalist reading of the modernist short story underscores the ways states of living are dependent on political states – and hints at the internationalism shaping modernism. The modernist short story genre is one of the few adequate to the peculiar nervous tension generated by the 'armed' war readiness of turbulent twentieth-century politics. The Irish have taken to the form, she suggests, because of their experience of war nervousness, from Great War through War of Independence and Civil War to World War II. The modernist short story captures the specific ways war history assaults and stuns the imagination. As she argued later in 'The Short Story in England' (1945), 'the art of the short story showed itself [in the 1930s] truly to *be* art in that it felt compulsions from the outside world' (313).

The Anglo-Irish and the Gendered Death Wish

If Bowen argued for filiation between short story formal fracturedness and war-modernist nervousness as both predicament and style, her short stories push this to extremes, goaded on by her Irish sense of the event-assaulted imagination. 'Sunday Afternoon' (1941) is a story about a middle-aged man, Henry Russell, back from blitzed London where his flat has been destroyed, visiting his aunt, Mrs Vesey, at her grand house on the outskirts of Dublin. He registers the ways the group of old people taking tea with his aunt still relish the old manners of Anglo-Irish society at the same time as being in fearful denial of the war's realities. In their midst is Maria, Mrs Vesey's niece, who identifies with the energy of the new world inaugurated by modern warfare. The story therefore concerns itself with Irish neutrality and post-Ascendancy Ireland: the ageing remnant of Anglo-Irish culture is struggling to comprehend the brutality of wartime conditions at the old imperial centre, London, from their neutrally becalmed vantage point. Bowen contrasts this bankrupt generation's self-marginalisation in dead space-time with the younger Irish generation's scorn for their past and hunger for sensation imagining the distant war. The impulsive Maria has an ungovernable restlessness which combines wild adolescent sexual adventurousness with a war-driven nervousness that feeds off the destructiveness of the Blitz. The story dramatises the contradiction between this hunger for sudden violence and her family's dreamy retreat into the past, a defeated self-mesmerising deadness identified with the Anglo-Irish beached by Irish politics, still probing the lineaments of old desire. They live according to 'fastidious, stylized melancholy', as though locked into the theatricality of another age; they have 'an air of being secluded behind glass' – museum pieces, stuffed or inanimate relics. They sit 'at this sheltered edge of the lawn' (616), pastorally inert, a circle closed off from the historical events and blastwaves of London's war.[1] It is these blastwaves that excite Maria in their radical power to destroy the past and its hold on her, raising sexual turmoil in her mind and heart, tempting her to flee to London and to seduce Henry who navigates between London and Ireland, holding the secret of the war in his own mind and heart.

The story dramatises this struggle between the generations, then; but moves on to think through the gendered forces at play, the struggle between the sexes. Maria is the returned spirit of Mrs Vesey's youth, liberated from Victorian values and *politesse*. Savage with the destructive energy of the war, she signifies the newly powerful female of the twentieth century, scaring the middleman Henry who identifies her with the brutes running the war. To tame her free warlike energy, he must typify her within a patriarchal tradition; so calls her Miranda. He thus fashions her as innocent in Ireland as Prospero's island, fascinated by the violence of the storm of war, but really just simply in need of a lover. The comparison has a choking effect on her radical spirit, but also threatens to redound on him, for it makes him into a 'half-old' father and lover: Prospero and Ferdinand.[2] But Bowen's own strategic scening suggests Maria has a Caliban energy too: if she is 'young and savage', then she might have Caliban's anti-colonial 'brute' imagination also, despite the hold Prospero-like Anglo-Irish patriarchy has over her language, emotions and body.

The text has its own self-reflexiveness, presenting itself as inherited from the Victorian tradition with its attention to a specific class and mores, a Jamesian mix: indeed, the name 'Vesey' signals this, used by James for a socialite schemer in his novella 'The Chaperon'.[3] As such it is fastidious in its language, stylised as it tracks the stiff speech patterns of this leisured caste, their melancholy related to their inward, closed-off seclusion. It is Jamesian in its display not only of upper-class coterie snobbery (Henry registers 'distaste' for the vulgar violence of the war among Mrs Vesey's guests, as well as difference from democratic Ireland) but also in its concentration on point of view: Mrs Vesey is said at one point, staring at Henry, to have 'eyes that penetrated his point of view' (617). The very brevity of the Victorian short story form is figured in Mrs Vesey's sheltered lawn, and we are asked to reflect how this sheltered form harbours an antiquated style (an Edwardian, Anglo-Irish politesse, with its 'dryness', 'distaste', 'aesthetic of living' (616–17)) that is pre-modernist, pre-twentieth century, pre-war, obsolete. At the same time, the short story is also a modernist tale: it is stricken through with war nervousness, staged in the erotic charge linking Henry's Blitz stories to Maria's sexual unconscious and vibrant destructive energy. The modernist story is troped spatially as the path leading to the gate and the bus and world beyond – Henry and Maria wait in this transitional space and enter into a battle of wits about the meaning of the house behind them, and the meaning of the war beyond the gate. The modernist story is similarly suspended between its lost past contexts and its uncertain future: in this space are registered the dying manners of previous styles of life and art (the Jamesian intensities of the now derelict Anglo-Irish) and the fearful void and destructive/revolutionary future which might or might not ever happen. It harbours a state of living in which events assault the imagination relayed by way of a short story form favouring violent emotion, sudden, abrupt, sexual energies; a war-cultivated apocalyptic style. The path to the gate is in short story time, a force field registering the assault of the events across the Irish Sea, triggering psychological fear and lusts as subtle and inward mental events concealed in Henry and Maria; and encouraging either ruthless indifference to, or yearning nostalgia for, the past that is being destroyed. Without a clear past or conclusive future, the tale gestures backwards to the radical break that was 1940, and forwards to some unnameable destructiveness. Bowen's innovation, in all the tales in *The Demon Lover* wartime collection, is to have fused the Jamesian and modernist short story into one Janus-faced compound. As Jamesian, it is a sheltered lawn staging an upper-class caste where class feelings and manners can be leisurely explored, complex points of view on repressed desires/fears staged. As modernist, it takes place on a roadway-transitional space suspended between violently abandoned past and undecidable future, registering sexual warlike forces in psyche and culture that are played out in a struggle between generations, genders and ideologies.

The struggle is ideological, for Henry at least, because he senses a parallel between Maria's impulsive glorying in the fact his flat was destroyed, and fascist war culture. He marvels at how quickly she forgets what has just occurred, the 'ruthlessness of her disregard of the past, even the past of a few minutes ago' (619). Maria's contempt for the past parallels the radical break enabled by the modernist short story, cutting to the quick without prehistory. Henry then identifies that ruthlessness, through Jamesian point of view, with the fascist enemy. Maria at table upsets her tea, rubs the cloth with her handkerchief, shakes 'a petal from a Chinese peony in the centre bowl' onto a plate of cucumber sandwiches: 'The little bit of destruction was watched by the older people with fascination, with a kind of appeasement, as though it were a guarantee against something worse' (620). Maria is being seen by Henry as a Hitlerite spirit of destructiveness; and it is this which makes her desire to flee to London so dreadful – she wishes to relish the destruction of the city with a German ferocity borne of a *fascisant* warmongering. It is this analogy which also motivates Henry's disciplining of her as Miranda at the gate. He scorns her modernism: even her impulsive scorn for the past is a creature of Anglo-Irish society. Bowen had spied on neutral Ireland and had reported to London, in secret communiqués to the Dominions Office in 1940, about the potential of the country to identify with fascist Germany.⁴ Here Henry is doing the same thing: he has identified a pro-German war lust in the younger generation freed from the constraints of the Pale and Anglo-Irish civilising manners. If she has Hitlerite forces within her and is being appeased by the Anglo-Irish – stuck in a 1938 Munich time warp due to their neutrality – then her desires, for London, for the war, for Henry as violently free of all his past, can be figured as 'destructive and horrible' (621). And yet heavy irony is triggered, partly through the very ridiculousness of his reading of the petal on the cucumber sandwich as destructive in the first place.

What is really at play at the gate, the irony implies, is Henry's own nostalgia for Anglo-Irish culture, his fear of and attraction to the girl, his own dismay at his own nihilist attachment to the 'zone of death', London under the Blitz (621). These mixed feelings concentrate into one complex affect: 'This moment he had been dreading, returning desire, flooded him in this tunnel of avenue, with motors swishing along the road outside and Maria standing staring at him' (ibid.). The time of suspense is revealed as the active and terrifying *present*, the 'moment' of being which fuses the past ('returning desire') and future ('the motors swishing along the road outside') to the present ('Maria standing staring'). It is this complex trifold present tense which Maria inhabits as a modernist-futurist Caliban-Miranda: a manifold present which holds within itself both the life force of 'returning desire' even when privileging past/future death forces in the zone beyond.

The conjunction of defunct Jamesian form with violent, psychologically unstable modernist form is made to parallel the balance between Henry's masculinist point of view and Maria's radicalism. How we read Maria depends on whether we buy into Henry's focalised judgement of her as dangerously launching herself into an identity-free future. Yet whether we read his judgement of her (proto-fascist, savage, naïve, ruthless, silly little girl, scornful, etc.) ironically or not, Bowen does sow a seed of doubt as to the motivations that might be running her relish for the destruction in London. As a Caliban-Miranda she may be revelling in the annihilation of the imperial-patriarchal capital of the old Anglo-Irish arrangements, foundation of the imprisoning past she despises. This surmise, based on nothing more than the airy consequences of the irony playing over Henry's over-emphases, is considered with more weight and heft in another story from the wartime collection, 'Mysterious Kôr' (1944).

The story is about Pepita's fascination for the empty moonlit city of London under Blitz threat when all Londoners are hidden away, signifying for her a zone free of human attachments and life forms. This fascination is contrasted with Callie's 'virginal' romantic dream of love;

this contrast is at once political (a war-dream of death to London contrasted with a longing for peace) and internal (the worlds of death and love as ambivalent images in a dreamy interior world). Bowen stages a De Chirico-surreal dream-cityscape with the visionary image of the white night-time deserted capital under a bomber's moon, intimation of an uncanny afterlife in the weird here and now. It is a ghost city of the moon, a city of the unconscious and of the dead. Pepita quotes from Andrew Lang's poem inspired by Rider Haggard's *She* as she stares at the moonlit London alongside her lover Arthur: 'Mysterious Kor thy walls forsaken stand, / Thy lonely towers beneath the lonely moon'. The lovers discuss her hallucination of the city as Kôr, Arthur implying that even Lang's poem implies Kôr is unreal; whereas for Pepita the war's violence is a fiat that realises the unconscious destructive realm, ('If you can blow whole places out of existence, you can blow whole places into it' (730)). Part of the difficulty in interpreting Kôr turns on the representation of the sexual unconscious in the story. In the terrible crowded conditions of wartime London, there is no place for this couple to come together through sex: they dare not in the park, and Callie's flat is impossible due to Callie's presence and ignorance of the ways of all flesh. Kôr is an imaginary romantic zone within the mind, where Pepita and Arthur can be together. That is what we assume Pepita's hallucination is all about; and Pepita's cruelty towards Callie when they share a bed seems to imply how much sexual frustration is behind her feelings about lack of loving privacy. Consciously, Pepita is determined to punish Callie for her virginal idiocy in not allowing the couple the run of the flat ('Pepita felt she owed a kind of ruin to her' (731)). So when we return to Pepita's point of view after time spent in Callie's mind that night, the vision she has of herself and Arthur seems to stand for a sexual-romantic vision of Kôr as lovers' lonely city:

> She still lay, as she had lain, in an avid dream, of which Arthur had been the source, of which Arthur was not the end. With him she looked this way, that way, down the wide, void, pure streets, between statues, pillars and shadows, through archways and colonnades. (739)

Yet already the note is struck: Arthur is *not* the end of the avid dream. The vision of the couple climbing the stairs 'down which nothing but moon came', treading the dust of the endless halls, looking down on the statued squares and streets, does not need Arthur: 'He was the password, but not the answer: it was to Kôr's finality that she turned' (740). Callie has intuited the inhumanity of Pepita's imagination, felt it in the heartlessness of her rebuke to her in bed, the 'kind of ruin' intended to her romantic love of love. Arthur too senses how Pepita's hallucination unsettles his own grasp of his very being in the world ('I woke up just now not knowing where I'd been' [738]). The radical inhumanity of Pepita's dream not only relishes a London stripped clean of Londoners, it targets friends and lovers as victims of its annihilating gaze, a finality as terminal death-zone spreading out from her unconscious interiority. This avid dream is a lust not for another but for the *void* with which it half rhymes ('avid' reaches 'void' through 'wide'). And it also raises this speculation: the dream of the void may be motivating the deepest female creative drives in wartime, drives familiar and personal to Bowen herself.

For Bowen based Pepita's dream of Kôr on her own obsession with Rider Haggard's novel *She* (1887). In a BBC talk broadcast in 1947, Bowen remembers the impact of first reading the book:

> Kôr, Kôr, the enormous derelict city ... I saw Kôr before I saw London ... London as Kôr with the roofs still on. The idea that life in any capital city must be ephemeral, and with a doom ahead, remained with me. ('She' in *Mulberry Tree*, 248–9)

Bowen is confessing to a deep desire to see London derelict, ephemeral, doomed, free of its people. To dream of the capital 'as high as cliffs and as white as bones, with no history' (729) is to dream of the whiteness associated with imperial England (the white cliffs of Dover, Albion). But she dreams it as sign now of death, generating a vision of blitzed London, stripping it of population to allow ghosts of other cultures to roam. The name 'Pepita' hints at her foreignness within the Empire's capital city – as foreign, unreal, fantastic and un-English as a deracinated Anglo-Irish girl.[5] Deeper than this identification of Spanish Pepita with Irish Elizabeth goes the common attachment to She as moon-female creative power. The ferocious, avid dreamer Pepita inherits Bowen's own vision of She:

> What her powers were I knew ... Her proud, ambitious spirit would be certain to break loose and avenge itself for the long centuries of solitude. In the end, I had little doubt, she would assume absolute rule over the British dominions, and probably the whole world ... ('She' in *Mulberry Tree*, 250)

Bowen wonders then whether she aspired to 'She's' role, and thinks not, since She was her vision of the adult female ('outsize absolute of the grown-up') transfigured by violent history ('She had entered fire'), inhabiting the psychoanalytic space of the inner powerful mother: 'no face – I saw her as I preferred her, veiled, veiled; two eyes burning through the layers of gauze' (250).

The internal mother-force as annihilating power to topple Empire in vengeance, zoned within Kôr, enormous derelict city, becomes for Bowen the symbol of the creative unconscious. But it is not She-who-must-be-obeyed who controls the magic, but the male narrator, Horace Holly – for *She* was her first revelation of the power of writing:

> Writing – that creaking, pedantic, obtrusive, arch, prudish, opaque and over-worded *writing* . . . what it could do! That was the revelation; that was the power in the cave. . . . The power of the pen. The inventive pen. (251)

The short story comes out of Bowen's double sense of the impact of the novel: releasing a vision of a female revengeful power as death wish to Empire and male dominion; yet controlled by a prudish scribal power. The double sense is thematised in the contrast between Pepita and Callie, and their rival interpretations of the moon and of Arthur. Pepita's moon is the bomber's moon, a killing revengeful spirit of bitter enquiry and judgement, looking down on London with an enemy imagination. For Callie it is the moon of romance, 'exonerat[ing] and beautif[ying] the lateness of the lovers' return' (734), shining on her little world. At one moment, waiting for Pepita and Arthur to return, she lies in bed and watches the moon bleach her hand as it lies on Pepita's side: 'She lay and looked at the hand until it was no longer her own' (ibid.). The moon can shape-shift her own body, making her occupy her friend's flesh as Arthur's lover. Pepita's moon aims to kill this romantic dream with the power of She: her moon resembles wartime searchlights, but also the eye of female destructiveness. In Callie's focalisation, it reveals a ring, then the Victorian mantelpiece 'of that lost drawing room', then the photograph of Callie's parents, then the housecoat, in other words, revealing Victorian marriage for Callie (ibid.). But to Pepita, it reveals Kôr, a city without men, a free space for female destructive creativity.

The struggle between the two young women's unconsciousnesses touches on something like the difference between the Jamesian story of repressed 'virginal' passion, and the modernist story of sexual feeling and destructive energies. This in turn can be aligned with the two kinds of short story Bowen admired, the Maupassant story of 'sharp actuality', 'direct emotions', 'hallucinatory and macabre' ('Guy de Maupassant' 249) and the Chekhov story of mood, '[i]solating some perhaps quite small happening, [emphasising] its significance by giving it emotional colour' ('The Short Story in England' 314). 'Mysterious Kôr' combines Callie's Chekhovian mood and tender detail, a throwback to Jamesian tales of innocent Daisy Millers, with a darker visionary-modernist story of destruction and surreal hallucination: Pepita's Maupassant-inspired brutal and hallucinatory actuality. And as with 'Sunday Afternoon', these 'moons' or styles of unconsciousness are fused as spatial vectors. As Bowen remarked in her postscript to the US edition of *The Demon Lover*, 'It seems to me that during the war the overcharged subconsciousnesses of everybody overflowed and merged' (*Mulberry Tree* 95). That merging occurs between Arthur and Pepita at the entrance of the gateless park: they look in 'but did not go in', then face around 'to look back the way they had come' (729). At this juncture, the two 'subconsciousnesses' meet as rival cities, Pepita's London, the moon's capital, Kôr-killing timeless zone of void, and Arthur's London, social, peopled, romantic. They meet just as Bowen's styles, Chekhovian and Maupassant-esque, overflow and merge. In Callie's flat, too, Bowen spatialises the double coordinates of her hybrid short story style: it contains both Callie's romantic, prudishly old-fashioned imagination, coloured by romantic idealism, loving mood, detail of her world, she content with a story of innocence and experience; and it holds Pepita's futurist-surrealist-modernist vision of the city zapped by the feminist and postcolonial death wish, dreaming of the finality of apocalyptic She. The tiny little flat figures the tight controlled space of the short story, yet contains both pre-war and wartime manners, claustrophobically domestic yet expanding over the whole world. The modernist short story as a space kills off any past and future, leaving only the suspense of imminent finality, exhibiting wartime as style. At the same time, it remembers Edwardian girlhood and nineteenth-century mores, dreams of romantic futures, in Jamesian hypermnesia. It both unleashes She's power, and controls it with Callie's 'prudish' script.

Hailing the Modernist Taxi: 'The Demon Lover'

The hybrid short story Bowen develops for the wartime collection acknowledges that the imagination may have been technologised by the twentieth century – Pepita's moon as searchlight – yet it still pertains as romantic dream power with the moon as transfiguring loving creativity. Those two forms of imagination blend nineteenth century with modernist forms of short story telling: trace memories of older patterns, a Jamesian complex of conduct codes, repressions, rituals combining with the abrupt, fragmentary and cryptic style that can capture modernity's war nervousness. In one style, we still read the traces of the love plots, the courtship ceremonies, the enigmatically veiled moods; in the other, sexual and violent psychology combines with brutal inhuman history and its technology. The doubling that the hybrid fusion of modernist with nineteenth-century short story entails is thematised, as we have seen, in the spatial coordinates of key scenes, the enclosed lawns and rooms or the gateways, presided over by twin moons, holding-places both for the futureless, pastless modern moment, and still operative forms of nostalgia and manner. The war nervousness that threatens to destroy everything through dreams of finality is countered by Romantic visions of relationship. The net effect of the hybridising of the styles is unsettling: a Gothic sense of the instability of the world under threat from '[s]omething more immaterial' (728), a shadowing of crowded London by Kôr, an inhabiting of both the objective and subjective worlds by the void. The implications of this existentialist crisis, the *voiding* of wartime Gothic, are spookily explored in the title story of the collection, 'The Demon Lover'.

The story is consciously Jamesian, reprising psychological ghost stories like 'The Jolly Corner' (1908) or *The Turn of the Screw* (1898), featuring uncanny returns to abandoned houses and hauntedness which is ambivalently mental or supernatural. In 'The Demon Lover', Kathleen Drover returns in August 1941 to her 'shut-up house', under the gaze of 'no human eye', meeting the '[d]ead air' as she opens the door (661). The house exhibits 'traces of her long former habit of life' visible in the details, the 'bruise in the wallpaper', the 'ring left by a vase', etc. Every object is covered not so much with real dust as with 'a film of another kind' (ibid.) – and the double sense to this, as to all the other phrases, hints at the presence of the 'demon'. She receives a mysterious letter and begins more consciously to sense 'someone contemptuous of her ways' in the space. The letter comes from the deep past, a lover of twenty-five years back arranging a rendezvous: it triggers a nervousness in her that drives her to the mirror to check on her identity in time. The story shifts then back to the past moment being summoned by the writing: August 1916 and the time she said farewell to her soldier fiancé – this moment takes place in a transitional space at the end of the garden, her looking back to the house and family, making a 'sinister troth' with him that they will meet no matter what (664). The story returns to the present moment and Kathleen realises it is the war that has created the crisis, sapping all intervening memory from the house: 'The hollowness of the house this evening cancelled years on years of voices, habits and steps' (ibid.). In order to stave off the fear of the supernatural, she takes comfort in the mundane reality of ringing for a taxi to carry her and her parcels to the train station. But the crisis bites too deep, and she begins to be seduced by the uncanniness, losing herself in fearful forms of memory (the remembered lover has no face). The comforting sense of the taxi driver emboldens her, but this feeling alternates with being spooked by the certainty that someone is heard leaving the house.

Outside, there are signs of 'the ordinary flow of life' and she takes a taxi that seems strangely to know where she is going. The taxi is stopped suddenly, and the driver turns to stare at his passenger, then drives off as 'Mrs Drover' screams and screams.

The taxi might be taken to signal the modernist short story: its urbane mobility, the brevity of its journeys, the tight space, the sense of being controlled by something driving you, its combination of technology and transitional power. Key moments in modernism turn on the taxi, especially in the work of Virginia Woolf – the famous glimpse of a couple getting into a taxi in 'A Room of One's Own' (1929), Clarissa's 'perpetual sense, as she watched the taxi cabs, of being out, out, far out to sea and alone' in *Mrs Dalloway* (1925), the awful sense of Katherine being swallowed up by the speed and suddenness of the taxi in *Night and Day* (1919) ('She instantly was conveyed away from him, and the cab joined the knotted stream of vehicles'), the long taxi ride through London Katherine and Mary take in the same novel when somehow the city and the cab conspire to release deep feeling.[6] This sensibility, combining the taxi's technology with the transitional female affect being stirred by the age and the metropolis so associated with modernist Woolfian feminism, was darkened for Bowen by Woolf's suicide in 1941.[7] The voiding occasioned by wartime Gothic turns on the double spaces we have seen Bowen working up to thematise pre-war and wartime styles: we have the garden-gate transitional space and the house as evacuated memory-box. The two spaces coalesce in the taxicab itself, as Kathleen is forced to confront the faceless terror of death itself in a city of inhuman forces. In that taxi, Bowen concentrates her hybrid sense of the short story as both tight realist prosaic space of Jamesian encounters and supernaturally expansive force field for unconscious dreamwork. The death wish that colours the female imagination at war, destructive of Anglo-Irish patriarchy in 'Sunday Afternoon', postcolonial-feminist in the Kôr fantasy of She-dominated dead London, is in 'The Demon Lover' turned on modernist feminism itself as dark response to Woolf's suicide. The struggle between a brutal modernity and female psychology under war compulsions is given nightmare figuration in the vision of the taxi driven by the demon, fusing the Jamesian ghost story with the techno-feminism of Woolf's fiction to create an unmistakeable Bowen hybrid: 'After that she continued to scream freely and to beat with her gloved hands on the glass all round as the taxi, accelerating without mercy, made off with her into the hinterland of deserted streets' (666). The hybrid attends both to the scary claustrophobia of the psychological modernist short story, and to the female death wish held tight within a form that witnesses the killing off of pre-war and nineteenth-century manner and style (those 'gloved hands'). The glassed-in subject figures the hybrid short story itself, former habits of life being abandoned, accelerating within techno-history towards a nameless future, the enclosed textual space breaking to reveal dark hinterlands.

Notes

1. 'Blastwaves' is Shafquat Towheed's term for the effects of the Blitz bombardment on surrounding culture in this story. Cf. 'Territory, Space, Modernity: Elizabeth Bowen's *The Demon Lover and Other Stories* and Wartime London' in *Elizabeth Bowen: New Critical Perspectives* (2009).
2. This is Neil Corcoran's argument in his fine discussion of the story in *Elizabeth Bowen: The Enforced Return* (2004).
3. Though at Lucan along the Liffey, there is a demesne which was owned by the Vesey family, the most notable 'Mrs Vesey' being the eighteenth-century intellectual 'Bluestocking'; her husband had Lucan House built in the Palladian style in 1770 – alluded to in the story ('a villa in the Italian sense' (616)).
4. Cf. Robert Fisk, *In Time of War: Ireland, Ulster, and the Price of Neutrality* (1983).
5. Based on Vita Sackville-West's grandmother, Pepita, the half-gypsy from Malaga, dancer in Madrid, celebrated by Sackville-West in her 1937 *Pepita*. Pepita and Sackville-West's mother are 'too Latin, somehow; too unreal; too fantastic altogether; too un-English' (*Pepita* [London: Virago, 1986], 225).
6. See Virginia Woolf, *Mrs Dalloway* (9) and *Night and Day* (302).
7. Her letter of condolence to Leonard Woolf, 8 April 1941 stated: 'a great deal of the meaning seems to have gone out of this world. She illuminated everything, and one referred the most trivial things to her in one's thoughts' (8).

Works Cited

Bowen, Elizabeth (1944), 'The Short Story', *The Faber Book of Short Stories* [1936], Stockholm: A/B Ljus Förlag, pp. 7–19.

Bowen, Elizabeth (1999), *The Collected Stories of Elizabeth Bowen*, London: Vintage.

Bowen, Elizabeth (2008), 'Guy de Maupassant' [1946], *People, Places, Things: Essays by Elizabeth Bowen*, ed. Allan Hepburn. Edinburgh: Edinburgh University Press, p. 249.

Bowen, Elizabeth (2005), 'Letter to Leonard Woolf, 8 April 1941', *Afterwords: Letters on the Death of Virginia Woolf*, ed. Sybil Oldfield, New Brunswick, NJ: Rutgers University Press, pp. 7–8.

Bowen, Elizabeth (1999), *The Mulberry Tree: Writings of Elizabeth Bowen*, ed. Hermione Lee, London: Vintage.

Bowen, Elizabeth (2008), 'The Short Story in England' [1945], *People, Places, Things: Essays by Elizabeth Bowen*, ed. Allan Hepburn, Edinburgh: Edinburgh University Press, pp. 310–15.

Corcoran, Neil (2004), *Elizabeth Bowen: The Enforced Return*, Oxford: Clarendon Press.
Fisk, Robert (1983), *In Time of War: Ireland, Ulster, and the Price of Neutrality*, Philadelphia: University of Pennsylvania Press.
Sackville-West, Vita (1986), *Pepita* [1937], London: Virago.
Towheed, Shafquat (2009), 'Territory, Space, Modernity: Elizabeth Bowen's *The Demon Lover and Other Stories* and Wartime London', *Elizabeth Bowen: New Critical Perspectives*, ed. Susan Osborn, Cork: Cork University Press, pp. 113–31.
Woolf, Virginia (1986), *Mrs Dalloway*, London: Penguin.
Woolf, Virginia (1919), *Night and Day*, New York: Harcourt and Brace.
Woolf, Virginia (1929), *A Room of One's Own*, London: Hogarth Press.

Chapter 6

'Haunted, whether we like it or not': The Ghost Stories of Muriel Spark

James Bailey

Although she is better known as a novelist, Muriel Spark published over forty short stories between 1951 and 2000, achieving critical acclaim for her work within the genre years before the publication of her debut novel, *The Comforters*, in 1957. It was writing 'The Seraph and the Zambesi', the winning entry in *The Observer*'s Christmas short story competition in 1951, which Spark cited as 'the first real turning point of my career' (Spark 1992a: 198). That story, in which a celestial being appears before the performers of a nativity play, juxtaposes elements of the fantastic and the commonplace in a manner which would become a characteristic trait of the author's entire *oeuvre*, and particularly her ghost stories. Indeed, it was the ghost story, and tales of the uncanny and unexpected more generally, which appeared to preoccupy Spark in the years preceding and immediately after her first novel. Be it in the playful explorations of ghosts as symptoms of fractured psyches in 'The Leaf-Sweeper' (1952) and 'The Pearly Shadow' (1955), the eerie domestic drama of 'The Twins' (1954), or the sombre meditation on mortality and posthumous reputation that was 'The House of the Famous Poet' (1952), the ghost story offered Spark a special kind of freedom to experiment with narrative form and explore a diverse range of thematic concerns.

When asked in a 2003 interview whether her interest in the ghost story reflected her own belief in the supernatural, Spark responded with a degree of caution:

> Yes, I do [believe in ghosts]. But not in the sense that one could possibly describe it.... Ghosts exist and we are haunted, whether we like it or not in the sense that it can only be expressed by a physical presence, or a ghost, but in fact, I do believe in the presence of something that you can call a ghost but not in the physical outline. I don't see any other way in which you can express this actuality, and I can't deny this actuality simply because there is no other way to express it. (Devoize and Valette 247)

For Spark, then, the distinct 'physical presence' of the ghost served as a necessary means of articulating the otherwise inexpressible, intangible 'actuality' of being haunted. It is the nature and purpose of the hauntings in Spark's short fiction that forms the focus of this chapter, which explores four of the ghost stories written by the author during the 1950s:[1] 'Harper and Wilton' (1953), 'The Girl I Left Behind Me' (1957), 'The Portobello Road' (1958), and 'Bang-Bang You're Dead' (1961).[2] All of these stories concern hauntings enacted by and upon female characters, and explore the overlapping themes of spectrality, gender and narrative agency. The first of this chapter's two sections, 'Border-Crossings', concerns the female ghost's disruption of the text's ontological boundaries in her quest for narrative control. The second, 'Living Ghosts', explores Spark's unsettling depiction of the ghostly 'absent presence' of women within patriarchal society, and examines the author's use of the ghost story as a means of critiquing forms of patriarchal power.

Border-Crossings: Haunted Texts and Narrative Agency

In her 2004 poem, 'Authors' Ghosts', Spark imagines authors as spectral beings who return 'Nightly to haunt the sleeping shelves / And find the books they wrote' (13, ll. 2–3), before making alterations to their old works. 'The author's very touch', notes its speaker,

> is here, there and there,
> Where it wasn't before, and
> What's more, something's missing –
> I could have sworn . . . (ll.18–21)

By evading closure and even wrong-footing its own narrator, Spark's poem ends up *becoming* the kind of haunted, 'tampered with' (l. 16) text that it originally set out to describe. An abrupt shift in tone is detected in its penultimate line, where fanciful speculation gives way to wide-eyed bemusement as the speaker trails off, caught out by unforeseen changes to the text, unable to finish. What precedes this line is the poem as the speaker once knew it – something familiar, finished, and seemingly self-contained. In unravelling in the way it does, the poem performs what Gérard Genette calls metalepsis, the traversal of the 'shifting but sacred frontier between two worlds, the world in which one tells [the extradiegetic], the world of which one tells [the diegetic]' (236). The effect produced is thus one of ontological ambiguity; the poem no longer appears to belong to its speaker, its original ending having been erased by a meddlesome ghostwriter on another narrative plane. The reader is left to hover indeterminately between both narrative realms, displaced and disoriented by the ghostly textual intervention.

What is especially striking about 'Authors' Ghosts', Spark's final published work before her death in 2006, is that its twinned themes of haunting and ontological uncertainty can be traced back to some of her earliest short fictions including one of her first, 'Harper and Wilton'. The narrator of that story, an author attempting to complete a novel while house-sitting for friends in Hampshire, finds herself troubled by a 'feeling of chilling weirdness' (244). She attributes this to the behaviour of the resident gardener, Joe, who spends his days staring cross-eyed at the bedroom windows of the house. Unable to determine which of these rooms so intrigued Joe, or why he should be fixated on either one in the first place, the narrator returns to her work before being approached by two young women, 'dressed in Edwardian-type long skirts and shawls, with their long hair knotted up severely' (245). The women introduce themselves as the eponymous protagonists of a short story about a pair of Edwardian suffragettes, a story which the narrator had drafted and discarded long ago. Wilton announces that she and Harper have returned to their author because she 'cast [their] story away' without providing a satisfactory ending; 'Now you've got to give us substance', she threatens, 'otherwise we'll haunt you' (246). On rushing home to retrieve the draft (which is 'reproduced' in full in the text), the narrator revisits the farcical tale of Harper, Wilton and the cross-eyed young man who stares incessantly at the adjacent windows of their boarding-house bedrooms. Thrown by the stranger's squint, each woman suspects the other of being the complicit object of his desire, with Wilton accusing Harper of 'encourag[ing] the advances of a strange man' and Harper complaining to the Suffrage Committee that her friend has 'behaved in a manner prejudicial to [their] Cause' (248). When the young man climbs a drainpipe to reach the women's bedrooms, Harper and Wilton – squabbling loudly and still blaming one another for his advances – are arrested for disturbing the peace and each sentenced to a month's imprisonment.

'Harper and Wilton' (the story embedded *within* the story) is contrived and cartoonish, its protagonists badly drawn and its resolution unsatisfying; the stranger's advances go unchallenged and unpunished, while the women's noisy dispute only confirms the prejudices of the arresting constable, who is left sighing (as much to the intended reader as to himself), 'Suffragettes, eh?' (249). Given his unnerving fixation on the bedroom windows, the revelation that the stranger in the story is in fact Joe is hardly surprising. The young man, says Wilton, 'has given us no peace' ever since his author created him; 'He is molesting us', Harper concurs, 'It was he who should have gone to prison, not us' (251). In their quest for 'substance', Harper and Wilton demand that their author take their plight seriously by elevating their story beyond the level of farce, rewriting it 'in the light of current correctness' so that they 'were vindicated and it was the squint-eyed student who was taken off to the police'. When their creator complies, 'Harper and Wilton disappeared, evidently satisfied' (ibid.), while Joe is at last arrested. Despite being a playful and deftly told take on the traditional ghost story, however, the story retains a sense of vertiginous recursivity which raises more questions than its seemingly neat resolution cares to answer. Although the narrator is astonished at being greeted by her fictional creations, that she has already come to reside in a house so similar to the one she once invented (an environment she shares with Joe, who also turns out to be her fictional creation) indicates something altogether more complex. Not only does the narrator encounter characters who have made the ontological ascent from the pages of their story to the 'reality' she occupies, she has also descended, albeit unwittingly, into a realm resembling the storyworld she created and discarded long ago. In doing so, it is the narrator who returns, like the revenant authors in the poem Spark would write fifty years later, to haunt the manuscript that lay dormant and forgotten in her desk drawer.

Instead of presenting a singular metaleptic crossing from its embedded story to the extradiegetic realm occupied by its narrator, 'Harper and Wilton' thus resembles something more akin to a Möbius strip – a twisting, uncanny ribbon of fiction(s) in which a narrator 'descends' to haunt her characters, who in turn 'ascend' from their tale to stalk her. The recursive structure of the story, in which metaleptic crossings take the form of ghostly encounters, would inspire Spark's debut novel, *The Comforters* (1957), a similarly self-reflexive meditation on the eerie dynamic between author and character which Spark playfully described as 'a novel about writing a novel, about writing a novel sort of thing' (Kermode 79). Its protagonist, Caroline Rose, discovers that she is a character in a work of fiction after overhearing the clanking typewriter keys and omniscient narration of an authorial entity she calls the Typing Ghost. Like Harper and Wilton, however, she comes to antagonise her author by resisting the plot dictated to her: 'It is not easy to dispense with Caroline Rose', the Typing Ghost complains; 'Caroline among the sleepers turned her mind to the art of the novel, wondering and cogitating, those long hours, and exerting an undue, unreckoned, influence on the narrative from which she is supposed to be absent' (154). Unlike 'the sleepers' who comprise the novel's cast of stock characters, Caroline *Rose* is a restless character-turned-revenant, ascending from her storyworld to wrestle authorial control from her creator, dictating the remainder of the novel on her own terms.

As in 'Harper and Wilton', *The Comforters* draws upon tropes typically associated with the ghost story to depict the liminal states of characters and narrators crossing what Genette calls the 'sacred frontier' between diegetic levels. In doing so, Spark forges an explicit link between these metaleptic crossings and the eerily indeterminate position of ghosts, who traverse the threshold between life and the afterlife. In his seminal critical study, *Postmodernist Fiction* (1987), Brian McHale identifies this same sense of deathliness as an inherent feature of the 'self-reflective, self-conscious texts' he associates with the postmodern:

> insofar as postmodernist fiction foregrounds ontological themes and ontological structure, we might say that it is *always* about death . . . In a sense, every ontological boundary is an analogue or metaphor for death; so foregrounding ontological boundaries is a means of foregrounding death, of making death, the unthinkable, available to the imagination if only in a displaced way . . . Texts about themselves, self-reflective, self-conscious texts, are also, as if inevitably, about death, precisely because they are about ontological differences and the transgression of ontological boundaries. (231)

If, as McHale asserts, any text which foregrounds ontological boundaries inevitably evokes death, a text which deals directly with death and the afterlife – one which features a posthumous narrator, for example – is ideally suited to techniques associated with textual self-consciousness. For such narrators, who were once living characters occupying the diegetic realm of the story ('the world of which one tells', as Genette puts it), the journey to the afterlife constitutes a metaleptic crossing to an extradiegetic level ('the world in which one tells') from which the world of the living can be observed and narrated with a simultaneous sense of intimacy and estrangement.

This interplay between intimacy and estrangement is a characteristic feature of 'The Portobello Road'. The story is narrated by Needle, a ghost who announces early on in the text that she 'departed this life nearly five years ago', but 'did not altogether depart this world. There were those odd things to be done which one's executors can never do properly. Papers to be looked over' (498). Occupying a liminal position 'not altogether' rooted in the diegetic realm of the living, Needle can review her life story as though it were a completed text to be 'looked over' and narrated as she sees fit: 'I did not live to write about life as I wanted to do', she explains, 'Possibly that is why I am inspired to do so now in these peculiar circumstances' (501). The narrator's talk of 'Papers to be looked over' holds a secondary meaning, however; in the five years since her death, Needle has come to be remembered as the victim of what the newspapers named 'The Haystack Murder' (520), after the place from which her corpse was eventually retrieved. The grim fate suffered by Needle, who happened to acquire her nickname after discovering a needle buried within a haystack 'one day in [her] young youth' (495) many years before her murder, has since become fertile ground for bad jokes: 'when my body was found', she recalls disdainfully, 'the evening papers said, '"Needle" is found: in haystack!' (520).

'The Portobello Road' is thus a short story *about* a short story, concerning as it does a life cut short, a sense of potential remaining unfulfilled and a reputation reduced to a tiresome punchline. Needle's lifelong belief that she was somehow 'set apart from the common run' (495), a suspicion apparently confirmed by her chance discovery of the needle in a haystack, comes to bolster her 'ambition . . . to write about life' (500). This ambition is never realised, however; Needle meets her early death when she threatens to expose George, an old acquaintance, as a bigamist before his marriage to her close friend Kathleen. Terrified that the truth should be revealed, George proceeds to kill Needle in a manner that symbolises a chilling reversal of the formative instance in which she became aware both of her individuality and narrative agency:

> He looked as if he would murder me and he did. He stuffed hay into my mouth until it could hold no more, kneeling on my body to keep it still, holding both my wrists tight in his huge left hand. I saw the red full lines of his mouth and the white slit of his teeth last thing on earth. Not another soul passed by as he pressed my body into the stack, as he made a deep nest for me, tearing up the hay to make a groove the length of my corpse, and finally pulling the warm dry stuff in a mound over this concealment, so natural-looking in a broken haystack. (520)

By suffocating and silencing Needle, George attempts to eradicate the dissident female voice and thus uphold an oppressive 'master' narrative designed to ensnare women like Kathleen within a deceitful marriage plot. In burying his victim, George's use of Needle's corpse as a means of penetrating the haystack is connotative of an act of rape, in which the dead female body is appropriated, horrifyingly, as a phallic instrument to be 'pressed . . . into the stack'. Needle's nickname, which once signified her uniqueness, now suggests the violent, phallic mastery (and subsequent erasure) of a woman judged deviant for being 'set apart' from the dominant order.

Were 'The Portobello Road' to recount Needle's short life *without* including her posthumous narration, it might well have read as a cautionary and deeply conservative tale, warning women of the dangers of speaking freely and straying too far from their place among 'the common run'. Instead, the existence of a narrative afterlife offers Needle a second chance to fulfil her authorial ambition, allowing her to ascend to a diegetic plane from which her voice can at last be heard. The unique narrative capabilities of a posthumous narrator are explored at great length in Alice Bennett's recent study, *Afterlife and Narrative in Contemporary Fiction* (2012). This perspective, Bennett argues, poses a distinct challenge to the binary model of narrative possibilities proposed in studies including Richard Walsh's 'Who is the Narrator?' (1997), which contends that 'the narrator is always either a character who narrates, or the author', leaving 'no intermediate position' between the two (Walsh 505). As Bennett identifies, 'narration from the afterlife forces this categorisation to the surface by combining the characteristics of authorial omniscience with those of a fictional character narrator, as well as affecting the relationship between the levels of diegesis within the text' (128). These dual possibilities are afforded to Needle, who is able to recount her lived experience as character narrator might, while also witnessing, as if omnisciently, a number of subsequent events including her own post-mortem and the imprisonment of the man falsely accused of killing her.

Needle is not only a posthumous author, however, but a revenant one, and is thus eager to return to play an active role in the diegetic realm from which she was expelled by George. It is perhaps fitting that she chooses to greet George during his and Kathleen's visit to the Portobello Road Market, appearing among the displays of second-hand 'combs and hankies, cotton gloves, flimsy flowering scarves, writing-paper and crayons' (499) that make up the detritus of past lives, and thus presenting herself as a remainder and a reminder of the woman he killed. 'As I spoke', Needle notices, 'a degree of visibility set in' (500), allowing her to be seen by her murderer and consequently undoing the violent erasure she suffered at his hands. It is now George who is plunged into a state of deathly silence. Needle's seemingly offhand remark that the thick, light-coloured beard George has grown since she saw him last causes him to look 'as if he had a mouthful of hay' (522) is therefore far from innocent; by describing her newly silent murderer with reference to the material he used to silence *her*, she gleefully acknowledges the reversal of agency effected by her ghostly return. In this variation of the traditional ghost story, Needle's ascension to a narrative afterlife enables her to escape the prescribed role of the Gothic female victim by casting herself as its active, purposeful protagonist.[3]

Living Ghosts: (Anti-)Realism and Spectral Selves

As evinced by Needle's revelry in her newfound narrative agency, the ghost trope is no mere metafictional stunt, but a valuable means of reinstating a voice that had been violently erased. Far from being a fanciful addition to an otherwise realistic tale, the posthumous voice thus announces itself as an entirely necessary means of conveying truths that could not otherwise have been spoken. Addressing her fiction's unconventional pairing of realistic and supernatural elements, Spark describes her approach as follows: 'I treat the supernatural as if it was part of natural history. If I write a ghost story it wouldn't come under the heading of a ghost story necessarily because I treat it as if it was a natural thing' (Brooker 1036). Spark's advocacy for a 'natural' approach to the ghost story is in keeping with her wider distrust of conventional, restrictive notions of realism. 'Realistic novels', she told Robert Hosmer, 'are more committed to dogmatic and absolute truth than most other varieties of fiction' (147). To this end, the ghost trope is particularly effective, enabling Spark to introduce elements of the supernatural into otherwise realistic scenarios, and, in so doing, to subvert or undermine the supposedly stable structures of patriarchal authority depicted therein.

Spark's 'natural' treatment of the ghost story is nowhere more apparent than in 'The Girl I Left Behind Me', first published in a 1957 issue of *Ellery Queen's Mystery Magazine*. Its narrator, an unnamed office employee who appears to have been lifted from a work of kitchen-sink realism, recounts the end of a wearisome yet seemingly uneventful day at work, including apparently inconsequential details regarding her bus journey and boarding house lodgings. Her mood is one of despondency as she recalls feeling 'particularly anonymous among the homegoers' (278) as she boards the bus, 'depressed' when another passenger 'looked away' from her 'without response' (279) and later 'desolate' (281) after being ignored by her landlady. Her thoughts turn frequently to her manager, Mr Letter, who she had last witnessed in a trance-like state, clutching his necktie and whistling the folk tune with which the story shares its title. It is only when she returns to the office, convinced of there being something 'left unfinished' (280) there that must be attended to, that the narrator discovers her own body, 'lying strangled on the floor' (283). The 'trick' played by Spark, then, is to reveal her narrator's seemingly unimportant observations as vital clues to her murder and present spectrality. The presence of the corpse thus appears to offer a reassuring solution to the various ambiguities amassed in the story, accounting for the narrator's sense of isolation and invisibility in her new, ghostly state, as well as the unsettling behaviour of Mr Letter.

It is perhaps because of this shocking yet seemingly neat resolution that 'The Girl I Left Behind Me' is cited by Bennett as an example of a text in which 'the dead narrator is essentially a punchline', which 'shuts down possibilities rather than opening them up' (18–19). Rather than eliminating possibilities, however, the 'punchline' revelation of the narrator's death raises further questions about the ghostliness of her silent, passive presence while still alive. Indeed, what is perhaps even more unsettling than the narrator's murder is her subsequent failure to recognise that it happened. 'No one . . . took any notice of me', she remarks of her commute from work, 'of course, why should they?' (278); the impression produced here is that the narrator's present, spectral state is not entirely unlike her past, living one. The story is thus an example of what Aviva Briefel, in her study of films including Charles Vidor's *The Spy* (1929) and Alejandro Amenábar's *The Others* (2001), terms 'spectral incognizance' – a ghost story 'subgenre' which 'represents death as an event that can be overlooked' (96). Spark's narrator manages to overlook *her* death not because it is too traumatic to recall, but because, having grown so radically detached from her body over a prolonged period of time, the violence inflicted upon it merely fails to register.

'The Girl I Left Behind Me' can thus be read as a ghost story regardless of its protagonist's death and posthumous narration, suggesting as it does a slow, sinister process of self-alienation which was set in place long before her murder.[4] Quite how this came to be is never made explicit over the course of the story (one of Spark's shortest at only five pages long), yet the narrator's recollection of her interactions with Mr Letter acquire an unsettling resonance when interpreted in light of the ending. Read retroactively, for example, what the narrator had described as Letter's frequent 'dreamy states' and 'lapses into lassitude' (278) reveal themselves to be periods of murderous contemplation, while his incessant whistling of the story's eponymous folk tune takes on a chilling sense of foreboding. These and other habitual practices, including fits of anxiety-inducing mania in the office, leave the protagonist feeling perennially apprehensive, her mood and behaviour manipulated to such an extent that she becomes a stranger to herself and those around her. As his name indicates, Mr Letter stands for the masculine, authoritative discourse which imprisons women like the narrator within its patriarchal sentence, leaving no room for her own voice to emerge. Only this can account for the narrator's overwhelming sense of joy upon discovering her corpse at the end of the story, which she 'embraced . . . like a lover' (283).

Given its preoccupation with the ghostly presence of women within patriarchy, 'The Girl I Left Behind Me' bears a certain resemblance to

Spark's later work, *The Driver's Seat* (1970), a novel described by its author as 'a study, in a way, of self-destruction' (Gillham 412). The life of the novel's protagonist, Lise, has long been characterised by a similar sense of deadening rigidity, from the eerily symmetrical distribution of her work colleagues – 'she has five girls under her and two men. Over her are two women and five men' (9) – to her anonymous-looking, seemingly 'uninhabited' apartment, the furnishings of which are built from 'swaying tall pines', now 'subdued into silence and into obedient bulks' (15). Lise has come to resemble one of these lifeless bulks; she is subdued and dutifully silent, with even her lips remaining 'pressed together like the ruled line of a balance sheet' as she submits to her role within the rigid, gender-imbalanced office hierarchy 'where she has worked continually ... for sixteen years and some months' (9). In *The Driver's Seat*, however, it is the protagonist who actively seeks out her killer, who, she specifies, must be male and must implement as murder weapons the knife and necktie that she purchased for the occasion. In doing so, Lise offers her bound and brutalised corpse as a text designed to communicate the death-in-life she has already suffered; the man's necktie which renders her body immobile is connotative of the stifling patriarchal order that has denied her agency, while the knife with which she orders her killer to pierce her throat replicates the brutal silencing of her voice that occurred long before the narrative began. In this novel, which develops the themes explored tentatively in 'The Girl I Left Behind Me', death remains woman's sole means of gaining access to narrative agency, of communicating the sense of ghostly voicelessness and disembodiment endured in life.

Rather than being summoned from the dead by seances or spells (or haunting the text via metaleptic border-crossings, as explored earlier), Spark's living ghosts are characters whose vitality and free will have been occluded by manipulative relationships, deadening routines and inhibitive social conventions. Such is the theme of 'Bang-Bang You're Dead', perhaps Spark's most personal short story, in which the prospect of becoming one's own ghost is an ever-present threat. The story was inspired in part by an incident that occurred during Spark's life in colonial Africa in the late 1930s, in which her former schoolfriend and fellow expatriate, Nita McEwan, was murdered by her husband. As Spark recalled in an interview, the incident became all the more unsettling due to the uncanny resemblance the women shared:

> I was staying at the same place as the girl when I heard two screams, a bang and then another bang ... I was told my friend had been killed by her husband. He shot her and then himself. The next morning when I entered the communal dining room, a woman screamed and fainted, thinking I was

a ghost, because I looked so similar to the shot girl. There were quite a lot of shooting affairs at that time. It was quite savage. (Greig 9)

For Spark, who had been suffering for some time in an abusive marriage, Nita's murder appeared to foreshadow her own – a feeling compounded by the friends' physical similarities and Spark's consequent, ghostly appearance to the fainting woman.[5] The incident became the starting point for the story of Sybil, whose long and fraught relationship with her own near-double, Désirée, plays out as a series of ghostly interactions.

'Bang-Bang You're Dead' employs as a framing device a social gathering at the English home of Sybil, who entertains her guests by showing them home movies of her life in Africa eighteen years earlier. The films, which paint a rosy picture of colonial life, including Sybil's apparent friendship with Désirée, are placed in uneasy juxtaposition with flashbacks depicting the reality of their relationship. As children in 1920s England, one such flashback reveals, the girls stage imaginary gunfights, during which (and 'contrary to the rules'), 'Désirée continually shot Sybil dead . . . whenever she felt like it.' Despite disapproving of her friend's unruly conduct, the nine-year-old Sybil 'obediently' plays along, endlessly 'resurrect[ing] herself' to endure a 'repeated daily massacre' in uneasy compliance with Désirée's newly invented rules (88–9). The game, though seemingly innocent, sets a pattern for Sybil's later life and her continued, submissive relationship with Désirée when the pair are reunited in Africa years later. Against her better judgement, Sybil goes 'in obedience' to the home of Désirée and her husband, Barry Weston, where she feels compelled to participate in 'a game for three players', in which, 'according to the rules, she was to be in love, unconsciously, with Barry, and tortured by the contemplation of Désirée's married bliss' (106). Much like her compulsion to participate in the shooting games as a child, the adult Sybil is drawn repeatedly, as if by a 'magnetic field' (101), to occupy a role intended to silence, humiliate and tame her.

In keeping with her name, therefore, Désirée stands as a patriarchal construct, a depthless object of male desire designed to torment Sybil by goading her into complying with a heteronormative script of gender and sexuality. Despite possessing a 'superior' intellect and a 'brain . . . like a blade' (87), Sybil remains hopelessly drawn to the commands of her double, restlessly pursuing passionless affairs with men including David Carter (ironically, the manager of a passion fruit plantation). Conceding that these affairs were merely 'an attempt . . . to do the right thing', Sybil 'worked herself as in a frenzy of self-discipline, into a state of carnal excitement over the men' she meets, which she achieved 'only by an effortful sealing-off of all her critical faculties'. As if in an act of protest, however, Sybil's body succumbs to a bout of tropical flu, leaving her suffering a 'twilight of the senses' on a bed 'overhung with a white mosquito net like something bridal' (97–8). With its conflated imagery of marital customs and abject horror – the honeymoon suite and the sickbed; the bridal veil and the ghostly white sheet; the virgin bride and the vulnerable, feverish body – the period of illness becomes a grim omen for Sybil's fate should she bow to convention and pursue marriage. To do so, her sick body warns her, would be an act of self-destruction, a deadly *ghosting* of her real self from which there is no way back. Sybil's sickness thus appears an initial stage in the sinister process of woman's corporeal estrangement within patriarchy, which reaches its chilling completion in 'The Girl I Left Behind Me'.

As in the Freudian model of the uncanny, where the double operates as 'the uncanny harbinger of death' (Freud 235), Désirée represents the imminent, ghostly future that awaits Sybil should she go against her better judgement and adhere to a conventional, heteronormative script. In the end, it is Sybil's repudiation of this script that brings about her double's death. Incensed at Sybil's rejection of his marriage proposal ('it's your duty to me as a man' [114], he insists), David forces his way into the Weston's home and, mistaking Désirée for his former lover in the dim light, shoots her dead before killing himself. The scene rests, finally, on Sybil, who 'rose from Désirée's body' (118) like a spirit might from a corpse. The impression produced here is disturbingly ambiguous, suggesting at once that Sybil has finally rid herself of the ties that bind her to her double, yet also that she will live on as Désirée's ghost, condemned to exist forever in her image. If the scene does illustrate the protagonist's newfound freedom, however, it appears to have been short-lived; as she entertains the guests gathered at her home many years later, it becomes clear that Sybil has become caught once again in a tired performance of female subservience, offering tactful half-truths about her life in Africa, while agreeing politely to replay the film reels and allowing Désirée's spectral projected image to obscure her own.

Their subject matter aside, it is arguably the condensed, elliptical nature of the short story form that provides 'The Girl I Left Behind Me' and 'Bang-Bang You're Dead' with much of their power to unsettle. The necessary brevity of the genre, for example, makes the transitions between Sybil's past and present all the more abrupt and disorienting, leaving strange, spectral traces of Désirée in scenes from which she is absent. Similarly, the creeping sense of unease and uncertainty that permeates 'The Girl I Left Behind Me' is only exacerbated by the oblique, inconclusive narrative necessitated by the story's five-page length, which make its impressions indelible. It is perhaps for reasons such as these that Spark claimed the short story to be 'superior to the novel in many ways', arguing that each story's formal concision made it 'something by itself' and thus 'likely to have a longer life' (Devoize and Valette, 243). This perhaps accounts for the author's self-acknowledged preference for 'keep[ing] it short' (Gillham 412) when it came to her novels, favouring neatly plotted, laconic narratives over sprawling, excessively detailed description.[6] While formal concision enabled Spark to tell the eerie, claustrophobic tales of women like Sybil and the unnamed 'Girl', her experiments with metalepsis and textual self-consciousness in 'Harper and Wilton' and 'The Portobello Road' produced short stories that are deceptively expansive, with the latter enabling its deceased protagonist to return to the text as its narrator, now able to interrogate the narrow margins of her lived life. In assessing various aspects of Spark's fiction, from her experimental narrative techniques to the subversive quality of her work, the significance of the short story (and the ghost story in particular) cannot be underestimated. It seems appropriate, then, to conclude by returning to the scene of Harper and Wilton, characters from a short story tossed aside and long since forgotten, reappearing to remind their author (who is now preoccupied with writing a book, rather than shorter narratives) of their lasting importance.

Notes

1. All stories are included in *The Complete Short Stories* (2011) and all quotations are taken from this volume.
2. Although 'Bang-Bang You're Dead' was not published until 1961, when it appeared in Spark's collection of short fiction and radio plays, *Voices at Play*, records of the author's correspondence with the *New Yorker* reveal that the story was submitted to, and rejected by, the publication in 1958. 'The Portobello Road' was also turned down for publication in 1957, despite positive reviews from its editors. For a detailed study of Spark's relationship with the *New Yorker*, in which several of her short stories *were* published, see Lisa Harrison, '"The magazine that is considered the best in the world": Muriel Spark and the *New Yorker*' (2010).
3. It is entirely possible that Needle's subversion of her prescribed role as Gothic female victim informed the content of Spark's artistic manifesto, 'The Desegregation of Art' (1970). Here Spark rejects any 'ineffective literature' concerned with 'the representation of the victim against the oppressor' (34) arguing that such representations only reaffirm the inertial positions of oppressor and oppressed. In place of this, Spark's manifesto calls for 'a less impulsive generosity, a less indignant representation of social injustice, and a more deliberate cunning, a more derisive undermining of what is wrong' (35). Where faithful depictions of suffering and tragedy serve merely to satisfy moral responsibilities and absolve readerly guilt, 'the art of ridicule

... can penetrate to the marrow. It can leave a salutary scar. It is unnerving. It can paralyse its object' (36).
4. 'You don't know how repulsive and loathsome is the ghost of a living man' (241), asserts the narrator of 'The Leaf-Sweeper'. Spark would go on to develop novels around this conceit of the living ghost. In her 1971 novel, *Not to Disturb*, for example, the Baron and Baroness Klopstock appear to their staff as 'insubstantial bodies', who 'haunt the house' (23). The novel that followed, *The Hothouse by the East River* (1973), turns the idea on its head by depicting a married couple, Elsa and Paul Hazlett, who live active, busy lives in 1970s New York, without realising that they both were killed at the end of the Second World War.
5. In his excellent biography of Spark, Martin Stannard writes that Nita McEwan's death 'seemed like an omen' (50) for the author's fate should she remain in her own abusive marriage.
6. The notable exception in Spark's *oeuvre* is her expansive 1965 novel, *The Mandelbaum Gate*. The author later criticised the novel for being 'out of proportion' (Gillham 412) and embarked upon a sequence of novels, spanning *The Public Image* (1968) to *The Hothouse by the East River* (1973), that were among her slightest and most elliptical.

Works Cited

Bennett, Alice (2012), *Afterlife and Narrative in Contemporary Fiction*, Houndmills; New York: Palgrave Macmillan.

Briefel, Aviva (2009), 'What Some Ghosts Don't Know: Spectral Incognizance and the Horror Film', *Narrative*, 17:1, pp. 95–108.

Brooker, James, and Margarita EstévezSaá (2004), 'Interview with Dame Muriel Spark', *Women's Studies*, 33:8, pp. 1035–46.

Devoize, Janette, and Pamela Valette (2003), 'Muriel Spark – b.1918 [Interview]', *Journal of the Short Story in English,* 41, pp. 243–54.

Freud, Sigmund (1955), 'The Uncanny' [1919], *The Standard Edition of the Complete Psychological Works of Sigmund Freud*, Vol. 17, ed. James Strachey, London: Hogarth Press, pp. 218–52.

Genette, Gérard (1980), *Narrative Discourse: An Essay In Method*, trans. Jane E. Lewin, Ithaca, New York: Cornell University Press.

Gillham, Ian (1970), 'Keeping it Short: Muriel Spark Talks about Her Books to Ian Gillham', *The Listener*, 24 September, pp. 411–13.

Greig, Geordie (1996), 'The Dame's Fortunes [Interview]', *The Sunday Times Books,* 22 September, pp. 8–9.

Harrison, Lisa (2010), '"The magazine that is considered the best in the world": Muriel Spark and the *New Yorker*', *Muriel Spark: Twenty-First Century Perspectives*, ed. David Herman, Baltimore: The Johns Hopkins University Press, pp. 39–60.

Hosmer, Robert Ellis (2005), 'An Interview with Dame Muriel Spark', *Salmagundi*, 146/147, pp. 127–58.

Kermode, Frank (1962), 'The House of Fiction: Interviews with Seven English Novelists', *Partisan Review*, 30, pp. 61–82.

McHale, Brian (1987), *Postmodernist Fiction*, New York; London: Methuen.

Spark, Muriel (2004), 'Author's Ghosts', *All the Poems*, Manchester: Carcanet, p. 13.
Spark, Muriel (1961), *The Comforters* [1957], New York: HarperCollins.
Spark, Muriel (2011), *The Complete Short Stories*, Edinburgh: Canongate.
Spark, Muriel (1992a), *Curriculum Vitae*, Harmondsworth: Penguin.
Spark, Muriel (1992b), 'The Desegregation of Art' [1970], *Critical Essays on Muriel Spark*, ed. Joseph Hynes, New York: G. K. Hall, pp. 33–7.
Spark, Muriel (1974), *The Driver's Seat* [1970], Harmondsworth: Penguin.
Spark, Muriel (1973), *The Hothouse by the East River*, Harmondsworth: Penguin.
Spark, Muriel (1971), *Not to Disturb*, London: Macmillan.
Stannard, Martin (2009), *Muriel Spark: The Biography*, London: Weidenfeld & Nicolson.
Walsh, Richard (1997), 'Who is the Narrator?', *Poetics Today*, 18:4, pp. 495–513.

Chapter 7

Disaggregative Character Identity and the Politics of Aesthetic In-betweenness in Angela Carter's Short Narratives

Michelle Ryan-Sautour

In the documentary 'Angela Carter's Curious Room', filmed shortly before her death in 1992, Angela Carter proclaimed her opposition to the illusion of character, describing, with her typical edge, how the idea of characters taking over a narrative is 'self-indulgent' and 'dumb', and explaining how her own characters 'leap off the page' in the process of 'telling something' to the reader (Carter 1992: n.p.). Carter has indeed underlined narrative as being an argument stated in fictional terms that allows her to explore ideas: 'I like creeping up on people from behind and sandbagging them with an idea that maybe they hadn't thought of for themselves' (ibid.). Such provocation is dangerous territory, and Carter was estranged from many feminist circles in the 1970s for her controversial engagement with feminism, as is evident in her embracing of Sadeian principles: 'Women do not normally fuck in the active sense. They are fucked in the passive tense and hence automatically fucked-up, done over, undone. Whatever else he says or does not say, Sade declares himself unequivocally for the right of women to fuck' (Carter 2001: 27). Carter's revisionist tales and speculative fiction indeed solicit the reader through defiant modes of ideological exploration, and her characters serve as a central pivot in this process. However, despite her aforementioned suggestion of allegorically saturated characters in a landscape of postmodern flatness, her stories actually play with the reader's literary faith, that is his or her active suspension of disbelief, through subtle shifts in the status of characters.[1] The result is a complex interplay of illusion and ideas.

Charles May has commented on how a fictional character can range between the respective poles of metonymy and metaphor within the short story, balancing between the illusion of individuality and the collective dimension of myth: 'Goodman Brown alternately acts as if he were an allegorical figure who must make his journey into the forest as an inevitable working out of the preordained mythic story of which he is a part, and as a psychologically complex, realistic character who, although obsessed with his journey, is able to question its wisdom and morality' (May 2002: 20). Carter's stories expand upon and amplify this tendency in the fusion of 'sign and sense' of 'short narrative' (Carter 1987a: 132) to create characters who, when held up to critical light, are revealed to have multiple facets. Her ideological beings resonate with the reader as persons, while echoing the political and cultural discourse that underlies much of her fiction. This chapter will address the complexity of the character images constructed through this process in a selection of Carter's short fiction and will propose hypotheses about their effect on the reader.[2]

Character instability appears first and foremost in the play with generic borders that characterises Carter's short narrative. Her stories often layer and juxtapose the modes of autobiography, news reports, biographical sketches, historical narrative and literary criticism with the Gothic, the fairy tale, and standard fiction, blending the likes of Baudelaire and Poe with Shakespearean characters and infusing speech with a flickering of intertextual resonances. As Karima Thomas suggests in her study of Carter's fictionalised news piece, 'The Fall River Axe Murders' (1985), characterisation hinges upon a self-conscious questioning of fictional modes (n.p.). In her well-known 'Afterword' to *Fireworks* (1974), Carter's first collection of short narratives, Carter confesses to a strong aversion to verisimilitude, and thus explains her attraction to the form of the 'tale':

> Formally, the tale differs from the short story in that it makes few pretenses at the imitation of life. The tale does not log everyday experience, as the short story does, it interprets everyday experience through a system of imagery derived from subterranean areas behind everyday experience, and therefore the tale cannot betray its readers into a false knowledge of everyday experience. (Carter 1987a: 133)

These 'subterranean areas of everyday experience' are examined in Thomas's essay, as she demonstrates the subtlety and variability in Carter's application of these principles. Thomas shows how Carter challenges the modes of realism in the historically inspired text, downplaying any 'false knowledge of everyday experience' by exposing the discursive strategies behind portrayals of 'fact' and 'truth' through Carter's clever doubling of the real Lizzie Borden (accused in 1892 of killing her father and stepmother) and her fictional counterpart (n.p.). The result is a deliberate, politically charged blurring of fact and fiction. Indeed, because Carter's 'tales' walk a tightrope of generic borders, they trouble traditional modes of characterisation. Although her professed preference for the Gothic modes of Poe where 'Character and events are exaggerated beyond reality' and style 'operate[s] against the perennial human desire to believe the word as fact' is not ultimately enacted in all of her short texts, many of her characters do retain the 'singular moral function' she sees as lying at the heart of the genre, 'that of provoking unease' (Carter 1987a: 133). This unease stems in part from the troubling complexity of beings who are positioned at the borders of fiction.

In his introduction to *The Postmodern Short Story* (2003), Farhat Iftekharrudin refers to Mary Rohrberger's use of the term 'anti-story' to address the way 'Postmodern stories are complex in form and content and make use of a variety of styles including parody, self-conscious fictionality, grotesquerie, and fantasy' (20).[3] The title of the first section in this collection of essays, 'Fictional Nonfiction and Nonfictional Fiction', addresses the manner in which postmodern anti-stories test the limits of the fictional contract in a wavering that, according to Michele Morano, affects the reader's engagement with the text:

> Presenting a piece of short prose as an essay or a story means offering the reader a set of parameters for receiving the work, a contract of sorts ... From the reader's perspective, a work's label of short story or essay sometimes competes with other information – be it intra- or extratextual – that complicates genre. (36)

Although most of Carter's short narratives are published as fiction, the subtitle to her *Fireworks* collection, *Nine Profane Pieces*, reflects a self-consciousness with regard to generic labels, as the word 'piece', suggests non-fiction, whereas 'story' implies fiction. An alternative subtitle in a later edition of the same collection, *Fireworks: Nine Stories in Various Disguises* (1981), also plays with generic ambivalence, but from another angle, as it indicates that the texts are simply parading as stories. This generic ambiguity sets up a sense of uncertainty in the reading contract.[4]

In Carter's semi-autobiographical texts in *Fireworks*, for example ('A Souvenir of Japan', 'Flesh and the Mirror', 'The Smile of Winter') the reader is led to hesitate between perceiving the first-person narrator as Angela Carter, or as a fictional being. Correspondences between Carter's own biography and the 'pieces' foster an illusion of authorial presence and authenticity in the texts that affects the reader's perception of the narrator's first person 'I'. Similarly, Carter's version of what Michael Orlofsky calls 'historiografiction', a term used to 'denote the literary treatment of persons or events from the past' (Orlofsky 2003: 47), plays with and cultivates hesitation in the reading contract. Texts such as Carter's 'The Cabinet of Edgar Allan Poe' (Carter 1987b) which depicts a stylised representation of Poe's life as a study of identity, accompanied by verbal play and parodies of his works, draw forth the biographical for semi-fictionalised reflection. Similarly, 'Black Venus' (Carter 1987b) represents Baudelaire's companion Jeanne Duval and thus functions in an intertextual/historical mode of bringing the silent voice of the muse to the surface of history. The first person 'I' of 'Our Lady of the Massacre' (Carter 1987b) provides the reader with a historically/intertextually charged account of a British woman captured by 'Indians' in the 'New World'. As a Lancashire woman imprisoned at Newgate Prison and then sent by boat to Virginia, the story's protagonist is connected implicitly with Daniel Defoe's *Moll Flanders*, as she appears to be the eponymous character's mother.[5] The beginning of the short story overlaps uncannily with that of Defoe's novel, as both characters open the works with discussions of naming and identity:

> My true name is so well known in the records or registers at Newgate, and in the Old Bailey, and there are some things of such consequence still depending there, relating to my particular conduct, that it is not be expected I should set my name or the account of my family to this work; perhaps, after my death, it may be better known; at present it would not be proper, no not though a general pardon should be issued, even without exceptions and reserve of persons or crimes. (Defoe 1722: n.p.)

> My name is neither here nor there since I used several in the Old World that I may not speak of now; then there is my, as it were, *wilderness* name, that now I never speak of; and, now, what I call myself in *this* place, therefore my name is no clue as to my person nor my life as to my nature. (Carter 1987b: 41)

Carter recuperates the inherent self-consciousness of Defoe's character, and exploits Moll Flanders' association with duplicity and shifting identity. In Defoe's novel, the protagonist's narrative is often unreliable. Her disregard for and easy abandonment of her children in order to climb the social ladder, also creates ambivalence around her character. Her life is depicted as a series of social performances, an intertextual theme that carries over into the reflections on identity embedded in Carter's stories and heightens the speculative potential of the story.[6]

Orlofsky sees historiografiction as being concerned primarily with character, and not as much with plot, setting and details (Orlofsky 2003: 47), and Carter's texts demonstrate a similar preoccupation. Her aforementioned character, Lizzie, who appears not only in 'The Fall

River Axe Murders' but also as a child in Carter's later story, 'Lizzie's Tiger' (1993), becomes the centre of an uneasy navigation between Carter's speculative realm and the historical 'facts' of the original crime. Similarly, the anachronistic appearance of nineteenth-century Australian outlaw, Ned Kelly, in 'Alice in Prague *or* The Curious Room' (1993), a story openly set at the end of the sixteenth century, draws the reader to superimpose this figure upon the historical figure of Edward Kelly, a sixteenth-century alchemist, resulting in a playful layering of identities: 'He always wears the iron mask modelled after that which will be worn by a namesake three hundred years hence in a country that does not yet exist, an iron mask like an upturned bucket with a slit cut for his eyes' (Carter 1994: 126). Such is the blurring of history, fact and fiction in narratives that are juxtaposed with the flagrant fantasy modes of 'The Loves of Lady Purple', 'Peter and the Wolf' and 'Penetrating to the Heart of the Forest', for example, or the jubilatory parody evident in 'Overture and Incidental Music for *A Midsummer's Night's Dream*' and 'In Pantoland'. The reader of Carter's 'pieces', or 'tales', is indeed faced with a collage of narrative modes that often interact in a dynamics of intertextuality that fuses the historical with the personal and, as I have argued elsewhere, leaves the reader wondering about Carter's speculative and political agenda.[7]

Carter's characters indeed evolve in universes that experiment with the contours of fiction, cultivating a floating, in-between reading posture, between the customary 'suspension of disbelief' one adopts in relation to the fictional text, and the seeking of truth and fact fostered by traditional non-fiction or autobiography. This is familiar territory for critics of postmodern fiction. However, in Carter's politically saturated writing, this generic complexity, and the resulting ontological instability of her fictional worlds, produces variable beings with a striking potential to destabilise the reader. This functions as a form of literary militancy that is further complicated by the layering of speculative, intertextual, historical identities within single characters, transforming them into discursive entities who seemingly function as pawns in a game of interpretation. In this respect, it is tempting to lean towards the allegorical pole of reading when engaging with Carter's texts. It is certainly for this reason that Thomas insists upon the discursive dominant of Carter's characters in 'The Fall River Axe Murders'.[8] However, the role of affect cannot be evacuated from the scene of characterisation. On the contrary, narrative techniques and cultural codes that privilege affective reactions on the part of the reader colour Carter's beings with sympathy and foster a commingling of aesthetic effects. As Carter comments in relation to her novel *Nights at the Circus* (1984):

it does seem a bit of an imposition to say to readers that if you read this book you have got to be thinking all the time; so it's there only if you want it. From *The Magic Toyshop* onwards I've tried to keep an entertaining surface to the novels, so that you don't have to read them as a system of signification if you don't want to. (Carter 1985: 87)

Carter's subtle forms of 'entertainment' in her short stories indeed expand upon May's suggestion that different levels of identity can coalesce within an individual character. Her stories seek to move beyond the mythical signification May suggests, rather than reify myth.[9] However, her characters do display a similar complexity, as they are composed of layers of conceptual discourse and affective details, that '"defamiliarize" the everyday' (May 1994: 133).

Vincent Jouve in *L'effet personage dans le roman* (*The Character Effect in the Novel* 1992) has created a reading model that can address certain aspects of this complexity. He emphasises the central role of the character in literary communication and studies the possible links between textual structure and a reader's reception of a character (50). In a manner similar to Charles May, he identifies two poles in character identity, the referential and the discursive and explains how characters oscillate between these poles, even within the same work.[10] According to Jouve, characters can range between the dominant of individuality (the character is seen as a person) and the collective or discursive modes of intertextuality or allegory (the character is seen as a figure to be interpreted). Carter's short narratives explore the relationship between these two poles and thus lead the reader to identify with figures of shifting, evasive contours, always on the fringes of readability. She sets up various levels of ontological seriousness in her characters through a careful manipulation of narrative technique, intertextuality, focalisation, stylistic density, and onomastics.[11] The image and identity of these beings undergo fluctuations, as the illusion of character, according to Jouve, is a complex, dynamic configuration, constructed progressively throughout the reading process.[12]

In order to address this process of construction, Jouve proposes a model based on Michel Picard's *La Lecture comme jeu* (*Reading as a Game* 1986), and identifies three different levels of reading in relation to the fictional character, that of the *lectant* (the intellectually aware reader who reads from the perspective of the author and sees the characters as pawns in a game), the *lisant* (the reader who is drawn into the illusion proposed by the text, who believes and plays the fictional game in the spirit of Coleridge's famous 'suspension of disbelief') and the *lu* (the passively 'read' reader who interacts on a more instinctive level with the text via erotic or violent scenes, for example) (Jouve 82). Jouve's model, although primarily addressing characters in the novel, provides a practical basis to examine the varying levels at which the reader is led to relate to Carter's characters in her short fiction. It is indeed difficult to purge even the most challenging of Carter's 'anti-stories' of the desire for affective identification. As Elaine Jordan observes, Carter's writing is more than self-conscious, critical enquiry: 'Carter's fictions make a spectacle of themselves, in great style; the critical distance invited can leave a reader more free than empathy. However, empathy may conceivably have a place' (1992: 167). I will sketch a few examples to suggest how this works within the restricted space of short narrative.

In Carter's speculative story, 'Reflections', the reader is placed in a densely layered fantasy, an *Alice in Wonderland* space, where the 'I' character of the narrator is led to pass into a world on the other side of a mirror. The names of the characters are saturated with allegorical meaning, as the two figures are labelled respectively as 'the androgyne' and 'Anna'. The 'androgyne' proposes a metafictional discussion of their sexual identity: '"The name of my niece is Anna," she said to me, "because she can go both ways. As, indeed, I can myself, though I am not a simple palindrome"' (Carter 1987a: 97–8). Philippe Hamon has commented on the form of *etiquettes* or 'labels' that underline the semiological status of the character.[13] Likewise, he extends this idea to the changeable status of the character: 'The illusion of life is first linked to the way the character is designated' (110, my translation).[14] In 'Reflections', names are undeniably linked to a reflection on indeterminate identity in relation to the binary suggested by the mirror. The narrator's reflection on the pronoun 'she' in relation to the androgyne, reinforces a self-conscious reflection about labels and the self: 'It is a defect in our language there is no term of reference for these indeterminate and undefinable beings; but, although she acknowledged no gender, I will call her 'she' because she had put on a female garment' (Carter 1987a: 95). The story is indeed suggestive of themes identified by Charlotte Crofts in relation to Carter's radio plays: 'Carter challenges the concept of the "self" as fixed and whole, offering alternative paths in the construction of identity' (2003: 25–6).

Carter's shifting labels succinctly examine the contours, the borders of the 'self' as incarnated in character. This is also evident in 'Elegy for a Freelance' (1985) where characters are reduced to the status of simple letters:

> I sterilized my nail scissors in the gas jet and A held his wailing son in his arms after I cut the cord. But, however pleased A was to be a father, he insisted on a fair trial for X. Perhaps, even then, B and C didn't quite trust me; I'd been a rich girl. But X confessed everything to us all quite freely. (Carter 1987a: 124)

Here characters represent an instrumental role in a reflection on revolutionary, anarchist culture. They appear less as people than as figures. However, the use of first-person narrative tempers the speculation invited by the other characters in this story, and in 'Reflections', and thus also invites empathetic responses on the part of the reader.

The first-person narrative is particularly well known for its invitation to reader identification, and Carter plays upon this effect through a mingling of speculative discourse and the violence of rape as experienced through the narrating 'I' in 'Reflections':

> Parting the air with the knives of her arms, she precipitated herself upon me like a quoit on a peg. I screamed; the notes of my scream rose up on the air like Ping-Pong balls on a jet of water at a fun-fair. She raped me; perhaps her gun, in this system, gave her the power to do so ... I felt such outrage I beat in the air behind my head with my helpless fists as she pumped away indefatigably at my sex, and to my surprise, I saw her face cloud and bruises appear on it, although my hands were nowhere near her. (Carter 1987a: 107–8)

The rape takes place in an inverted world on the other side of a mirror. The affective dimension of such violence ties in with the speculation to create an emotionally charged realm of critical enquiry where the reader is led to hover between the speculative and the personal, making of identity crisis an arena of both collective and individual anxiety: 'I once again advanced to meet my image in the mirror. Full of self-confidence, I held out my hands to embrace my self, my anti-self, my self not-self, my assassin, my death, the world's death' (Carter 1987a: 111). The effect is vertiginous, as the reader is led to inhabit the inherently incomplete image of the 'I'. As Jouve contends, the 'I' is the least determined of all characters and thus intensifies reader identification (52).[15] This heightens the sense of violence in the aggression. The result is a dynamic and subtle stratification of reading levels. If one follows May's logic, the short story foregrounds the *lectant* and the *lu*. In this story, the layering of signification heightens the short story's metaphorical dimension in its appeal to the *lectant* while also harnessing the primal forces May sees as being inherent to the short story (139) by soliciting the *lu*. The combination potentially shifts the reader out of comfortable perceptions of reality and identity. As May observes: 'The short story is closer to the nature of reality as we experience it in those moments when we are made aware of the inauthenticity of everyday life, those moments when we sense the inadequacy of our categories of conceptual reality' (1994: 142). In the above scene, this is accomplished through an emphasis on the distanced *lectant* in the reader, who perceives the allegorical reflection on the mirror, alterity, and identity, in combination with a heightened role for the *lu*, who can be affected by the rape scene, and the sense of imprisonment. The interaction between these reactions is, of course, much more complex that Jouve's model can possibly explain, but the *lectant/lisant/lu* triad allows for a richer imagining of how Carter's discursive, political strands are wrapped through characters that are loaded with affect and interpellate the reader on multiple levels.

In the overt, fantasy universe of 'Reflections' Jouve's model works well to describe the mechanisms of fictional belief. In Carter's autobiographical pieces, however, the 'I' of the narrator/fictional character lies too close to the borders of the authorial 'I' for Jouve's model to truly fit. The result is that the oscillation between a perception of autobiography and fiction is added to the fluctuations in reader identification, as the narrative stages personal crisis: 'It was midnight and I was crying bitterly as I walked under the artificial cherry blossoms with which they decorate the lamp standards from April to September' (Carter 1987a: 68). This crying narrator is depicted through conceptually dense discourse that colours the narrative with a meditative intention:

> During the durationless time we spent making love, we were not ourselves, whoever that might have been, but in some sense the ghosts of ourselves. But the selves we were not, the selves of our own habitual perceptions of ourselves, had a far more insubstantial substance than the reflections we were. (Carter 1987a: 71)

The reader is left to imagine the 'I' as either Carter, or a fictionalised, speculative counterpart. The resulting ontological status of the character image is unstable, metamorphic throughout the narrative as Carter's conceptually elusive being vacillates between tears and rueful, self-conscious comments about the theatricality of existence: 'The most difficult performance in the world is acting naturally, isn't it? Everything else is artful' (Carter 1987a: 77). In their fluctuating representation and incompleteness Carter's characters evade definition, as the multiple levels of engagement they invite intensify unease and confusion in the construction of their image. They exist as individuals, persons that allow the reader to engage in the reading of her texts, however shaky the generic status, yet also continually test the borders of this individuality, extending beyond the textual frame into the realms of intertextual, literary, historical and ideological reflection. The ultimate impression is one of unfixed identity traits loosely grouped around the single pronoun or name as an ideological nexus.

The reader is thus led to see *through* the character, to use the character as a tool by which to gain access to a universe in flux, where idea and person coalesce in the shifting image of the same being. As such, the characters in Carter's fiction resist being reduced to an integral image. On the contrary, they acquire a changeable autonomy that moves beyond authorial and narratorial control, much as Bakhtin has described Dostoevsky's characters:

> all the concrete features of the hero, while remaining fundamentally unchanged in content, are transferred from one plane of representation to another, and thus acquire a completely different artistic significance: they can no longer finalize and close off a character, can no longer construct an integral image of him or provide an artistic answer to the question, 'Who is he?' (48–9)

Although Dostoevsky's forms of resistance to identity are quite different from Carter's, the idea of 'integral image' is central, especially if the linear nature of the reading process is taken into consideration. The character is shown to be an open being, created through a process of image building/modifying/breaking that is specific to reading, and is of utmost relevance for reading Carter's short stories. The temporality of image-making in reading Carter's short story enacts, in some ways, Judith Butler's well-known concept of performativity, of identity as an ongoing process of construction: 'performativity is not a singular act, but a repetition and a ritual, which achieves its effects through its naturalization in the context of a body, understood, in part, as a culturally sustained temporal duration' (Butler 1999: xv). In engaging the reader in a process of construction through discursively layered characterisation and politically charged images, Carter is making of her texts an arena of emotionally charged reflection, a reflection that, through wilful play upon the suspended world of literature and its conventional postures, opens up characters to the possibilities of an identity in flux.

Through her characters, Carter thus creates dynamic images of ideas that, in their intertextual and discursive echoing, foster the processes of resignification defended by Butler: 'it is only *within* the practices of repetitive signifying that a subversion of identity becomes possible' (185). Carter creates a signifying space that points presciently to identity as an incomplete, ongoing process, thereby reflecting Butler's assertion that, 'there is no self that is prior to the convergence of who maintains "integrity" prior to its entrance into this conflicted cultural field. There is only a taking up of the tools where they lie, where the very "taking up" is enabled by the tool lying there' (ibid.). Such tools can appear in the form of characterisation conventions and intertextuality. Carter's experimentation also inadvertently signals a questioning of selfhood as being essential for a politics of re-evaluation. This ties in with Denise Riley's conception of feminist solidarity being situated in provisional identity, a point of view that corroborates that of Judith Butler's:

> This essay is, in part, a defence of having nothing to say for oneself. It wonders why the requirement *to be* a something-or-other should be so hard to satisfy in a manner which is convincing to its subject; it decides that hesitations in inhabiting a category are neither psychological weaknesses nor failures of authenticity or solidarity. Instead, it suggests that as mutating identifications, sharpened by the syntactical peculiarities of self-description's passage to collectivity, decisively mark the historical workings of political language, a more helpful politics will recognize a useful provisionality in the categories of social being. (2000: 1)

The reader is indeed faced with 'mutating identifications' and the foregrounding of provisionality as an aesthetic and political end in Carter's texts where characters defy firm definition, either in generic, conceptual, political or individual terms. Riley argues for the need to avoid the 'ossified massifications' evident in some manifestations of feminist militancy (176), and she proposes to open up the self through strategies such as irony, so as to displace meaning and a sense of shared identity, and to privilege what she describes as a 'solidarity of disaggregation' (175).[16] Such practices would resist the processes of 'homogenisation' and refuse the silent subjugation of interior differences (ibid.). The unorthodoxy and prescience of Carter's brand of feminism has been the object of many critical articles, and, as mentioned above, often resulted in her marginalisation, perhaps because of her uncanny anticipation of the 'disaggregative' political modes championed by Riley (ibid.). Maggie Tonkin has indeed remarked how Carter's use of irony 'thwarts the desire of many feminist critics for art that offers a clear-cut and suitably indignant representation of patriarchal injustice' (Tonkin 19). Carter's characters challenge easy categorisation and, in their disaggregative forms, point to alternative forms of aesthetic militancy, as Riley suggests: 'Identities may first have to be loosened or laid aside for the sake of solidarity' (177).

Jouve has commented on the inherent fragmentation and instability of the character image, in that it is composed through a series of successive syntheses of traits (50).[17] This is accentuated in Carter's short narratives, where a reader's reflex to construct the unified image of person is manipulated so as to continually defer meaning, much in the spirit of irony: 'There is an ordinary potential for irony to quietly interrogate damagingly rigid categories, including their predictable syntax' (Riley 156). In 'The Merchant of Shadows', for example, the character labelled 'The Spirit' incarnates vacillations in identity through a process of inter/extratextual reiteration, as the masks of various film directors, actresses and writers flicker across the character throughout the story, until the narrator ultimately realises that 'The Spirit' before him is, in fact, the director Hank Mann(heim):

Perhaps, having constructed this masterpiece of subterfuge, Mannheim couldn't bear to die without leaving some little hint, somewhere, of how, having made her, he then *became* her, became a better she than she herself had ever been, and wanted to share with his last little acolyte, myself, the secret of his greatest hit. But, more likely, he simply couldn't resist turning himself into the Spirit one last time. (Carter 1994: 84)

As identities appear to flicker across the characters in this story they produce a cinematic metafictionality. The actress 'The Spirit' is associated with different roles, and the director is rumoured to have died in a reiteration of the ocean drowning death of Norman in *A Star is Born* (1937). The narrator refers self-consciously to the hazy existence of these people he characterises as 'beings': 'I was trapped helpless among these beings who could only exist in California, where the light made movies and madness' (Carter 1994: 81). Such metafictional asides suggest the flatness associated with the movement of an image on a screen, and indicate limited, conceptual beings. However, the vertigo experienced by the narrator in his quest for knowledge of the other, and his attempts to fix identity, is saturated with affect that draws the reader in, as he or she is led to identify with the narrating 'I'/Eye: 'And out of the dark it came to me that dreamy perfume of jasmine issued from no flowering shrub but, instead, right out of the opening sequence of *Double Indemnity,* do you remember? And I suffered a ghastly sense of incipient humiliation' (ibid. 79).[18] The narrator/researcher's attempts to penetrate to the 'truth' of the identity of 'The Spirit' is set forth as a reading quest that thoroughly explores the contours of cinematic and fictional characters as intertextually layered and exceedingly unstable.

In 'The Merchant of Shadows' the character therefore appears as a construct that plays upon the reader's desire to perceive the other, and is exploited by Carter to create figures who live on the edge of personhood, beings that the reader could not meet on the streets, in the world outside the text, as they occupy a shadowy borderland of discursive identity. This is an uncanny twist on Frank O'Connor's famous comment about 'outlawed characters wandering about the fringes of society' in the short story (1963: 19). Carter's characters are indeed positioned in the fringes of social and conceptual identity.

Liliane Louvel has evoked the term *tiers pictural* (pictorial third) to describe the in-between 'image' constructed by visual representation in a text 'The pictorial third is this vibrant in-between space of text and image, a manifestation of the oblique bar that separates the two. It is an activity played out in the middle, midway between two poles' (Louvel 2010: 260, my translation), explaining how the reader's internal space could be conceived of as a 'dark room'.[19] In this space, images are projected in a 'performance' of affect, meaning and experience in flux:

> In these dark machines that we are, the dynamic of the pictorial third is played out in movement, an energy that results in destabilization, a surplus of meaning and affect, a dream that dances between the two. Neither one nor the other, it is a simultaneous incarnation of both in the fluctuating image. It is a mode that belongs to the realm of the dynamic, of movement, of desire, of felt experience, of the event in the sense of what happens. It is also an operation, a performance. (Louvel 260, my translation)[20]

As Jouve observes, character performance explores the boundary between the optical image and dream image to create the 'literary image' (42). This is perhaps what troubles the reader the most in the construction of Carter's beings in their 'dark room'. One might even say that the 'character effect' moves beyond the visual with tropes such as synesthesia that play with sensorial stimulation, thus contributing to a sense of lived experience in a suspended world. Louvel's concept, which was created for the advancement of intermedial studies, suggests how we might further conceive of Carter's characters as occupying an 'in-between' space as conceptually explosive beings, who far from being relegated to the status of flat figures, appeal to the reader on intellectual, emotional, sensorial, visual levels and thus move as vibrant, evanescent, lived images in the mind of the reader.

It is such moments that short narrative stages so well with its characteristic density and complex temporal layering. Carter's stories suggest that the true power of words can be found in their ability to feed the imagination. This power translates into the perpetuation of performances of conceptually charged characters, that is the force of Carter's living 'puppets' who live on and thrive in the 'as if' realm of the reader's internal 'dark room' of the imagination.

Notes

1. Carter's relationship with postmodernism is an area of controversy in Carter studies. Some critics find it difficult to reconcile her political militancy with her postmodern re-writing practices, an aspect of her work, as Maggie Tonkin (2012) observes, that remains difficult to resolve: 'It is obvious that there can be no final word on the vexed issues of either Carter's, or indeed of feminism's, relation to postmodernism. And far from wishing to fetishize the seemingly endless debates on these subjects, I want simply to acknowledge their contentious, and perhaps ultimate unresolvability, and return to my starting point, which is that of Carter's alleged fetishism' (11).

2. As the question of characterisation in the fairy tale warrants an in-depth genre specific approach, I have decided not to focus on *The Bloody Chamber* (1979) in this essay.
3. Many readers are certainly familiar with Mary Rohrberger's collection *Story to Anti-Story* (1979): 'Contemporary writers find no guarantee as to the authenticity of the "real" world; consequently their stories often (1) merge reality and illusion in such a way that the extensional or everyday world and the dream world cease to be separate realms (2) abandon reality and move to fantasy, games, mimicry, parody, and self-parody, (3) call attention to themselves as artifice in an attempt to make authentic the act of knowing, (4) use the apparently disconnected and incongruous as techniques for creating coherence. So that what we get are stories, strange and sometimes dizzying in their effects; plots are truncated, distorted, or abandoned (thus anti-story); metaphors and symbols convolute, turning in upon themselves' (7).
4. I have also commented on this generic ambiguity in an earlier essay about autobiographical estrangement in three of Carter's semi-autobiographical anti-stories, 'Autobiographical Estrangement in Angela Carter's "A Souvenir of Japan", "The Smile of Winter" and "Flesh and the Mirror"' (Ryan-Sautour 2007).
5. 'But the case was otherwise here. My mother was convicted of felony for a certain petty theft scarce worth naming, viz. having an opportunity of borrowing three pieces of fine holland of a certain draper in Cheapside. The circumstances are too long to repeat, and I have heard them related so many ways, that I can scarce be certain which is the right account.

    However it was, this they all agree in, that my mother pleaded her belly, and being found quick with child, she was respited for about seven months; in which time having brought me into the world, and being about again, she was called down, as they term it, to her former judgment, but obtained the favour of being transported to the plantations, and left me about half a year old; and in bad hands, you may be sure' (Defoe 1722).
6. Moll Flanders reappears elsewhere in Carter's fiction as a means by which to explore the theme of identity. Consider, for example, the character Fevvers in Carter's *Nights at the Circus*.
7. 'Revisiting the "Intentional Fallacy" as a Political Mechanism in Angela Carter's "The Loves of Lady Purple"' (Ryan-Sautour 2010).
8. 'Loin de tout projet d'authentification véhiculé par une épaisseur référentielle ou un effet de réel qui présente le personnage comme une personne, Carter opte pour une densité intertextuelle, des variations narratives et énonciatives, et une sélection de dominantes sémantiques qui tantôt brouillent la lisibilité du personnage, tantôt attirent l'attention du lecteur sur l'encodage discursif qui sature le récit. Dans un cadre Ô combien structuré, le personnage devient une fonction discursive, puisque ses actions, ses pensées et la façon dont il est décrit véhiculent une dominante sémantique allant de paire avec le discours féministe défendu par l'auteur dans ses écrits.'

    'Far from any project of authentification fostered by referential development, or an effect of the real that presents the character as a person, Carter opts for intertextual density, narrative and enunciative variations, and a selection of semantic dominants that alternately blur the readability of the character, and draw the reader's attention to the discursive coding with which the narrative is saturated. In this highly structured framework, the character becomes a discursive function, as his or her actions, thoughts and the manner in which he or she is described, expresses a semantic dominant that is connected to the feminist discourse expressed by the author in her writing' (Thomas 2010: Paragraph 62, my translation).

9. 'If the novel creates the illusion of reality by presenting a literal authenticity to the material facts of the external world, as Ian Watt suggests, the short story attempts to be authentic to the immaterial reality of the inner world of the self in its relation to the eternal rather than temporal reality. If the novel's quest for extensional reality takes places in the social world and the material of its analyses are manners as the indication of one's soul, as Lionel Trilling says, the field of research for the short story is the primitive, antisocial world of the unconscious, and the material of its analysis are not manners, but dreams. The results of this distinction are that whereas the novel is primarily a social and public form, the short story is mythic and spiritual' (May 1994: 133).

10. Jouve comments on how a character can be situated between the referential pole and the discursive pole: 'The character image, as shown above, is caught between the referential (it refers to an external world), and the discursive (it is composed of discourse). It is therefore developed in relation to these two poles according to methods that vary from one novel to another' (50, my translation).

'L'image-personnage, nous venons de le voir, s'avère prise entre le référentiel (elle renvoie à une extériorité) et le discursif (elle est constituée par le discours). Elle se développe donc par rapport à ces deux axes selon des modalités très variables d'un roman à l'autre.'

11. Expression borrowed from Jouve to describe the degree to which a character appears to represent a real human being (67).

12. 'The identity of the character is constructed progressively through processes that are relatively complex' (50, my translation).

'L'identité de ce dernier ne se construit que progressivement au travers de processus relativement complexes.'

13. Philippe Hamon, in his well-known essay, 'Pour un statut sémiologique du personnage' (For a Semiological status of the character) underlines how the form of the proper name reflects the characteristics of the character: 'Le lecteur a presque toujours tendance à isoler, à l'intérieur du nom propre, des radicaux, suffixes, préfixes, morphèmes divers qu'il analysera, par *rétroaction*, en fonction du signifié du personnage ou qui, inversement, lui serviront, s'il les reconnaît d'emblée, de référence *prospective*, d'horizon d'attente pour "prévoir" le personnage.'

'The reader almost always has the tendency to isolate roots, suffixes, prefixes and diverse morphemes in the proper name that he or she will analyse *retroactively* according to the signifier of the character, or which, on the contrary, will serve, if he recognises these elements immediately, as a *prospective* reference that creates a horizon of expectations and allows him or her to "predict" the character's development' (Hamon 1977: 149, my translation).

14. 'L'illusion de vie est d'abord liée au mode de désignation du personnage' (110).
15. 'The "I" is the least defined of characters. For this reason the "I" plays a privileged role in the processes of reader identification' (52, my translation). 'Le "je" est le personnage le moins déterminé qui soit. Pour cette raison, il est le support privilégié de l'identification.'
16. 'The backward turn of decomposition can also be an aspect of solidarity. So to recognise internal differences within some larger grouping may entail what we could christen "a solidarity of disaggregation": an insistence on the political advantages of reformulation' (Riley 175).
17. 'L'image mentale, toutefois, ne se satisfait pas d'une addition de traits: c'est au travers de synthèses successives effectuées par le lecteur qu'elle se développe.'
    'The mental image, however, is not a simple accumulation of traits: it is through a series of successive syntheses made by the reader that it develops' (50, my translation).
18. I have commented on this 'flickering' effect in 'Flickering Wor(l)ds: The Quest for Identity in Angela Carter's "The Merchant of Shadows"' (Ryan-Sautour 2003: 73–90).
19. 'Le tiers pictural est cet entre-deux vibrant entre texte et image, à l'instar de la barre oblique qui séparerait les deux. Moyen terme, il est une activité qui se joue entre-deux.'
20. 'Dans ces "machines obscures" que nous sommes, joue la dynamique du tiers pictural: mouvement, énergie qui entraîne une perturbation, un surplus de sens et d'affect, une rêverie qui danse entre les deux. Ni l'un ni l'autre, il est l'un *et* l'autre en tours et retours de l'image. Il s'agit vraiment d'une modalité qui est de l'ordre du vivant, du mouvement, du désir, de l'expérience ressentie, de l'événement au sens de ce qui advient : une opération aussi, une *performance*.'

Works Cited

Bakhtin, Mikhail (2006), *Problems of Dostoevsky's Poetics*, ed. and trans. Caryl Emerson [1984], Minneapolis: University of Minnesota Press.
Butler, Judith (1999), *Gender Trouble* [1990], New York: Routledge.
Carter, Angela (1994), *American Ghosts and Old World Wonders* [1993], London: Vintage.
Carter, Angela (1987a), *Fireworks: Nine Profane Pieces* [1974], New York: Penguin.
Carter, Angela (1981), *Fireworks: Nine Stories in Various Disguises* [1974], New York: Penguin.
Carter, Angela (1992), Interview, *Angela Carter's Curious Room*, dir. Kim Evans. BBC 2, 15 September, Film Documentary, BFI Film archives, London.
Carter, Angela (1985), Interview by John Haffenden, *Novelists in Interview*, London: Methuen, pp. 76–96.
Carter, Angela (1993), *Nights at the Circus* [1984], New York: Penguin.

Carter, Angela (2001), *The Sadeian Woman* [1979], New York: Penguin.
Carter, Angela (1987b), *Saints and Strangers (Black Venus)* [1985], New York: Penguin.
Crofts, Charlotte (2003), *'Anagrams of Desire': Angela Carter's Writing for Radio, Film, and Television*, Manchester: Manchester University Press.
Defoe, Daniel (1722), *The Fortunes and Misfortunes of the Famous Moll Flanders &c*, Project Gutenberg, March 19, 2008 [EBook #370] [Last accessed 20 April 2014.]
Hamon, Philippe (1977), 'Pour un statut sémiologique du personnage', *Poétique du récit*, ed. Gérard Genette et Tzveton Todorov [1972], Paris: Seuil, pp. 115–67.
Iftekharrudin, Farhat (2003), 'Introduction', *The Postmodern Short Story: Forms and Issues*, ed. Iftekharrudin, Farhat et al., Westport, CT: Praeger, pp. 1–22.
Jordan, Elaine (1992), 'Down the Road: Or, History Rehearsed', *Postmodernism and the Re-Reading of Modernity*, ed. Francis Barker et al., Manchester: Manchester University Press, pp. 159–79.
Jouve, Vincent (1992), *L'effet-personnage dans le roman*, Paris: Presses Universitaires de France.
Louvel, Liliane (2010), *Le Tiers pictural: pour une critique intermédiale*, Rennes: Presses Universitaires de Rennes.
May, Charles (1994), 'The Nature of Knowledge in Short Fiction', *The New Short Story Theories*, ed. Charles May, Athens, OH: Ohio University Press, pp. 131–43.
May, Charles (2002), 'Why Short Stories are Essential and Why They are Seldom Read', *The Art of Brevity: Excursions in Short Story Theory and Analysis*, Columbia: University of South Carolina Press, pp. 14–25.
Morano, Michele (2003), 'Facts and Fancy: The "Nonfiction Short Story"', *The Postmodern Short Story: Forms and Issues*, ed. Iftekharrudin, Farhat et al., Westport, CT: Praeger, pp. 35–46.
O'Connor, Frank (1985), *The Lonely Voice*, New York: Harper and Row.
Orlofsky, Michael (2003), 'The Fictionalization of History in the Short Story', *The Postmodern Short Story: Forms and Issues*, ed. Iftekharrudin, Farhat et al., Westport, CT: Praeger, pp. 47–62.
Picard, Michel (1986), *La lecture comme jeu*, Paris: Minuit.
Riley, Denise (2000), *The Words of Selves: Identification, Solidarity, Irony*, Stanford: Stanford University Press.
Rohrberger, Mary (1979), *Story to Anti-Story*, Boston: Houghton Mifflin Company.
Ryan-Sautour, Michelle (2007), 'Autobiographical Estrangement in Angela Carter's "A Souvenir of Japan", "The Smile of Winter" and "Flesh and the Mirror"', *Etudes britanniques contemporaines*, 32, 57–76.
Ryan-Sautour, Michelle (2003), 'Flickering Wor(l)ds: The Quest for Identity in Angela Carter's "The Merchant of Shadows"', *La nouvelle anglo-saxonne contemporaine*, Poitiers: Presses de la Licorne, pp. 73–90.
Ryan-Sautour, Michelle (2010), 'Revisiting the "Intentional Fallacy" as a Political Mechanism in Angela Carter's "The Loves of Lady Purple"', *Journal of the Short Story in English*. 54, pp. 81–100.
Thomas, Karima (2010), 'Quand la personne s'avère être un personnage: la mise

à nu de la construction discursive du personnage dans le fait divers', *L'atelier*, 2:1, <http://ojs.u-paris10.fr/index.php/latelier/article/view/40> [Last accessed 5 June 2013.]

Tonkin, Maggie (2012), *Angela Carter and Decadence: Critical Fictions/ Fictional Critiques*, Houndmills, Basingstoke: Palgrave.

Chapter 8

New Waves of Interest: Women's Short Story Writing in the Late Twentieth Century
Ailsa Cox

In the introduction to his *Penguin Book of Modern British Short Stories* (1987), Malcolm Bradbury celebrates a 'new wave of interest in short fictional forms' (12). Several of the younger writers whose work he included – Angela Carter, Graham Swift, Clive Sinclair, Ian McEwan, Adam Mars-Jones, Rose Tremain – had already published well-received collections. Amongst other contributors, Beryl Bainbridge, Fay Weldon and Edna O'Brien were also publishing short story collections alongside their novels in the 1970s and 1980s.

Yet by 2002, the English and Scottish Arts Councils were launching a 'Save Our Short Story' campaign, defending what was now perceived as an endangered species. This chapter asks what was happening to short story writing by women in the years between Bradbury's assertion and the launch of the campaign. It draws on my own experiences as a short story writer, reader, publisher and teacher to give a personal view of short story writing and publishing at this time. In the first section, I give an overview of the publishing context; in the second, I describe my own experiences as I began to write and publish short stories in the 1980s and 1990s. I conclude by looking at stories by two important short story writers who emerged during this period, A. L. Kennedy and Janice Galloway, showing how they integrated orality into their fiction while also challenging notions of realist representation.

Short Story Publishing and Women's Writing in the Late Twentieth Century

In his introduction, Bradbury draws formal analogies between the twentieth-century short story after modernism and the poem, identifying its potential for experimentation and stylistic virtuosity. He expresses some ambivalence towards the place of short story writing in the British literary canon, but also suggests that the revival of interest signals a postmodern artfulness and exploration of fictional form that is diversifying literature culture more broadly in the UK. Clare Hanson's book, *Short Stories and Short Fictions, 1880–1980* (1985, reprinted 1987) also celebrates 'a resurgence of interest and confidence', claiming an increase in magazine outlets and the number of single author collections (159). Like Bradbury, she argues that 'the short form is the form for innovation, and many of the best young writers are turning first to short fiction' (ibid.). This revival of interest was also marked academically by the foundation of the *Journal of the Short Story in English* in 1983, the first international conference of the Society for the Study of the Short Story in English in 1992; and the publication of important critical texts, including Hanson's own volume, Susan Lohafer's *Coming to Terms with the Short Story* (1983) and Valerie Shaw's *The Short Story: A Critical Introduction* (1983).

The coming generation, heralded in Bradbury's anthology, did indeed come to dominate British fiction in the late twentieth century, and into the twenty-first – notably Julian Barnes, Martin Amis, Ian McEwan, Salman Rushdie; and, despite her early death, Angela Carter, whose influence on the form outshines her male contemporaries. Carter is represented by 'Flesh and the Mirror', from her first collection, *Fireworks* (1974); her second, *The Bloody Chamber* (1979), was to become one of the most widely studied and influential texts of the twentieth century. Indeed, Adrian Hunter describes *The Bloody Chamber* as 'one of the most important works of British fiction to have appeared since the Second World War' (2007: 125). However, it was the novels, more than ever, that secured the literary status of these writers. Richard Todd's 1996 monograph, *Consuming Fiction: The Booker Prize and Fiction in Britain Today*, identifies a synergy between the major prizes, the media and bookshops such as Waterstones, which raised the game for literary culture, writing that:

> Today's serious literary novelists in Britain . . . unlike those of sixty to seventy years ago, are alive to commercial possibilities that for the most part of the twentieth century have been available only to writers deliberately aiming at the best-selling, genre-fiction end of the market such as crime and science fiction. (59)

Todd's illuminating study demonstrates how commercial factors in the book trade and the media contributed to canon formation in the 1980s and 1990s. A polemic written by Peter Lewis for the literary magazine *Panurge* in 1993 takes a more abrasive tone, bemoaning 'the extraordinary transformation that has overtaken British publishing in a short space of time, especially since the Thatcher phenomenon ... with its privileging of market forces' (39). Lewis is far from nostalgic for the gentlemen's cliques of old-fashioned publishing, but he does lament the dominance of multinational conglomerates such as Random House, along with a cult of money and celebrity, which he claims, have made publishing 'sexy' (39) and turned the televised Booker Prize ceremony into 'the publishing equivalent of the Grand National and the Cup Final' (41). The inevitable result is that commercial publishers concentrate their efforts on the 'dead certs' and 'star players' of the literary world, leaving minority pursuits – such as the short story – to the small presses which are mostly, like Lewis's own Flambard Press, based outside London.

As Todd's study demonstrates, pedagogical practices and fashions in literary criticism also play a part in building readership, and the inclusion of a contemporary text in the curriculum may be the decisive factor in its longevity and the career of the author. The 1990s was a period of expansion in higher education in the UK, following the transformation of the polytechnics into universities. Charles E. May's contention that 'in great short stories, the hidden story of emotion and secret life, communicated by atmosphere and tone, is always about something more enigmatic and unspeakable than the story generated by what happened next' might help account for the disappearance of the short story from the fast-emerging canon of late twentieth-century literature (2011: 158). According to May, the short story poses problems for the pedagogue because it does not lend itself so easily to clear-cut discussions of 'themes', which may be driven by a social agenda. Derek Attridge's study, *The Singularity of Literature* (2004), also argues that instrumentalist approaches to literature have come to dominate the academy, noting that 'literature's powerful effects, and the high estimation it is accorded in cultural formations, inevitably lead also to its being appealed to and utilised when a political and ethical cause is being fought for' (80). While Attridge does not deny that such an approach may sometimes be both necessary and productive, he suggests that reading the text as an illustration of ideological assumptions denies a resistance to fixed meaning, derived from its aesthetic properties.

The elusiveness and fragmentation integral to the literary short story makes it harder to commodify than longer forms. The narrative drive of the conventional novel can be integrated into the postmodern novel without sacrificing the artfulness which Bradbury admired in the younger generation. These interrelated factors, commercial and educational, may account for the submergence of Bradbury's 'new wave of interest' under the tide of the postmodern novel. By 2002, the English and Scottish Arts Councils were launching a 'Save Our Short Story' campaign, defending what was now perceived as an endangered species. A report by Jenny Brown Associates, published in 2004, provided evidence of a decline in the mainstream publishing of single author collections, falling from 215 in 2000 to 135 in 2002. Meanwhile titles from the small presses had grown from 203 in 2000 to 287 in 2002. The report laments the lack of publishing data over a wider period; as any statistician knows, figures can fluctuate from year to year, and a two-year decline cannot be taken as conclusive evidence of a long-term trend. Perhaps more tellingly than the figures alone, the testimony of authors, publishers, booksellers and others in the book trade confirmed the view that the historical neglect of the short story form was more likely to accelerate than to be reversed.

The health of the short story, as pointed out by many commentators, most recently Dean Baldwin (2013), is directly related to the availability of publishing outlets. The popularity of the general interest magazine outlets in the late nineteenth and early twentieth century would never be repeated, but the glossier women's magazines had been publishing short stories in the 1980s and the early 1990s. Fay Weldon's contribution to the Bradbury anthology was a story first published in a mass-market women's magazine, *Cosmopolitan*. A. S. Byatt's story 'Medusa's Ankles' first appeared in *Woman's Journal* and Helen Simpson's first published story, 'The Bed', was published in *Vogue*, where she was working as a journalist. Interviewed by Katherine Orr in 2011, Simpson remembers Angela Carter also publishing in *Vogue*:

> Women's magazines like *Good Housekeeping* or *Cosmopolitan* used to have serious fiction departments running stories by writers like Rose Tremain and William Trevor. Can you imagine? Kate Figes was the fiction editor at Cosmo. She used to organize a Book Day every year, [a sort of] literary festival . . . (Orr 2011: 111)

The situation had changed by the start of the twenty-first century; when *Woman's Journal* closed in 2001, its former editor claimed that women's magazines were 'all the same and have the personalities of dead rats' (Gibson 2001: n.p.). Commercial markets such as these were becoming less available to the writer of literary short stories. The biggest market for the British short story was, and remains, BBC Radio. Radio's contribution to the aesthetics of the form in the late twentieth century is manifested through a preference for an inclination towards arresting and ironic narrative voices, and the dramatic monologue in writers such as Jackie Kay or Anne Enright.

During the last two decades of the twentieth century, women writers continued to publish in Arts Council funded literary journals such as *Panurge, Stand* and the *London Magazine*. These were joined by women-only publications, notably *Writing Women*, based in Newcastle. There were also annual anthologies such as *Best Short Stories* (1984–96), edited by writer David Hughes and agent Giles Gordon, both of them well-loved figures who embodied the convivial and benevolent side of traditional publishing, mourned by Peter Lewis in his piece for *Panurge*. Briefly, in the mid 1980s, Penguin published an anthology, *Firebird*, which included stories by writers such as Elizabeth Baines and Marina Warner alongside poetry and extracts from novels. This was soon overtaken by the quarterly *Granta*, established by Cambridge University students in the Victorian era, but now relaunched by Penguin as a major force in literary debate. The first new-style *Granta* was dedicated to American writers; one of the legacies of the editor, Bill Buford, was the coining of the term 'dirty realism', applied to the likes of Raymond Carver, Richard Ford and Jayne Anne Phillips. Another was his inclusion of travel writing, the essay, photo journalism and other forms of non-fiction, whose power might equal or even surpass that of fiction, especially since in Britain, at least, fiction was tired and inward looking. In an editorial published in 1980 he asked 'can the British writer be anything but provincial?' (Buford 1980: 11).

Storia, the women's-only anthology published four times by Pandora, an imprint of Routledge and Kegan Paul, was more firmly committed to fiction, with contributors including Jeanette Winterson, A. S. Byatt, Kathy Acker and Kate Pullinger. *Storia 3: Consequences* (1989), edited by Eva Figes, was constructed as a chain of texts, each writer responding to the previous story's characters, setting or themes. Other feminist publishers included Honno in Wales, The Women's Press, Onlywomen Press, Sheba and, of course, Virago. Virago's greatest contribution towards short story writing was the establishment of a female canon through its publication of volumes by Grace Paley, Paule Marshall, Elizabeth Taylor, Katherine Anne Porter and others. Angela Carter's Virago anthology, *Wayward Girls and Wicked Women*, first published in 1986 and still going strong, gave us an eclectic collection, including the surrealist Leonora Carrington, the Ghanaian author Ama Ata Aidoo and the Indian-born Suniti Namjoshi, whose *Feminist Fables* were published by Sheba in 1981. The Sheba co-operative also published anthologies of lesbian erotica under the title *Serious Pleasures*. The co-operative's re-statement of its principles, available now as an online archive, echoes Buford's attack on a stagnant literary culture from a rather different angle.

The new feminist presses turned their backs on the high-modernist clique then firmly in control of the British book scene, and looked instead at what that world literally couldn't see: the writing of women who hadn't been to Oxford or Cambridge, and who weren't necessarily white or heterosexual or middle-class, and who didn't speak with the polished vowels of Bloomsbury. The new writers weren't seduced by the pastoral English idyll of haywains and cottages and servile, cap-doffing peasantry. They wrote instead about what it was like to live as an ordinary, non-privileged woman in post-imperial Britain in the second half of the twentieth century. ('About Sheba Feminist Press')

One example of fiction that addresses 'what it is like to live as an ordinary non-privileged woman' might be Moy McCrory's collection, *The Water's Edge*, first published by Sheba in 1985. McCrory draws on her Liverpool Irish background to create incisive and vivid stories, full of comic incongruities. In 'The Vision', the appearance of the Virgin Mary in a Toxteth backyard leads to religious insubordination; the title story explores the troubled identity of an Irish immigrant, haunted by memory and leading a liminal existence in a London boarding house. The exact target of Sheba's polemic is unclear; which writers, 'high modernist' or not, were being seduced by 'haywains and cottages' in the late twentieth century? (Perhaps the writers are thinking of the Merchant Ivory version of E. M. Forster's *A Room with A View*, released in the same year as *The Water's Edge*.) What is more important is the insistence, shared with Buford, that other voices should be heard, voices excluded from representations of a culture now in terminal decline. As a fragmented form, written with intensity and immediacy, the short story is well suited to a fast changing world which may have moved on by the time you have finished, let alone published, your novel.

Becoming a Writer

This is where my story comes in. I am white and heterosexual, but I certainly do not, in Sheba's words, 'speak with the polished vowels of Bloomsbury'. I was born in Walsall in 1954 to working-class parents who both left school at the age of thirteen. My dad worked as a baker and confectioner, my mother first as a bookkeeper and then a shop assistant. We lived on the newly built Gypsy Lane Estate, soon to be renamed the Beechdale. All the streets were named after scientists and inventors – Faraday, Cavendish, Gurney, Stephenson. I was one of four children at the Beechdale Primary School who passed the eleven-plus and went to grammar school; the only one of those four to get a degree. I arrived at university with a comical accent; by the time I left I had, if not exactly polished, modified those guttural Black Country vowels. There are thousands of women like me, who were educated out of a certain type of 'respectable' working class, but will never feel entirely comfortable amongst their 'betters'. The title of Alice Munro's story, 'Who Do You Think You Are?' (*The Beggar Maid*, 1978), spoke to me at once, although Munro is in fact closer to my mother's age than my own.

The university I chose was Lancaster, on the basis that it was one of the very few universities that offered a module in creative writing. When I got there, I was too shy to sign up. I only started writing seriously after my son was born, a few years later, which was when I realised my time was not my own, and that I would never get anywhere without becoming disciplined and focused.

The first time I showed my writing to anyone was at a women's writing group, which was called Home Truths. The workshop was run by Commonword, a community publisher based in Manchester, which was funded by the regional arts association. Rebecca O'Rourke's *Creative Writing: Education, Culture and Community* (2005) provides an overview of the emergence of creative writing in the UK from schools, community projects and adult education in the second half of the twentieth century. As Mark McGurl also points out in his detailed analysis of the impact of university-based creative writing programmes on literature in the US, the workshop method was partly driven by the radical pedagogies of the 1960s and 1970s, inspired by thinkers such as Ivan Illich and Paulo Freire. Such pedagogies champion free expression and empowerment, challenging existing hierarchies. I had already become involved in the women's movement, spending much of my time after leaving university volunteering for Women's Aid and campaigning on domestic abuse, health issues and so forth. The support I got from the women's writing group gave me the confidence I did not feel at university literary societies, where most of the writers were flamboyant young men.

Commonword was a member of the Federation of Worker Writers and Community Publishers, its other groups including Centreprise in Hackney, Queenspark in Brighton and the Scotland Road and Liverpool 8 groups on Merseyside. Commonword still exists, and so does the Federation, promoting diversity in writing and offering an outlet for marginalised voices. At that time, in the early 1980s, class-consciousness was most definitely the cornerstone of the Federation, an organisation with strong affiliations to the trade unions and the Marxist Left. I began working for Commonword part-time, running writing projects, organising readings and painstakingly piecing together publications using a golf-ball typewriter, stencils, glue and scalpels. Our illustrations favoured stark black-and-white images, reminiscent of German expressionist woodcuts from the Spartacist era. The iconography of working-class masculinity, the romance of iron, steel and coal, was still pronounced in both the writing and the covers produced by Commonword and by the Federation magazine, *Voices*, which was also produced from Manchester, and which I helped edit. A *Voices* editorial by Wendy Whitfield describes the Home Truths workshop where I first shared my writing based in 'a suburban library in a well-lit area'. (The 'well-lit area' is an unspoken allusion to the Yorkshire Ripper murders, still a haunting presence for women on the streets at night.) She explains the necessity for a new group, distinct from the original Commonword workshop:

> It's a city-centre workshop, with a membership of three men to every woman. Real attendance is almost exclusively male. When women do make an appearance, they rarely, if ever, return. What is obviously an ordinary workshop discussion to the men, feels like aggression to some women. (Whitfield 1981: n.p.)

She finds this a particular problem for writing she identifies as 'feminist', by which she means women who write more intimately about personal experience. Whitfield's less-than-strident editorial and the introduction of women-only writing groups caused a furore in the Federation, the traces of which may still be tracked through the archived issues of *Voices*. Amongst those opposed to separate groups there was a fear that working-class solidarity might be fractured; and also that the purity of the movement was being undermined by middle-class infiltrators. The Liverpudlian Jimmy McGovern, who has become by far the best-known writer to emerge from the movement, was one of the fiercest critics of women's and, later, gay writers' groups. Interviewed by Tom Woodin in 2001, he articulates the defensiveness felt by writers who perceived themselves under attack by the feminist movement:

> 1979–1989 was a bloody awful time to be a white working class male . . . The trade unions (built largely by white working class males) were smashed. The factories and mines and shipyards (staffed largely by white working class males) were closing. Feminists were telling us we were sexist pigs. Blacks were telling us we were racist bastards. Gays were telling us we were homophobic bigots . . . The trendy left . . . had a mental image of us: a foul-mouthed fascist skinhead with a tattoo on his arm and a spanner in his hand
> . . . And quite a few people in the Fed thought something similar. . . . I think that's why I packed the Fed in . . . In the future, I decided, my identity would be 'white, working class male'. I would still attack racism and sexism and homophobia, yes, but I would be a white, working class male and other

decent, white working class males would be my true brothers. (McGovern 2001: n.p.)

Some of the men in the Commonword group Whitfield refers to were bewildered by the kind of comments she published in her *Voices* editorial. They were angry when their workshop was listed as 'the Monday Night Group', downgraded, as they saw it, from its position as the original Commonword Writers. Thirty years later the pain has faded and there is still a workshop meeting as the 'Monday Night Group'.

Looking back, from a distance of more than thirty years, I can see the wider cultural shifts at work in these squabbles, which affected my own progress as a short story writer, acquiring my identity and shaping my own practice. Back in those old issues of *Voices*, a letter from the poet Lotte Moos expresses her irritation with sloppy working-class writing, claiming that 'the lack of interest in writing discipline and skill may carry the risk that once the worker-writer has exhausted his own, after all, limited store of autobiography, without having acquired an interest in the business of writing (his own and other writers'), he may stop writing altogether' (Moos 1982). She questions whether a simple declaration of the author's working-class credentials should validate anything they might produce, regardless of artistic merit.

The type of writing we were publishing in this period tended to be limited to varieties of social realism, including the oral historical. McGovern's affirmation of an embattled identity, both individual and collective, at the core of his own practice, highlights the importance of personal authenticity for those who were challenging mainstream literary values. Questions of personal authenticity and representation also preoccupied many women writers in this period. Elizabeth Baines' essay 'Naming the Fictions' dramatises an imaginary dialogue with an alter ego, The Feminist Writer, who asserts the importance of 'setting the record straight' (Baines 1987: 175) and of 'Positive Images' (176): 'And here again was this concept of Fiction as testimony, confession or reportage. Being honest about who you are intellectually and emotionally had slipped over somehow into proving your credentials, proving your life matched up to your art' (175). Influenced by French feminist thinkers such as Julia Kristeva and Hélène Cixous, some women began to think about identity as something far more slippery and difficult to contain; and about the connections between writing, the unconscious and the female body. In her *Voices* editorial, Whitfield wrote about women's writing as self-exposure; in her essay 'Shelving the Self' Sue Roe argued that 'the house of fiction does not readily admit the self' (Roe 1994: 51). The self must in some way be erased in the writing process, balancing the intensity of a personal vision with artistic detachment.

So far as my own fiction was concerned, I became dissatisfied with models of writing that valorised personal testimony and an unproblematic authenticity; I also wanted more stringent criticism of my work than I was getting in my workshop. And so I finally made it to a creative writing course at Lancaster; I got a place on the MA there in 1984, just after an experimental story, 'Twentieth Frame', was shortlisted for the *Stand* short story prize. I had outgrown those first, confidence-building groups at the library. But I would never have published anything without them. My involvement in the worker-writer movement, in community publishing and also in reminiscence projects with older people, sharpened my awareness of a continuity between speech and writing. Each story, for me, begins with the struggle to tune into the right voice; like many other writers I edit by reading aloud. And because the short story is a compressed, intensive form, orality and the rhythmic elements of language are especially pronounced in short fiction. This does not necessarily mean that the writing duplicates everyday speech, but it does promote immediacy and stylistic precision.

I also began to think of my stories as a type of collage. In the days before word processors and computers I used scissors and paste to reorder the narrative. Even now, very few of my stories run in chronological order. They shift back and forth in time, sometimes juxtaposing different voices with each other. My story, 'Into the Sun' (Cox 2009) was written in the early 1990s, at the time of the first invasion of Iraq. As we moved seamlessly from peace to war, I was struck both by the echoes and the contrasts with familiar images and voices from the past, and I introduced some of those incongruities into the story through news bulletins, station announcements and quotations from World War I poetry. The intercutting and the temporal shifts were influenced by film, especially the work of the British director Nicolas Roeg. His 1973 film *Don't Look Now* is, of course, an adaptation of Daphne du Maurier's short story; but this aspect was less important to me than the elliptical visual imagery and the broader generic affinities between film and short fiction. Elizabeth Bowen refers to both film and the modern short story as 'an affair of reflexes, of immediate susceptibility, of associations not examined by reason' (256). In my own work, I was also responding to the layers of time you can see in the fabric of a city like Manchester, which is constantly being demolished, reassembled and renovated.

When fellow short story writer Elizabeth Baines and I decided to found a fiction magazine we called it *Metropolitan* because the urban nature of short-fiction writing seemed so evident to us. With Arts

Council and Manchester City Council backing, we ran as a quarterly from 1993 to 1997, publishing a mixture of new and established names, including Tamar Yellin, Livi Michael, Ravinder Rhandhawa and Lesley Glaister.[1] We began our journal because there were so few outlets for our own work. We also wanted to produce a literary magazine that would reach a wider readership through arts centres and bookshops, rather than relying on subscriptions from potential contributors; and for that reason we tried to make *Metropolitan* as stylish and visually appealing as it could possibly be on a limited budget. We chose an A4 magazine-style format, rather than the more usual A5 with a spine. We used photographs as a counterpoint to the stories rather than illustrations (though our choice of photographers was limited; we discovered photographers demanded higher fees than writers). We sent out review copies and were noticed by the *Sunday Times* and *Independent* and by literary agents who sent us their clients' work and rang us up about contributions that had interested them.

These were the days of brown envelopes, international reply coupons and multiple trips to the post office. The more successful the magazine, the harder we worked to keep up with it. We noticed that women writers whose submissions we rejected would rarely be heard from a second time – unlike some male writers who sent us another story almost by return of post. For that reason we took special care with the feedback for women whose work was promising. A literary journal should be a community. Although for most of us the act of writing will always be a solitary business, driven by our own inner resources, belonging to such communities legitimates and professionalises that inner compulsion. Such communities might be based around a publication or a workshop or an educational course or groups of like-minded friends; the best of them also nurture a shared or at least a compatible sense of poetic practice.

The short story is always an endangered species; and the tides run back and forth with 'new wave[s] of interest'. The championing of the form by Bradbury and others in the 1980s did not herald a time of public triumph. But this was not an entirely fallow period either. The steady development of writing groups and workshops, both in community groups and in more formal educational settings, helped sustain the form and strengthen it through a diversity of voices. I have already discussed the contribution made by the feminist press, but other independent presses also promoted short story writers, notably Serpent's Tail and the two Edinburgh-based presses, Canongate, and Polygon, which published A. L. Kennedy's first collection, *Night Geometry and the Garscadden Trains* (1990). Kennedy's collection won three major awards – the Scottish Arts Council Book Award, the Saltire First Book Award and the *Mail on Sunday* John Llewellyn Rhys Prize. Her success embodies the gradual incorporation of the marginal into the mainstream, a process which is far from complete for short story writers, but has been made possible by the grass-roots activities of the 1980s and 1990s. Kennedy herself worked in community arts projects; her work is marked by urgency, concentration and a storytelling voice that seems rooted in orality. The stories engage with 'ordinary' people, without the burden of having to fully define or represent or ventriloquise the lives of others:

> This is no more than a story about Grandmother, because it cannot be the truth. If you and I were there to see it now, it might be the truth, but as it is, this is a story. Time divides me from my mother and her mother and beyond them there are lines and lines of women who are nothing more than shadows in my bones. So this is a story. (Kennedy 1990: 42)

New Writing in the 90s: A. L. Kennedy and Janice Galloway

Kennedy's contemporary, Janice Galloway, whose first book was also published by Polygon (*The Trick is To Keep Breathing*, 1989) shares her concern with orality and with voicing those experiences traditionally excluded from the mainstream. Despite these similarities, each has a unique and distinctive approach to the form. Kennedy's style is cryptic and detached, often seeming to distrust her own facility with descriptive detail. Galloway, on the other hand, revels in sensuous imagery, using stream-of-consciousness techniques to simulate the flow of thought, nurturing empathy with her mostly female protagonists. In Kennedy's work, this interiority is much more problematic. Even though her narrators conduct a conversation with the reader, apparently confiding in her, the voice seems speaks through a mask. The very title of the collection, *Night Geometry and the Garscadden Trains*, encapsulates a clash between artifice and orality. The reference to the trains is very localised, made comic and incongruous because it has been removed from its context in the Glasgow rail timetable. The title story begins like a dramatic monologue, in stylised colloquial language reminiscent of Pinter or Beckett:

> One question.
> Why do so many trains stop at Garscadden? I don't mean stop. I mean finish. I mean terminate. Why do so many trains terminate at Garscadden? (24)

The rhythms and repetitions of this fragmented opening add emphasis and clarity, as they might on stage; they also recontextualise an ordinary word such as 'terminate', activating its many connotations. Throughout the story, Kennedy plays with the multiple meanings of that word, including the association with terminal illness.

'Night geometry', by contrast, is an overtly literary image, somewhere between metaphor and metonymy because it not only represents the precise configuration of the sleepers' bodies and the pattern of their breathing, but also something less tangible in the couple's relationship:

> The positioning, our little bit of night geometry, this came to be important in a way I didn't like because it changed. I didn't like it then, as much as I now don't like to remember the two of us together and almost asleep, because, by fair means or foul, you can't replace that. (27)

The clumsy syntax suggests the untrammelled flow of thought. The repetition here is much less poised and musical than in the opening paragraph. This apparent spontaneity is reinforced by the story's numerous digressions, for instance the banal observation that 'you can never be sure that anything is unique' (28), illustrated by a seemingly random comparison between her relationship with her husband, Duncan, and that of the Inca people with the conquistador Pizarro. Earlier in the story, Duncan is introduced with the observation, 'Esau was an hairy man', followed by the comment, 'I only mention Esau now, because Duncan wasn't hairy at all' (25). Such inconsequentialities disrupt narrative progression and symbolic unity, disguising a highly artful text as an unmediated personal confession. However, the piece of misdirection concerning the biblical Esau signals the withholding of information, rather than its revelation.

Kennedy breaks the conventional rules of creative writing – for instance, 'show not tell', the avoidance of passive constructions – often summarising relationships rather than re-enacting events mimetically: 'It was tactfully assumed that the going to bed had happened with other partners in other times, but they had never managed to reach the same conclusion' (30). This sentence is typical Kennedy. It is a distinctive voice that recurs across her work, including the non-fiction – dry, ironic, even arch, and coy about specifics. When it surfaces in this story it builds an emotional barrier between the reader and the traumatic events it describes: 'there they were in bed with the fire on, nice and cosy: Duncan and a very young lady I had never met before. They seemed to be taking the morning off' (33). Clichés such as 'nice and cosy' and 'fair means or foul' (27) are used parodically. Although this text is, like so much of Kennedy's writing, fragmented and resistant to unitary meaning, it uses the conventional plot device, the 'twist in the tale'. The constant references to the trains tie the narrative together symbolically, as a meditation on death and bereavement. They also build up tension, ultimately misleading the reader to expect an accident or even a suicide involving the trains directly: 'Then, one Monday morning, there was an incident involving my husband and a Garscadden train' (33). In fact, it is revealed that problems with the trains have made the narrator turn back on her journey to work, which is how she discovers her husband in flagrante. She grabs a kitchen knife to attack him, but only succeeds in injuring herself so badly she is taken to hospital for the night.

On a second reading, narrative patterns emerge, linking the imagery of the trains to the narrator's loss of her mother and the end of her marriage to a theme of survival, 'proof of my existence ... There are too many people alive today for us to notice every single one' (34). The closing image, however, is not the trains at all, but something which nowadays requires an explanatory footnote:

> But the silent majority and I do have one memorial, at least. The Disaster. We have small lives, easily lost in foreign droughts, or famines; the occasional incendiary incident, or a wall of pale faces, crushed against grillwork, one Saturday afternoon in Spring. This is not enough. (Ibid.)

This is the final digression, the introduction of material which has no obvious connection to what has come before. The 1989 Hillsborough disaster, when ninety-six Liverpool fans were trapped and suffocated in a football stadium, was a very recent at the time of writing, but even so, the image reads as a coded reference. Discussing this collection as a whole, Kaye Mitchell argues that Kennedy's work advances 'a politics of the marginalised and dispossessed via a poetics of particularity' (58). Kennedy does, indeed, scrutinise the relatively small-scale trauma of everyday existence, but she often avoids the particular in favour of indeterminacy.

This is evident if we compare the opening story from this collection, 'Tea and Biscuits' with the title story of Galloway's *Blood* (1991). Blood was a potent cultural image during the late 1980s and early 1990s because of the fear triggered by the AIDS pandemic. 'Tea and Biscuits' is constructed from a series of ellipses, some no more than a paragraph in length, most of them capturing moments from a love affair with an older man, Michael. The final fragment in this jigsaw gradually reveals itself as an account of a blood donation. The use of the iterative once again means this is a generalised description, but the experience is given immediacy by vivid sense impressions:

> They would talk to you and find a vein, do it all so gently, and I would ask for the bag to hold as it filled. The nurse would rest it on my stomach and I would feel the weight in it growing and the strange warmth. It was a lovely colour, too. A rich, rich red. (7)

As in the title story, 'Tea and Biscuits' ends with a revelation, inviting the reader to re-evaluate her previous assumptions. But it is only a partial revelation; following a more recent donation, the narrator has been told 'there might be something wrong with my blood' (8). Once again, the narrator analyses her situation in parallel with a seemingly random example: 'I have a clock now, they told me that. A drunk who no longer drinks is sober but he has a clock because every new day might be the day that he slips' (ibid.). A further image is introduced in the final paragraphs, the image of a Native American tribe; 'they thought we all went through life on a river, all facing the stern of the boat and we only ever looked ahead in dreams' (ibid.). These digressions allude to a dilemma that is never made explicit, though we might assume she has contracted the HIV virus, possibly from Michael himself.

In an interview with the *Scottish Review of Books*, Janice Galloway identifies herself as someone who is especially interested in the 'visceral': 'we are human beings, bags of bone and blood and viscera' (Galloway 2009). This visceral quality is very much apparent in the title story of her first collection, 'Blood', which describes a teenager's visit to the dentist in gruesome detail:

> He put his knee up on her chest, getting ready to pull, tilting the pliers. Sorry, he said. Sorry. She couldn't see his face. The pores on the backs of his fingers sprouted hairs, single black wires curling onto the bleached skin of the wrist, the veins showing through. She saw an artery move under the surface as he slackened the grip momentarily, catching his breath; his cheeks a kind of mauve colour, twisting at something inside her mouth. The bones in his hand were bruising her lip. And that sound of the gum, tugging back from what he was doing, the jaw creaking. Her jaw. (1)

Despite the use of past tense, events seem to unfold in real time, as the character's thoughts and impressions register moment by moment. Galloway dispenses with speech marks, integrating direct speech with the inner speech of her characters, and thereby adding to a heightened sense of orality in her fiction.

In the *Scottish Review of Books* interview, Galloway also questions the whole concept of 'ordinary' life, suggesting that documentary realism will always be an over-simplification of lived experience. 'Blood' resorts to a kind of hyperrealism, describing with nightmare intensity the horrors of trying to staunch the bleeding after an extraction while also menstruating. The protagonist really is a (heavily leaking) bag 'of bone and blood and viscera', but, in the richness of her interior life, she is much more than the sum of those parts. She tries to transcend her shame and self-consciousness through music: 'the Mozart she'd been working on, something fresh and clean' (5). She almost succeeds until some one asks her what she is playing: 'and she opened her mouth not able to stop, opened her mouth to say Mozart. It's Mozart – before she remembered' (8). In a mortifying final image, the blood spills from her mouth onto the white piano keys.

This is quite a contrast with Kennedy's understated ending. Both writers make demands of their readers; Kennedy by restraint, Galloway by excess. Kennedy forces the reader to decipher clues, while Galloway immerses the reader in heightened subjective experience. The staging of intense, even hyperbolised, subjectivity characterises Galloway's short fiction. The collection *Blood* is punctuated by five numbered story scripts, 'Scenes from a Life'. Formatting the story as a performance detaches the reader from the events and highlights human interaction, even the individual self, as something that is under construction. 'Scenes from a Life No. 27: Living In', Galloway introduces her protagonist through a lengthy 'Note for the Actor': 'TONY is entirely suggested through improvised movement. NEVER SPEAK' (127). Act 1 begins with a slowly paced account of Tony rising from bed, performing his ablutions and getting dressed before leaving the large room with toilet facilities, described with realist attention to detail in the opening pages. As in 'Blood', the action seems to unfold in real time:

> Next, he selects a bottle of aftershave to dash some into his hands and slap into his face and neck (neck only if bearded). He may also add a discreet touch to his pubic hair as an afterthought – gingerly. (119)

Act 2 provides a kind of interval in the empty room, illustrated by a numbered list of offstage sounds evoking urban nightlife – including traffic noises, wolf whistles, drunken scuffles and football chants. Time is condensed until Act 3, when Tony returns from work, reaching the room through the audience. Real time is resumed with the evening routine: drinking a beer, listening to music, switching on the large TV – 'the man, the can and the radio make a soothing triangle for at least ten minutes' (121). Finally he completes another set of ablutions and goes to bed: 'Everything is still for a long time' (122).

During Act 3, narrative time is accelerated, and the conceit that we are reading a viable stage play begins to collapse. Nonetheless, Galloway continues to invoke theatrical devices: 'Next to the recumbent figure, the lumps in the duvet move. Minutely at first, then more noticeably they move towards TONY then undulate in small rhythmical patterns above his body' (122). Eventually a naked woman 'emerges in one sweep to stand at the end of the bed' (122). Suddenly a story which has appeared to be a piece of social observation, documenting a purely external reality, is transformed by this mysterious figure taking her place by a mirror under the starlight specified by the stage descriptions. This character has no name and in a final note to the actress the narrator specifies 'extreme stillness . . . The audience must never be sure whether she is substantial or not' (123). The description of her slow, steady actions by the mirror, 'the white contours of her body . . . curving out of the darkness' (ibid.) leaves us in no doubt that she is masturbating. A story which has begun by chronicling the minutiae of masculine experience closes by reinstating female experience which has been erased from the record, affirming the centrality of subjective experience, that something extra that is grounded in the body but not entirely contained by the 'bag of bones'.

Both Galloway and Kennedy are experimenting with voice and form during what might be regarded as a fallow period for the short story. The artfulness Bradbury praises in the up-and-coming writers he published in his anthology is just as evident in these writers. But they are also responding to debates about identity, gender, class and access to literary culture for those groups traditionally excluded from the mainstream. The complexity of these responses is made possible by the short story's combination of virtuosity with accessibility, its ability to make demands on the reader which might be difficult to sustain at a longer length. This also explains the short story's appeal to writers themselves, and its endurance, despite its fluctuating fortunes in the marketplace.

Note

1. A full list of contents is available on Elizabeth Baines' website. <http://www.e.baines.zen.co.uk/other.htm> [Last accessed 12 August 2014.]

Works Cited

'About Sheba Press' (n.d.), <http://mith.umd.edu/WomensStudies/ReferenceRoom/Publications/about-sheba-press.html> [Last accessed 12 August 2014.]

Attridge, Derek (2004), *The Singularity of Literature*, London: Routledge.

Baines, Elizabeth (1987), 'Naming the Fictions', *Feminist Literary Theory: A Reader*, ed. Mary Eagleton, Oxford: Basil Blackwell, pp. 175–6.

Baines, Elizabeth (n.d), 'Other Work', <http://www.e.baines.zen.co.uk/other.htm>

Baldwin, Dean (2013), *Art and Commerce in the British Short Story, 1880–1950*, London: Pickering & Chatto.

Bowen, Elizabeth, 'The Faber Book of Modern Short Stories', *The New Short Story Theories*, ed. Charles E. May, Athens, OH: Ohio University Press, pp. 256–62.

Bradbury, Malcolm (ed.) (1987), *The Penguin Book of Modern British Short Stories*, London: Viking.

Jenny Brown Associates (2004), 'The Short Story in the UK' (Report for Arts Council England, North East; Scottish Arts Council, New Writing North.)

Buford, Bill (1980), 'Introduction', *Granta* 3, pp. 7–16.

Byatt, A. S. (1990), 'Medusa's Ankles', *Woman's Journal*, 182–3; 185–9.

Carter, Angela (ed.) (1986), *Wayward Girls and Wicked Women*, London: Virago.

Cox, Ailsa (2009), *The Real Louise and Other Stories*, Wirral: Headland.

Don't Look Now, film, dir. Nicolas Roeg. UK; Italy: Casey Productions, 1973.

Galloway, Janice (1991), *Blood*, London: Secker & Warburg.

Galloway, Janice (2009), 'The SRB Interview: Janice Galloway', *Scottish Review of Books*, 5:2. <http://www.booksfromscotland.com/Books/Scottish-Review-of-Books> [Last accessed 12 August 2014.]

Galloway, Janice (1989), *The Trick is to Keep Breathing*, Edinburgh: Polygon.

Gibson, Owen (2001), 'Ex-editor claims Woman's Journal closure was inevitable', *The Guardian*, 14 November. <http://www.theguardian.com/media/2001/nov/14/ipc.pressandpublishing>.

Hanson, Clare (1987), *Short Stories and Short Fictions, 1880–1980*, Basingstoke: Macmillan.

Hunter, Adrian (2007), *The Cambridge Introduction to the Short Story in English*, Cambridge: Cambridge University Press.

Kennedy, A. L. (1990), *Night Geometry and the Garscadden Trains*, Edinburgh: Polygon.

Lewis, Peter (1993), 'The Death of the Publisher', *Panurge*, 19, 38–50

Lohafer, Susan (1983), *Coming to Terms with the Short Story*, Baton Rouge: Louisiana State University Press.

May, Charles E. (2011), 'Why Teaching the Short Story Today is a Thankless Task', *Teaching the Short Story*, ed. Ailsa Cox, Basingstoke: Palgrave, pp. 147–60.

Mitchell, Kaye (2008), *A. L. Kennedy*, Basingstoke: Palgrave.

McCrory, Moy (1985), *The Water's Edge and Other Stories*, London: Sheba Feminist Publishers.

McGovern, Jimmy (2001), email interview with Tom Woodin. Cited in Tom Woodin, 'Muddying the Waters: Changes in Class and Identity in a Working Class Cultural Organisation', *Sociology*, 39:5, pp. 1001–18.

McGurl, Mark (2009), *The Programme Era: Postwar Fiction and the Rise of Creative Writing*, Cambridge, MA: Harvard University Press.

Moos, Lotte (1982), 'Not Interesting' (letter), *Voices* 28, <http://www.mancvoices.co.uk/issue_28.htm#NOT_INTERESTING_> [Last accessed 12 August 2014.]

Orr, Katherine (2011), 'Overturning the Narrative: An Interview with Helen Simpson', *Short Fiction in Theory and Practice*, 1:1, 109–18.
Roe, Sue (1994), 'Shelving the Self', *The Semi-Transparent Envelope* by Sue Roe, Susan Sellers, Nicole Ward Jouve, with Michèle Roberts, London: Marion Boyars, pp. 47–92.
O'Rourke, Rebecca (2005), *Creative Writing: Education, Culture and Community*, Leicester: NIACE.
Shaw, Valerie (1983), *The Short Story: A Critical Introduction*, London: Longman.
Todd, Richard (1996), *Consuming Fictions: The Booker Prize and Fiction in Britain Today*, London: Bloomsbury.
Whitfield, Wendy (1981), 'Editorial', *Voices* 23, <http://www.mancvoices.co.uk/issue_23.htm> [Last accessed 12 August 2014.]

Chapter 9

Feminist F(r)iction: Short Stories and Postfeminist Politics at the Millennial Moment
Emma Young

The 1990s was a decade overrun with conflicting feminist discourses, most notably, the rise of third-wave feminism and its 'sister' discourse, postfeminism. While third-wave feminism is generally acknowledged by proponents as a continuation of the second wave, often thereby invoking the mother-and-daughter metaphor, and is defined by its reclamation and renegotiation of the 'personal narrative' (Yu 875), cultural understandings of postfeminism are far more complex.[1] In part, the ambiguity and subsequent inconsistency in usage which plagues postfeminism arises from the undifferentiating double deployment of the label. On the one hand, 'postfeminism suggests that the breadth of feminist issues is now much broader than ever before and intersects with a number of theories about gender, race and ethnicity, sexuality, class, corporeality and popular culture' (Braithwaite 341). In this usage, then, postfeminism denotes a conceptual shift in which issues of multiplicity, plurality and difference are prioritised, and thus the influence of poststructuralist and postmodern thought is embraced. Simultaneously, however, postfeminism is also employed to 'describe the "end" of feminism, complete with its supposed current rejection by young women; a moment when feminism is perceived as no longer relevant' (Braithwaite 337). Although this second meaning of the term is best articulated as post-feminism (with the hyphen emphasising the 'after' meaning), the slippery, semantic overlap and the interchangeable usage in which some critics use *postfeminism* to articulate *post-feminist* ideas is clearly problematic.[2] It is in the context of these competing feminist discourses that this chapter explores the short stories of two profoundly feminist writers, Michèle Roberts and Helen Simpson, and suggests that the short story collections of these authors, both published at the turn of the millennium, reflexively critique the feminist politics of this cultural moment.

The temporal marker of the millennium heightens the awareness of change, reaffirms the notion of generations, instigates deeper reflection about the past, and brings to the fore the question of what happens afterwards; a point highlighted by the rhetoric of destruction and demise interwoven in the 'Y2K' hyperbole which circulated in this period. In other words, the uncertainty of the future is foreground and the millennial moment in particular illuminates the relevance of being 'post-' something. Just as the turn of the nineteenth century fostered a climate of change and uncertainty, which resulted in a broader milieu of cultural fear for the future, the turn of the millennium is haunted by similar sociocultural anxiety. Extending these affinities between the two periods, the increase in feminist debate in the millennial moment echoes the rise of first-wave feminism, women's suffrage and the New Woman writer of the nineteenth century. The short story genre became a literary medium through which the New Woman writer could fabulate the social transgression at the heart of her burgeoning feminist politics. With the open-ended narrative structure and the emphasis upon specific temporal moments, or instances, this alternative mode of narration 'offered flexibility and freedom from the traditional plots of the three-decker Victorian novel, plots which invariably ended in the heroine's marriage or her death' (Showalter viii–ix).[3] An example of this is Sarah Grand's 'The Undefinable: A Fantasia', published in *Emotional Moments* (1908), a feminist allegory about women's liberation and men's subsequent enlightenment. The male artist is visited by a young woman, a muse, who subverts all of his (patriarchal) expectations. Towards the story's ending the artist realises that his muse is 'a free woman, a new creature, a source of inspiration the like of which no man has even imagined in art or literature' (287). Culminating in this moment of feminist revelation, Grand's story exhibits the narrative tendencies often associated with modernist experimentation. In considering the feminist politics of contemporary women's short story writing, it seems important to acknowledge the precedent of this relationship in an earlier, yet culturally analogous, moment.

This chapter is structured around two distinct yet overlapping discussions. The first section considers the short stories 'Fluency' and 'Just One More Saturday Night' from Roberts's short story collection *Playing Sardines* (2001). By focusing on these two narratives I consider how Roberts embraces the figure of the middle-aged woman, who (via her age) is affiliated with the second wave, to readdress the emphasis placed on younger women in 1990s (post)feminist debates. 'Fluency' and 'Just One More Saturday Night' assert the importance of women's reclamation of space and of having a public identity and voice.

Subsequently, I propose, it is through these narratives that Roberts revives, and even inserts second-wave feminism into a decidedly (post) feminist moment. Following on from this, the second section of this chapter considers Simpson's *Hey Yeah Right Get a Life* (2000) and the way in which this collection engages with the 'Mummy Wars' of the 1990s. The comparative portrayal of parenthood offered in 'Hey Yeah Right Get a Life' and 'Burns and Bankers' suggests a need to move beyond the binary opposition of stay-at-home mother versus career woman as extenuated by the so-called Mummy Wars. Subsequently, Simpson's short story collection purports the importance of recognising a woman's right to choose for herself and eschews a feminist politic in keeping with that of the third wave. While these readings isolate unique strands of feminism they both also illuminate how the versatility of the short story genre (in reflecting cultural moments through its specific formal features) and the short story collection (with the ability to offer multiple perspectives on the same issues) are apt literary vehicles for these feminist writers.

Michèle Roberts and the Politics of Ageing

In 'Addressing Age in Michèle Roberts's *Reader, I Married Him*' (2013), Sarah Falcus notes the relevance of ageing to the short story 'Fluency', and suggests that the story 'articulates the invisibility of post-menopausal women very clearly' (4). This short story asks the reader to reconsider his or her cultural understanding of the ageing body and how this intersects with notions of belonging and sexual attraction. That the protagonist, Pauline, lives in hotels (spaces marked by their sense of transience) implies the ageing body is at least temporally homeless in contemporary society. Indeed, the sixty-year-old narrator lives a haunted existence as she spends her days in Paris in 'pursuit of particular beloved artist or writer ghosts, tracking down their flats and studios and favourite cafes' (61). Although undertaking this youthful pursuit in the present, a tension resides in the figure of Pauline as she continuously strives to recapture the past. However, this desire to relive the past contributes to new discoveries: 'Aged sixty, I still go for long walks around London, and of course continue to discover parts of it I haven't known before' (65). Thus, Roberts's narrative purports the relevance of the past, not as a purely nostalgic ideal, but because it offers discernible benefits to the lived experience of the present. With this treatment of time and the life trajectory, the story fosters ambivalence and tension while illuminating the *fluency* of identity.

The city is a continual locale of change in 'Fluency': 'Now the city has been restored, rebuilt, reinvented. It's an image, refurbished and repainted, of its former self' (64). As a place, London functions metaphorically to reflect the shifts that occur in Pauline's physical body. Like the refurbishment of the city, Pauline's body changes, ages, and is reinvented to reveal new possibilities. In other words, 'Fluency', as the title suggests, presents ageing as a site of reinvention as opposed to the assumed trajectory defined by degradation. Strolling around London like a traditional *flâneur*, thus subverting the gendered nature of this identity and emphasising Pauline's peripatetic existence, Pauline considers how, 'women of my age were not supposed to fall in love. I had been a widow for ten years, very well, but now I was a grandmother, I had put away childish things' (68). Crucially, it is the idea that Pauline is 'not supposed to' feel this way that Roberts emphasises. The possibility of Pauline falling in love is not denied, however, the narrative reveals how this pushes against social expectations. It is through such critique of the sociocultural representation of ageing bodies that 'Fluency' becomes a narrative in dialogue with feminist theory. Pauline reflects how:

> The culture shouted at me from every angle, every advertising boarding, every TV programme, every cinema screen, old women were invisible and should stay that way. Worse, they were obscene and disgusting if they entertained thoughts of love and sex. Women past the menopause should cut their hair and retire from the field. They should not want physical pleasures, they should not have desires. Their ageing, sagging, unspeakably ugly flesh should remain hidden. They should not be occasions of shame and embarrassment to the young. And so on and so on. (69)

While the young female body is often considered by feminists as a site of patriarchal control and a space in which the dynamics of sex, pleasure and the ideals of beauty figure, here, precisely the same cultural constructs regulate the ageing, or older body. Further, society positions the ageing female body in direct conflict with its younger equivalent and this establishes a binary whereby young equates with beauty and sexual attractiveness, and in which post-menopausal women are generally conceived as 'past it'. In this light, the ageing body becomes a grotesque body that should behave – or perform – in a certain manner. Pauline defies such social circumscription through her romance with Pierre, a painter who is fifteen years her junior. Pierre likes Pauline's pictures, the photographs of men and women over the age of fifty in which 'some of them naked and some clothed' (69). Pierre embraces the beauty of the older body and the sexual pleasure that it offers.

With this depiction of the female body in 'Fluency', Roberts articulates a similar argument to that put forward by Germaine Greer in *The*

Change (1991). Noting that, 'whether written by men or by women, middle-aged women are virtually invisible' (22), Greer connects this invisibility to society's understanding of menopause, that of a 'non-event' which signifies 'the menstrual period that does not happen' (25). Assuming that nothing happens at this time in life, fiction has neglected the middle-aged woman. In a similar vein, in *The Fountain of Age* (1993), Betty Friedan uses personal stories of aging men and women to subvert the belief that age equates with 'nothingness', and renders this discourse visible as 'The Age Mystique'. Friedan depicts men and women growing old with purpose, starting new adventures, and thereby shattering the myth of age-as-problem. Both of these texts were published in the early 1990s, which implies an increased preoccupation with the discourse of ageing. This focus on the ageing body, I propose, is directly connected to the feminist climate of the 1990s in which 'ladette' culture was rife, Tad Friend coined the phrase 'do-me feminism' in *Esquire* magazine, and later in the decade young women were screaming 'girl power'. All of these developments drew on the image of the sexualised young woman and were used metonymically to suggest women's empowerment and liberation and propagated a post-feminist sensibility. In response to this seemingly fresher, newer, yet often controversial development, figures strongly affiliated with second-wave feminism re-emerge in critical debates. By asserting the importance of ageing in gender debates and rethinking the representation of the middle-aged woman, these feminist critics uphold the relevance of their second-wave politics in the (post) feminist moment. This focus on the ageing female body is a reminder of both the existence of this class of women, but also of the ongoing significance of second-wave feminist discourses.

Similarly, 'Just One More Saturday Night', far from defining middle age by a 'lack of time', uses poetry and performance as a means of celebrating middle age. The protagonist Teresa is an experienced poet and is due to perform at a small library in Skillet, a town of 'dead geraniums, an empty market square . . . and a red-brick church surrounded by a treeless graveyard' (164). With the 'dead geraniums' invoking Eliot's 'Rhapsody on a Windy Night' in which his '[m]idnight shakes the memory / As a madman shakes a dead geranium' (16), Skillet is established as the epitome of decay and emptiness. However, unlike Eliot's poem, in which the male protagonist wanders into the streets at night to be faced with his own loneliness, Roberts reworks the original connotations of 'dead geraniums' and her protagonist Teresa ends up discovering, not losing, herself. Before this resolution, however, at the poetry evening Teresa encounters Gertrude, the event organiser and evening's compère who claims to be a poet herself (but too avant-garde for publishers), and who proceeds to belittle and undermine Teresa where possible. In introducing Teresa, Gertrude remarks 'how nervous Teresa was and how well she was hiding it' (168). Although this is untrue, Gertrude continues to declare how, women 'of Teresa's age ... did not normally tour around the country with poets so much younger than themselves' (ibid.). When Gertrude recognises that the women in the audience were about the same age as Teresa, and therefore 'bound to feel very shy', she explains that they can write questions on pieces of paper rather than speaking to ask them (ibid.). Thus, it is the slightly younger figure of Gertrude who reproduces social norms in assuming how Teresa and the other women are feeling. Her categorisation of these older women as shy, *retiring*, and less visible is symptomatic of the wider social invisibility of this group in society and culture. 'Just One More Saturday Night' reveals divisions in the women's bond because of Gertrude's individualistic attitude and the triumph of self-promotion, the narrative therefore illuminates the demise of 'sisterly' relationships which were a defining feature of the second wave. The generational tensions in this narrative mimic the uneasy relationship between second-wave feminism and an increasing individualism associated with post-feminism. Further, the focus on the ageing female body reminds the reader that it is 'strange how quickly one ages within feminism' (Braidotti 55).

Following the poetry performance, Teresa and the two other performers, Maggie and Damien, miss the final train home and so 'shepherded the audience into the pub' where the 'ten ladies quickly grew jolly and confiding' (169). Supplanting the earlier negativity, in the pub the women begin to bond and Roberts reminds the reader of the pleasure and strength that can be gained through women's mutual support. That night Teresa and Maggie share a room and as she lies in bed Teresa begins to laugh and think to herself, '[w]ell, old girl . . . you're not doing too badly. Fifty-two years old and you're still on the road. At least you're still getting the gigs' (170). Teresa's laughter here, far from the mocking humour of sexist jokes often associated with 'lad culture', combined with the affectionate, self-referential 'old girl' are gestures that celebrate her strength and success. The story's title is not a plea for another Saturday night, and therefore a little more time in the public eye; instead the title recognises that performing in public and making new friends is an everyday experience for women of any age. In the face of criticism and social condemnation Teresa does not change who she is or how she behaves, she is 'walking down her own street, hopping over dog turds and composing a poem. A performance poem, a sort of middle-aged rap', which she sings aloud joyfully (171). Poetry and celebration defy the marginalisation of the middle-aged woman's body as the inclusion of 'rap' – typically associated with youth culture – is yet another motif that Roberts invokes to blur the lines between young and old. In *Discourses of Ageing in Fiction and Feminism* (2012), Jeanette King suggests that women 'can only make themselves visible by "disguising" themselves as younger women, through their clothes, their hair colour, their make-up' (xi). This need to '"pass" as younger in order to be part of a more favoured group' (ibid.) is, for King, linked to the current trend in female body politics in which there is a need to create a 'lack' of ageing in the female body. With 'Just One More Saturday Night' Roberts counters this narrative around ageing and, through performance, renders visible the ageing, female body in order to destabilise the binary conceptualisation of women's bodies as young or old, sexually attractive or unattractive, and to illuminate the reality that the majority of life is spent 'in the middle'.

The subsequent effect of these narratives in *Playing Sardines* is to reveal the way in which strands of feminism were in dialogue in the late 1990s and into the new millennium. Clearly, Roberts understands contemporary feminist discourses to be decidedly post-feminist in nature whereby '[f]eminism is cast into the shadows, where at best it can expect to have some afterlife' (McRobbie 255). In this respect, the collection's stories reside at odds with the contemporary moment as it is a self-reflexive engagement with *and* critique of this period. More broadly, in *Playing Sardines* there are also narratives that highlight the importance of play (an activity typically associated with childhood) for women, and a story which uses identical, middle-aged twin sisters to critique the notion of women 'having it all' (yet another post-feminist line of argument). Therefore, it is by embracing the polyphonic and didactic nature of the short story collection – in which multiple narratives can reverberate around a similar theme and sit in conversation with one another – that Roberts is able to offer a multi-perspective depiction of the middle-aged woman and second-wave feminism in (post)feminist times.

Helen Simpson: Writing and Righting Domesticity

In *Hey Yeah Right Get a Life*, Simpson engages with the burgeoning personal politics of the third wave and (post)feminism in which the domestic sphere and parenthood re-emerge as contentious sites of debate. At the heart of this personal turn lies the discourse of New Traditionalism, a phenomena which is directly related to the explicitly post-feminist backlash. According to Stéphanie Genz, New Traditionalism 'articulates a vision of the home as women's sanctuary from the stresses of their working lives', and it 'centralises and idealises women's apparently fully knowledgeable choice to abstain from paid work in favour of hearth and family' (52). In this context the domestic sphere is re-encoded as a space of female autonomy and independence – a far cry from the site of oppression, or the problem without a name heralded by Betty Friedan in *The Feminine Mystique* (1963). Within these debates exists an even more specific conflict, coined the 'Mummy Wars', which perpetuates a division between the (so-called) traditional, stay-at-home mothers and their career-centred counterparts. The prevalence of this debate is symptomatic of the fact that '[d]uring the 1990s and 2000s feminists offered the most concentrated and sustained critiques yet of child rearing standards and their implications for mothers' (Kinser 127). In *Hey Yeah Right Get a Life*, Simpson offers an experiential, fictional intervention in these feminist debates.[4]

The 'Mummy Wars' developed in tandem with greater discussions of women's employment. Catherine Hakim's controversial article 'Five Feminist Myths about Women's Employment' (1995) set out to demystify gendered perceptions of the labour market and argues that 'feminist sociology has gone on to create a new set of feminist myths to replace the old patriarchal myths about women's attitudes and behaviour' in relation to work (430). In fact, Hakim summarises, this feminist scholarship has merely offered a 'narrow range of acceptable conclusions' in which 'women are victims' (448). In many ways Hakim's work is a response to publications such as Arlie Hochschild's *The Second Shift* (1989), a study highlighting the gendered implications of domestic work and parenthood in which most women feel 'the second shift was *their* issues and most of their husbands agreed' (6). According to Hochschild, time is the pre-eminent issue of the moment for women as family lifestyles and marriages 'bear the footprints of economic and cultural trends which originate outside' (11). It is the awareness that there is 'no more time in the day', despite economic changes and working patterns demanding individuals 'speed up' (Hochschild 8), that concerns Simpson in these narratives about parenthood. Crucially, as a genre defined by its temporal constraints, the short story is a particularly relevant medium to engage with these issues.

In 'Hey Yeah Right Get a Life' the protagonist Dorrie is an archetypal stay-at-home mother. Having had three children in the space of four years, 'she had broken herself into little pieces like a biscuit and was now scattered all over the place' (153). Nonetheless, Dorrie 'felt a sick thud of relief that it was not two years ago when she had been racing against the clock to get to work pretending to them that all this had not just happened' (159). Throughout the story Dorrie's daily life is presented as stressful and both emotionally and physically draining. However, it is portrayed as a blessing in comparison to her previous attempts to juggle children and work; a point which reflects Hochschild's claim that 'women more often juggle three spheres – job, children, and housework – while most men juggle two' (8–9). Dorrie's self-perceived inability 'to keep both worlds up in the air' prompts her feelings of failure (159). Implicitly, Dorrie measures her success as a woman against contemporary notions of women 'having-it-all'; the sympathetic portrayal of Dorrie results in a critique of this post-feminist discourse. From standing outside the school gate through to interactions with her husband, 'Hey Yeah Right Get a Life' offers a gritty, realist exploration of everyday life for Dorrie. In this short space the snapshot of her life illuminates the spectrum of issues and ordinary topics with which she is confronted. For example, at the school gate she overhears two women talking: '"Look at her nails," said the one directly in front of Dorrie. "You can always tell. Painted fingernails mean a rubbish mother"' (166). Spending time on oneself is viewed with contempt and correlates with bad mothering in this scene. This conversation causes Dorrie to reflect on her own choices and the confession to Patricia (the mother who made this comment) that, in fact, Dorrie was thinking of painting her own nails that night. However, Patricia vindicates Dorrie from the label of 'bad mother' because it is an exceptional situation, her wedding anniversary, and Patricia sees Dorrie's activity as supporting her own point. It is not only other mothers enforcing life advice onto Dorrie, but sitting in the doctor's surgery the 'tattered covers of the waiting room magazines smiled over at them [Dorrie and the children] in a congregation of female brightness and intimacy' (169). The magazine titles all reverberate with Dorrie's life, yet the sense of sisterly solidarity which they promote is positioned in stark contrast to her daily experience of being unable to 'exchange more than a sentence or two of any interest because of our children' (ibid.). Despite a shared experience with other women, in Dorrie's daily life there is little time to act upon this communality. Ignoring the magazines with lead titles about hairstyles and orgasms Dorrie surveys those with 'words like juggle and struggle across the covers, these were for her and her like' (170). Upon reading an article entitled 'Doormat etiquette: are you too nice?' Dorrie bemoans how even being nice is an attribute that women should feel guilty about or ashamed of. Echoing the conduct manuals of the eighteenth and nineteenth centuries, these magazines instruct Dorrie on how to live her life as a woman. Accordingly, Simpson emphasises how mothering is a 'historically constructed *ideology*' (Hays x; original emphasis).

Following a day in which Dorrie has not had any '*proper* time' (176; original emphasis) to herself, the story culminates with her wedding-anniversary dinner. However, when the narrative perspective switches to her husband Max, the evening unfolds in an unexpected manner. Looking at Dorrie, Max

> appraised her worn face, free of make-up except for an unaccustomed and unflattering application of lipstick, and the flat frizz of her untended hair. She was starting to get a double chin, he reflected wrathfully; she had allowed herself to put on more weight. Here he was on his wedding anniversary sitting opposite a fat woman. And if he ever said anything, *she* said, the children. It showed a total lack of respect; for herself; for him. (182)

Max's concern here is not for his wife but for how Dorrie's appearance reflects negatively on him. As he says later on, 'I'm not exactly flourishing either, you know. You're getting to me' (187). Dorrie is represented as being responsible for the well-being of the entire family. This sudden shift to Max's perspective, after the entire preceding narrative being from Dorrie's point of view, unsettles the reader. Having established a rapport with Dorrie, and feeling aligned with her, Max's comments sit at a disjoint to that position in which the reader has been coerced. Further, Max's apparent disregard for the daily pressures his wife faces is reinforced when he informs her that he has sacked his full-time assistant, Naomi. Upon finding out Naomi is pregnant, Max has offered her a part-time job instead (184–5). When Dorrie jumps to Naomi's defence and explains to Max how much Naomi will need the money now she is pregnant, he retorts: 'If she could combine it with another part-time job. Beggars can't be choosers. I mean, if she chooses to have a baby, that's her choice' (185). The repetition of the word 'choice' here is important because it chimes with the post-feminist notions of women having 'free choice' in a (neo)liberal society. Max goes on to inform Dorrie that she can pick up the remaining part-time hours that Naomi cannot do by fitting it around the edges of her current life, after all 'other women do' (186). While all of this contributes to the reader realising that Max fails to understand his wife's daily existence, and that they live in two separate worlds, it is his response to her apologising for feeling 'dreary' that truly jolts the narrative: 'That's what I mean. Such a victim. Makes me want to kick you', before he concludes that this 'makes me hate you' (188). This section of the story closes and the narrative resumes with the couple back at their family home. The rituals of daily life resume and this snapshot has been left hanging, without any real resolution. In the compact space of the story, then, Max is not validated or criticised for his comments, it is left open.

Notably, Simpson leaves it up to the reader to respond and to make a judgement.

This emphasis upon the reader deciding for him or herself is also relevant to the wider collection because another story, 'Burns and Bankers', offers an alternative narrative of motherhood. At the Burns Night celebrations the working-mother Nicola views herself as a social interloper as she 'had a foot in both camps. Not only had she borne four children but she also earned as much as her husband and more than Iain Buchanan [another guest]' (201). Whereas the other couples around the table are formed of a highly paid working man and his housewife, Nicola and Charlie have both achieved high-status roles in their respective industries. Nonetheless, while Nicola may appear a far cry from the Dorrie this is revealed as a falsity:

> And why is it always down to me, thought Nicola, this talk of having it all and so on? I took the top first in my year. I'm cleverer than him though I don't rub it in. We have four children. But there's no question of him adapting his hours to the family or helping manage the nanny and the house and all that *that* involves. (218)

Regardless of her employment status, as a mother Nicola is shown to encounter the same demands on her time as the stay-at-home mother Dorrie. Indeed, just like Dorrie's husband Max, who fails to grasp the pressures his wife faces in organising the family daily life, here too it is taken as a given that Nicola, rather than Charlie, will be the flexible one in the relationship when it comes to the children. Moreover, through Nicola the notion of women 'having it all' is revealed to be a rhetorical spin and women's lives are shown to still be determined by broader factors, not the 'free choice' the discourse purports.

'Burns and Bankers' interrogates the image of the 'supermum' who, in a magazine picture, 'strides forward, briefcase in one hand, smiling child in the other' (Hochschild 1). Yet, in actuality, what this story attests to is that this is an 'upbeat "cover" for a grim reality' (ibid. 4). Sharon Hays develops Hochschild's work and considers the cultural contradictions of motherhood – which embroils both the stay-at-home and working mother. According to Hays, the culturally appropriate model of mothering in the late twentieth century takes the form of 'intensive mothering' which 'advises a mother to expend a tremendous amount of time, energy, and money in raising their children' (x). The contradiction emerges because this intensive mothering is being promoted in a society where 'over half of all mothers with young children are now working outside of the home' (ibid.). Furthermore, the value placed on unselfish nurturing sits in juxtaposition with the ideology of self-interest perpetuated by a capitalist society (ibid.). While Hays's study is located in the American context, like Hochschild's, its findings are also relevant to the British setting. Amid these competing ideologies, then, exists a cultural ambivalence about motherhood which subsequently leads to the supposed 'Mummy Wars'. However, Hays argues, this conflict 'is both exaggerated and superficial' (132) and ends up merely portraying 'all women as somehow less than adequate' (133). Indeed, this is the consequence of the ideology and actually provokes the oppositional tension between stay-at-home and working mothers as both categories of women attempt to justify their own choices in comparison to the other as a means of gauging how they fulfil the model of intensive mothering. As these two stories from *Hey Yeah Right Get a Life* illuminate, in reality the experience of the stay-at-home mother is not that dissimilar to that of the working mother as both women experience feelings of guilt and are subjected to the same demands on their time and emotions.

Talking about this collection, Simpson states, 'I really did not know whether I sympathised more with Dorrie, self-sacrificing maternal doormat, or Nicola, high-flying mother-of-four with a nanny' ('With Child', n.p.). When considering the interplay between these individual narratives within the context of a short story collection, a more nuanced relationship emerges than the suggested either/or of this statement. In actuality, what this selection of stories articulates is the need to think beyond a binary of working *or* stay-at-home mother and instead it scrutinises the sociocultural and economic factors that shape, impede and define the lives of women. Furthermore, it is notable that the original collection was published in 2000, the same year in which '*Cosmopolitan* magazine declared . . . that young twenty-something women had become the new "housewife wannabes", the relationship between domesticity and female/feminist emancipation seemed to have been reversed' (Genz and Brabon 57). While the feminist backlash proclaims that domesticity is a feminist choice per se, Simpson's narratives portray a conflicting tale. In fact, while *Cosmopolitan* magazine attempts to position itself as promoting feminist stories, through the narrative of Dorrie, Simpson highlights the negative impact that such magazines have with their 'advice' and 'knowledge' about how to be a woman and what being a woman means. Thus, at the moment when domesticity 'suddenly became a buzzword' (ibid.) Simpson invokes the 'buzzword', not to herald it as a liberating choice for women, but to explore the historical continuum of women's experiences, and at times ongoing subjugation, in the home sphere. In this respect, then, Simpson's righting of parenthood through her writing articulates a third-wave impetus to 'appropriate the personal mode to reveal the political and theoretical element in being a woman in the twenty-first century' (Yu 876).

While engaging with differing topics and themes, the individual short stories and short story collections of Roberts and Simpson both signal the complex, contradictory and confusing feminist politics that circulated in the late 1990s and into the new millennium. Angela McRobbie suggests that '1990 (or thereabouts) marks a turning point, the moment of definitive self-critique in feminist theory' (256) and these fictional writings should therefore be understood as part of broader social and political transformations. For Simpson, the short story genre offers a means of highlighting the competing demands placed on women and how, in particular, this relates to issues of time and selfhood. The compact space of the short story is used to emphasise the constraints women, and especially mothers, encounter. As Melissa Benn states, '[w]omen with children talk about time all the time: feeds, sleep, how many days they are at work, what they manage or don't manage to do at home. Time torments them: time is a treasure' (64). The ability of the short story to foreground notions of time then, because of its narrative brevity, allows Simpson to exploit the genre in order to fictionalise the everyday experiences of women. Similarly, Roberts draws on the short story's ability to exist as a site of tension, in the moment, to challenge the prominence of 'the category of "young women"' and in turn that 'feminism is decisively aged' (McRobbie 255). The short story as a narrative space suggests wholeness, a complete short story. However, simultaneously, short stories can be open-ended, ambiguous and omit a significant amount of information about characters, setting or plot. Furthermore, in general, narrative implies a forward-moving potentiality, yet short stories are often static and move vertically through character's memory or thoughts rather than horizontally via plot and action. Thus, in using this genre Roberts replicates the short story's formal qualities in the negotiation of feminist tensions that are at once related yet in disagreement with one another. What a reading of Roberts's and Simpson's short stories reveals is that the short story and feminism are both sites of tension and ambivalence.

In conclusion, Roberts and Simpson embrace the possibilities afforded by the short story collection in which multiple perspectives and contradictory experiences coexist in a shared narrative space in order to generate a dialogue between contemporary feminisms. This fictional dialogue replicates the conversations of the period, creatively responds and furthers contributes to these discussions, while all the time asking the reader to reflexively critique the motivations, constraints and wider social coercion that perpetuates these discourses. Benn notes that it 'is one of the most commonplace observations about feminism that at some undefinable point, like a river that spawns many tributaries, feminism became feminisms' (2). By the 1990s these feminisms were in clear dialogue and, as these stories reveal, women were attempting to negotiate their personal life choices and experiences in the context of multiple feminist ideologies.

Notes

1. Although, in comparison to postfeminism, as a label third-wave feminism has been more readily accepted, nonetheless this term still provokes questions about the development of contemporary feminist discourses. In particular, tensions between the second and the third wave are often depicted as marking the demise of second-wave feminism in light of the so-called rebellious daughter of the third wave. In *Not My Mother's Sister* (2004) Astrid Henry highlights the problems of over-emphasising the generational implications of feminist waves: 'When we remain stuck in feminism's imagined family, we lose sight of the myriad relations feminists have with one another as well as the possibility of cross-generational identification and similarities' (182).
2. For clarity, throughout this paper I will refer to 'postfeminism' and 'post-feminism' as defined by this overview. However, when making reference to this cultural period more broadly, when both discourses coincide, I will use '(post)feminism' for ease of reference and in order to maintain the important distinction between the two terms.
3. The focus upon instances, or moments, is exemplified by the titles of short story collections published by New Woman writers including Ella D'Arcy's *Modern Instances* (1895) and Sarah Grand's *Emotional Moments* (1908).
4. Kinser also notes that the 'number of websites and blogs alone that relate to mothers is astounding, and web community and social networking sites continue to proliferate' (131) in this period. While writing this chapter the website 'Mumsnet' promoted a blog post entitled 'Stop judging part-time workers – we're not lazy' which challenges the misconception that part-time working mothers have ample free time. <http://www.motherdiaries.com/2014/05/bloomin-part-timers-maintaining-work.html> [Last accessed 6 August 2014.]

Works Cited

Benn, Melissa (1998), *Madonna and Child: Towards a New Politics of Motherhood*, London: Jonathan Cape.
Braidotti, Rosi (1995), 'Generations of Feminists, or, Is There a Life after Post-Modernism?', *Found Objects*, 6, 55–86.
Braithwaite, Ann (2002), 'The Personal, the Political, Third-wave and Postfeminism', *Feminist Theory*, 2, 335–44.

Eliot, T. S. (2002), *Selected Poems* [1954], London: Faber and Faber.
Falcus, Sarah (2013), 'Addressing Age in Michèle Roberts's *Reader, I Married Him*', *Contemporary Women's Writing*, 7:1, 18–34.
Friedan, Betty (2010), *The Feminine Mystique* [1963], London: Penguin.
Friedan, Betty (1993), *The Fountain of Age*, London: Simon & Schuster.
Friend, Tad (1994), '"Yes!" (Feminist Women who Like Sex)', *Esquire*, 121.2, 48–56.
Genz, Stéphanie and Benjamin A. Brabon (2009), *Postfeminism: Cultural Texts and Theories*, Edinburgh: Edinburgh University Press.
Grand, Sarah (1993), 'The Undefinable: A Fantasia', *Daughters of Decadence: Women Writers of the Fin-de-Siècle*, ed. Elaine Showalter, London: Virago, pp. 262–87.
Greer, Germaine (1992), *The Change: Women, Ageing and the Menopause* [1991], London: Penguin.
Hakim, Catherine (1995), 'Five Feminist Myths about Women's Employment', *The British Journal of Sociology*, 46.3, 429–55.
Hays, Sharon (1996), *The Cultural Contradictions of Motherhood*, New Haven, CT: Yale University Press.
Henry, Astrid (2004), *Not My Mother's Sister: Generational Conflict and Third-Wave Feminism*, Bloomington: Indiana University Press.
Hochschild, Arlie (1989), *The Second Shift: Working Parents and the Revolution at Home*, London: Viking.
King, Jeanette (2012), *Discourses of Ageing in Fiction and Feminism: The Invisible Woman*, Houndmills: Palgrave Macmillan.
Kinser, Amber (2010), *Motherhood and Feminism,* Berkeley: Seal Press.
McRobbie, Angela (2004), 'Post-Feminism and Popular Culture', *Feminist Media Studies*, 4:3, 255–64.
Roberts, Michèle (2001), *Playing Sardines*, London: Virago.
'Stop Judging Part-time Workers – We're Not Lazy' (2014), Web. 22 May. <http://www.motherdiaries.com/2014/05/bloomin-part-timers-maintaining-work.html> [Last accessed 3 March 2014.]
Showalter, Elaine (1993), 'Introduction', *Daughters of Decadence: Women Writers of the Fin-de-Siècle*, London: Virago, pp. vii–xx.
Simpson, Helen (2001), *Hey Yeah Right Get a Life* [2000], London: Vintage.
Simpson, Helen (2006), 'With Child', *The Guardian*, 22 April. Web. <http://www.guardian.co.uk/books/2006/apr/22/featuresreviews.guardianreview3> [Last accessed 3 March 2013.]
Yu, Su-Lin (2011), 'Reclaiming the Personal: Personal Narratives of Third-wave Feminists', *Women's Studies*, 20, 873–89.

Chapter 10

Class as Destiny in the Short Stories of Tessa Hadley

Sue Vice

Tessa Hadley's two collections of short stories, *Sunstroke* (2007) and *Married Love* (2012), appeared after she had already published three novels, yet it is the shorter form with which the author is particularly closely associated. Extracts from her novels in progress have themselves been published in apparently self-contained form as stories, and it is this genre which constitutes the content of her courses on creative writing at Bath Spa University.[1] Hadley's short stories are often described as 'domestic', a term which is used to suggest both the interiors of the – for the most part – well-appointed homes in which events unfold, as well as the import of those events for the characters' interior worlds. In this chapter, I will examine the relationship between domestic and subjective interiors in Hadley's work, and thus the connections between her particular kind of social realism and its literary narration.

The critical reception of Hadley's work has focused on its class basis to the extent that the very features of middle-class British life with which it is concerned are used as literary terms with which to characterise it.[2] Patrick Gale (2007) notes that Hadley's tone is 'like a hand smoothing out the last wrinkle in a perfect set of bed linen, or minutely adjusting the silver on a dinner table' (n.p.), in phrasing which equates narrative with materialistic precision, while Edmund Gordon (2012) describes Hadley's stories as 'classy chronicles of contemporary emotions' (n.p.), managing to unite class concern and an assertion of literary value in a single adjective. However, as I will argue, all of Hadley's literary effects, including the representation of class, rely on a complex use of voice in an instance of Mikhail Bakhtin's notion of polyphony, which takes the form of what he calls 'a plurality of consciousnesses, with equal rights and each with its own world, [which] combine but are not merged in the unity of the event' (6). By this means, making it hard to establish precisely whose voice it is that we hear, and making the reader work hard to determine the nature of the stories' central 'event', Hadley's short stories are perhaps most clearly indebted stylistically to those of Katherine Mansfield, one of the writers frequently cited as an influence.³ In Mansfield's 'The Garden Party' (1922), for instance, such techniques are used to represent the struggle of Laura Sheridan, a young woman living in well-to-do circumstances, to determine which of the voices that surround her bear heeding: that of her family and the community of early twentieth-century New Zealand bourgeoisie, or that of her own social conscience. This is evident in relation to the fact that Laura's wish that the Sheridans' planned garden party be cancelled when a local working man dies in an accident is judged 'extravagant' by her sister Jose, a term implying both financial irresponsibility and dramatic self-indulgence. Their mother insists that the party must continue as planned, and lends Laura a beautiful hat which makes her want to take part in the festivities after all, as the free indirect rendering of her response reveals: 'Is mother right? she thought. And now she hoped her mother was right. Am I being extravagant? Perhaps it was extravagant' (543). The hat and the repeated word together represent Laura's suppression of her own independent thoughts, and their replacement with an ambivalence that allows her to go along with her family's wishes.

The construction of a plot centred on class is starkly apparent in Hadley's story 'The Trojan Prince' from the collection *Married Love*. Here, James McIlvanney is the bathetically designated eponym of a story that represents the intersection of class and sexual relations, a combination that, as we will see, is present throughout Hadley's *oeuvre*. However, the story is doubly removed from present-day class-related concerns, both because it is named after Virgil's mythic account of Aeneas' shipwreck in Carthage, and since it is explicitly set in 1920s Tyneside. Such a backward glance appears to offset the story's narrative motor being precisely that of starkly acknowledged class strictures. The story's setting early in the previous century defamiliarises its detail to the effect of implying comic distance, if not satire. For instance, James's visit to his well-to-do cousin Ellen Pearson begins with his concern that the maid who opens the door to the house, one that is more 'decent' than his own, might be 'a girl he'd known at school' (59). Thus we see the transitional nature of James's social position as his working-class education is placed in possible conflict with his aspiration. The nature of his 'interest' in Ellen is ambivalent; the reader learns that he is drawn by the 'mystery' of her 'blonde languor' (62), in a phrase which makes sexual lassitude indistinguishable from the leisure of privilege. As Ellen's companion, the more down-to-earth and lowly Connie Chappell, puts it to James, 'Ellen likes you ... you could get a job with her dad's firm' (72), emphasising the fact that sentimental interest can be used for material ends. Yet it is

Connie, also a distant cousin of James's, who awaits him on his return to Liverpool, after he survives a wreck at sea on his namesake, the cargo ship *The Trojan Prince*. James's perception of Connie also unites awareness of sexual with class identity. When he first sees her at Ellen's house, she wears 'pink, slinky pyjamas' but 'the soles of her bare feet are dirty', like those of 'a sloppy little cat' (65). As Hadley observes, James experiences 'attraction as repulsion' (Interview with Deborah Treisman, n.p.) in relation to Connie, and she argues that his not marrying Ellen after all is because the latter is simply not, in the end, equally attractive to him. Yet James's seems also to be a class-based romantic choice. He spends the days during which he is shipwrecked on an island off the Canadian coast 'making precise plans to better himself' (ibid.) and 'imagines telling all this to Connie' ('Trojan', 79). Thus James's final perception, 'He knows he ought to marry Ellen Pearson and get a house full of furniture. But he can't. He won't' (80), suggests a decision for aspiration rather than acceptance, as embodied by Connie's more familiar and 'homely' allure (Interview with Deborah Treisman, n.p.).

Although some of Hadley's stories, like her most recent novel *Clever Girl* (2013), are narrated in the first person, the majority rely instead on the modernist ambivalence of third-person narration that moves in and out of characters' voices. Even direct utterance is recorded without quotation marks. This is particularly significant when such a narrator is the mediator of class-related representation in the contemporary era. This third-person narrative voice, often too readily identified by critics with Hadley's, sometimes takes up what appears to be a stance of its own, self-consciously set apart from the characters. Although not established, as is 'Trojan Prince', in an era identified as long past, in a story such as 'Sunstroke' the narrator is distant in both time and space, an onlooker from a somewhat earlier time, with what appears initially as an almost personalised, opinionated voice. As if imitating a gradual and filmic move from a general panorama to particular detail, this narrator starts out with the description, equivalent to an establishing shot, of a Somerset beach on a summer's day, then claims that 'it's hard to believe' (2) contemporary, technology-focused children still enjoy seaside pleasures, and at last zooms in on the story's protagonists. Rachel and Janie are two young women sitting on the grass in what we are told is 'the Jubilee Gardens (that's Victoria's Jubilee, not the last one)', under 'the shade of an ornamental tree that neither can identify', and looking, 'if it still means anything, bohemian' (2). Being 'bohemian' is presented here as if it were an outmoded designation, but it is in fact the answer to an up-to-date question, about the women's class identity: although they 'don't look wealthy', it is clear 'even from the outward appearance' that they are not staying at any of the seaside resort's guest houses, and 'certainly not at the refurbished holiday camp' (2). Despite the narrator's implication that such matters are not reducible to cash, the reader thus learns that this is not a story about poverty. In a detail that is at once symbolic and irreducibly real, we are told that 'Rachel and her husband Sam have a cottage in Somerset where they spend their holidays' (3). As Anne Enright points out, several of Hadley's stories feature characters who own summer cottages, places 'where desire is born and a new future begins' (n.p.). In 'Phosphorescence', the Cooley family's 'primitive chalet' for visitors at their holiday cottage in Wales becomes an 'awful hut' (71) for their guest Claudia, the scene of her marriage's disintegration. As well as offering the occasion for characters to be freed from their habitual and workaday routines, such a symbol draws on a stark materiality. Enright observes that Hadley's recurrent theme of marital escape and betrayal, in three stories set in a holiday dwelling, is itself not neutral, since 'adultery is an expensive business' (n.p.). The image of the second home, as a supplement to everyday life and scene of its deconstruction, equally rests on an invisible financial and, particularly in the Welsh setting of the Cooleys' holiday home, ethically questionable underpinning.

A tone of what seems to be ironic detachment is thus set up from the start in 'Sunstroke', continued in the more finely grained account of Rachel and Janie's circumstances. Both do a 'token' amount of work outside the home; although, since before they had children their relationships 'showed every sign' of being 'modern' ones with shared domestic labour, both have been left with a sense of 'life unlived' (4). In this way, the narrator's superior knowledge of which jubilee is commemorated and, we assume, the name of the 'ornamental tree' of which the protagonists are ignorant, turns inwards to give an account of their financial and emotional well-being. The two realms are presented as inextricable. The very word 'token' acts simultaneously as an adjective that refers to the inessential nature of the women's work, and, as a noun, an empty signifier of substitution or exchange, in this instance a clue to the women's barely acknowledged malaise, personified in the story by the attraction both feel towards Sam's single friend Kieran. Later we learn that Janie's partner Vince refrains from pointing out that 'his work brings in money and hers doesn't' (15). Although Vince is thinking about the wage-value of his work as a lighting designer versus Janie's as an artist, the precise subject of his suppressed utterance is ambiguous: it is not just Janie's art, but all the rest of her work in the home, located in what the narrator calls 'the warm vegetable soup of motherhood' (4), that goes unpaid. As the narrator points out, now taking part in the women's own perceptions, their 'half involuntary' absorption into domestic life 'surprisingly resembles their own mothers' lives, thirty years ago'. The adverb is shared: both the narrator and the two women are surprised at this turn of events. Those elements of Rachel and Janie's lifestyle that resemble those of an earlier era, embodied by Janie's wearing a dress decorated with 'seventies-style pink paisley patterns' (2), are subject to the arbitrariness that applies to gendered household negotiations over waged and non-waged work, as analysed in the late 1970s by such second-wave feminist theorists as Michèle Barrett. Barrett argues that what she calls the 'family household system', by means of which women were pushed exclusively into the domestic sphere during the Industrial Revolution, has persisted into the present, as we see in Hadley's story, since such a system has 'become entrenched in the relations of production of capitalism' (249). The personal dissatisfaction or 'oppression' that results from such a formation, and which prepares for the story's denouement, is itself expressed in such a way that reveals the overlap of emotional and material. This is made clear by the narrator's repeated phrasing: the women share 'a sense of surplus, of life unlived', more specifically 'a sensual surplus' (4). In a version of the classical Marxist theory from which the term is drawn, the women are not sufficiently compensated in any sense for their labour, its 'surplus value' going to furnish the 'profit' of their menfolk. This takes the form of the men's exemption from cooking, housework and childcare in order to write novels, in the case of Rachel's husband Sam, and to plan lighting designs, in Vince's. The 'tokenly' limited nature of such profit in contemporary settings is signalled by the narrator's telling use of small details. Sam has 'actually been able to cook for fifteen years', the adverb 'actually' doing double duty here in expressing his own pride as well as an onlooker's incredulity; while the rendering of Vince's thought that he 'really does want to spend more time with [the kids]' (11) is nicely balanced between the genuine and compensatory senses of 'really'. Both perceptions are relayed indirectly to the reader through the narratorial device of free indirect discourse, allowing for a sense of the characters' self-awareness battling with self-delusion where gender and class are concerned.

The difficulty of deciding how to relate these literary structures to the class-related differences on which the narrator reports is evident in a contrasting pair of stories about female friendship. In a similar pattern to that in 'Sunstroke', the reader is introduced to Phil and Louie in 'Exchanges' in terms which make clear the narrator's initial distance – the women 'look interesting', yet remain nameless – while a closer look anatomises them in terms of their apparently high status (105).

The narrator claims that both are the kind of woman whose age, 'in good clothes, in a good light, after a good life of the privileged kind of work that doesn't weather or wizen you' (ibid.), is hard to determine, even though they are, 'without an Old Testament miracle', beyond child-bearing (106). The advantage of gentle work is thus shown to be compromised only by gender. As if in response to the narrator's hint in 'Exchanges' at the kind of work that might 'weather or wizen you' is the description in 'Friendly Fire' of Shelley's friend and fellow cleaner Pam, who is said to be 'fat like a limp saggy cushion, very short, with permed yellow curls that were growing out grey; her face was crumpled like an ancient baby's' (23). Both work and class have taken their toll on Pam, it appears. Although critics including Gale have identified such detail, including the protagonists' names, and the backdrop of the story as a whole, as characterised by class condescension, the significant difference in perspective between the two stories is narratorial. In contrast to the earlier story, 'Friendly Fire' opens with immediate access to Shelley's world and the story's focalisation through her: 'Shelley was helping out her friend Pam' (22). The perception about Pam's appearance is identified as Shelley's own via the third-person narrator, since the emphasis is on her gaze. Shelley is looking at her friend, 'lit up' inside her car, and imagining 'herself as Pam was seeing her'. Like Phil and Louie, Pam and Shelley are physically contrasting. However, our sense of this is presented from outside in 'Exchanges' – 'One is fine-boned, small ... the other is taller and more awkward' (105) – but arises from Shelley's viewpoint in 'Friendly Fire', when she considers the words of her husband: 'Roy said that Pam and Shelley side by side looked like Little and Large, because Shelley was tall and thin' (23). Later in 'Exchanges', we gain access to each woman's interiority in turn, as the title implies, while all of 'Friendly Fire' remains with Shelley. However, narrative standpoint does not entirely account for the class-based assumptions that go to construct these two stories. It is hard to ignore the fact that the reader's introduction to Phil and Louie takes place as they visit the Victoria and Albert Museum in London, while Shelley is waiting to help out Pam on an industrial cleaning job in King's Lynn.

Yet the focus of much of Hadley's writing on middle- and upper-middle-class characters and their lives is not simply a limitation or failure of imagination. There are indeed moments in which the reader might feel that they can detect something of this kind of endorsed or unquestioned privilege, for example in Christine's bourgeois dilemma, in 'Mother's Son', where she has found it hard to 'choose paintings for the walls' for her flat in a Victorian artist's studio that 'had been renovated and cost the earth' (22). Even here, however, there is a hint at self-consciousness in the narrator adopting what sounds like Christine's own wry phrase about the flat's price. The latter reflects that she is glad to have 'bought expensive chocolate biscuits' when her son visits unannounced (ibid.), as if expense conveys the same kind of maternal care as her allowing him to smoke in her flat. In 'Because the Night', Tom's distaste for his mother's protégé, her former pupil Simon, centres on the latter's 'puny' physique, in contrast to which we learn that, 'Red-headed Tom was small and hard and solid, invaluable in the rugby first fifteen at Dulwich College' (90). The reader might question the function of such a culturally specific detail here. In part, the location of Tom's physicality in a school rugby team serves to reveal not only his difference from the troubled, drug-taking Simon, but also his own sense of that difference. The narrator's tone might at first sound neutral, so that naming the private school itself is simply to endorse the story's upper-middle-class setting. However, the narrator seems rather to be delineating more of that world's detail, and the hint at a comic half-rhyme between 'solid' and 'College' itself acts to imply a narratorial distance from the sentence's meaning. As part of this delineation, the narrator sees both the specific and the general in relation to the story's family, the siblings Tom and Kristen and their parents Peggy and Jim, who are described as individuals but as typical, or even stereotypical, of their particular class position as well. This is clear equally in relation to the children's au pairs, named as the minimally identified series of women, 'Annegret then Bengta then Sylvie' (81), to their home, its location likewise unspecified, set 'on a hill at the edge of one of those minor towns in Surrey that are clustered up against the skirts of London' (82), and their father's work, which changes, as noted in parentheses, from a job at 'Anglia World to Transglobal Services' (88). In each case, what appears to be individually named or located detail is rather simply one of a metonymic string of interchangeable elements – to sinister effect, in the case of Jim's blandly named companies, which turn out to be indirectly linked to the arms trade. In the case of Tom's school, it seems that a specific signifier has been chosen to augment such a picture. As the description of Kristen's suggests – she 'didn't hate her girls' independent school' (84) – education for which you pay is presented as an inevitable part of this slightly unsympathetic-seeming social world. In this case as in Tom's, the detail is used to imply something personal, for Kristen a wish for solitude. Indeed, by such means the world of 'Because the Night' is carefully distinguished from that in the Culverts' Rectory in 'Buckets of Blood' and 'A Mouthful of Cut Glass', or Ally's apparently lower-middle-class home in 'She's The One'.[4] It is as if the very act of making such distinctions forces the reader to acknowledge the existence of inequality in the detail of social privilege versus its absence. In 'Friendly Fire', the working-class Shelley's children are not at private schools, nor, as Louie is said to do with her children in 'Exchanges', does she take them on 'the march against the war in Afghanistan' (107). Rather, her seventeen-year-old daughter Kerry has fallen pregnant and her son Anthony, after an adolescence characterised by pierced eyebrows and 'stinking to heaven of Lynx aftershave' (31), has joined the army and been posted to Afghanistan. Such juxtapositions do not just rely upon but reveal social difference.

A dilemma for the reader of an analogous kind which is perhaps less easily resolved arises in 'Surrogate', from *Sunstroke*. In this story a student, Carla, begins an affair with a man whom she serves in a pub because he resembles the apparently unattainable Patrick, the university lecturer in Early Modern Studies with whom she is besotted. It is through Carla's first-person narration that the reader learns that the differences between the two men possess what feels like an uncomfortably class-based element. On their first encounter at the bar where she works, Carla describes the surrogate, Dave, as lacking 'Patrick's concentrated excitement', that he 'asks for a pint of Stella in an ordinary accent, not like Patrick's educated one', and 'appears to be shy, and maybe not very clever' (98). First-person narrative here constitutes the reason for such effects as patronage, which is not simply an accidental side effect of the story's plot. These are the words of a narrator whose tastes and behaviour keep her at a distance from the reader, as Carla's description of a binary between 'ordinary' and 'educated' suggests. We might question whether the terms are in fact at odds, and what an 'educated' accent might sound like. The surrogate Dave is a 'gas engineer', and, as Enright argues, 'the story seems to assume that sleeping with a gas engineer is more "wrong" and, crucially, less interesting than sleeping with a lecturer in 17th-century poetry' (n.p.). Yet it is not clear that either the 'story' itself, in Enright's phrasing, or the reader, allies themselves quite so clearly with Carla. Her youthful enthusiasm for Patrick's scholarly demeanour, his 'bowed shoulders', 'small beer belly', eyes that 'squinted slightly' when he took off his glasses, is self-consciously idiosyncratic, while the story itself focuses in more detail on the affair with Dave than marriage to Patrick. Carla's fantasies about a relationship with Patrick turn real when she learns that her feelings are reciprocated, and although she claims to be 'genuinely happily married' to him in the present time of her narration (103), a reversal takes place at the story's conclusion. The 'little hunger of wasted opportunity' with which such a marriage has left Carla emerges in fantasies that are now about the surrogate instead, precisely in his role as a gas engineer who visits the house by chance. In both roles, as surrogate and then as fantasy, Dave remains a simulacrum, his job and class position enabling and determining this status. The story is more a revelation of Carla's eccentric inner world than an endorsement of it, although the class-based terms in which such eccentricity emerges might make the reader unsure about quite how to respond to her as a character.

Hadley has claimed in an interview that it is 'difference', including that of class, which fuels her literary practice, a feature formally and generically embodied by the concept of the short story collection. It is just this notion of class-based mismatch, implicit in 'Surrogate', that forms the plot of two linked stories. The first of these, from *Sunstroke*, is 'Buckets of Blood', about the teenage Hilary's visit to her sister Sheila at university and 'almost enviously' tending to her during a miscarriage (Anonymous 2010: n.p.); in 'A Mouthful of Cut Glass' from the later collection *Married Love*, the middle-class Sheila, daughter of a vicar, and her working-class boyfriend Neil, whose father is a toolsetter, visit each other's family homes. In 'Buckets of Blood', Hilary's viewpoint is so strongly presented that it is as if the story is titled after her recalling Sheila's explanation of her predicament, turning the naval imprecation into a literal description: 'It's a fine mess. Blood everywhere. Buckets of blood. You'll have to get rid of everything' (49). Hilary's susceptibility to the words of others is revealed anew in the narrator's free indirect use of her vocabulary. When we hear that Hilary was 'going to meet Sheila in the fleshpots, or at Bristol University, where Sheila was reading Classics' (40), we understand that the 'fleshpots' used to describe university life is a term picked up from Hilary's father's ironic – and, it seems, ironically apt – adult usage. However, the vicar's citation of the term derives from the sixteenth century rather than biblical sense of 'fleshpots', since he uses 'flesh' to imply sexual temptation, in contrast to the phrase's origin in Exodus where the wandering Israelites express regret for the lost culinary and domestic luxury of Egypt.[5] It is Hilary's similarly nostalgic view of the sisters' childhood that is shattered by Sheila's experience, which is embodied by the story's various synonyms for 'fleshpots', in its title and in Hilary's awareness of the distressingly literal object, 'something like a chamber pot' (49), that is crucial to her sister's misfortune. Hilary's customarily innocent view of the world is conveyed by a different kind of phrasing: 'a lady with blue-white hair' sits next to her on the bus to Bristol. The childlike designation of this woman, who is knitting for a grandchild, sums up the ambivalence of Hilary's position in relation to adult femininity, as the story reveals. Hilary's most challenging encounter presents, as we saw in 'Sunstroke', a fusion of sexual with class anxiety, since it is Sheila's relationship with Neil that threatens to drag the sisters back to the 'muffling dependencies of home and childhood' (49).

The description of Hilary's first encounter with Neil exploits free indirect discourse's ambiguity in rendering her perception as if objectively: we are told that 'he spoke with a strong northern accent' (44). Although it seems clear that this is Hilary's individual perception and not the narrator's description, as the emotive 'strong' and vague 'northern' imply, her words are not quoted directly. Such ambiguity of subject-position and uncertainty about the origin of utterance can have the radically destabilising effect described in Makiko Minow-Pinkney's analysis of Virginia Woolf, in which she argues that through the use of free indirect discourse, Woolf 'offers us a subject which has no simple unity, no clear boundary between itself and other' (61). Such a fictive version of the Kristevan 'subject in process' is also perceptible in 'Buckets of Blood'.[6] Hilary's narratorial error is corrected or answered by her sister, making clear not only her unworldliness but the unreliability of what we read, when Sheila asks:

– What did you think of Neil?
Hilary was cautious. – Is he from the north?
– Birmingham, you idiot. Couldn't you tell? Such a pure Brummie accent. (57)

Hilary's misrecognition is overdeterminedly personal and generalised in her sister's eyes. This is a perhaps more subtle example of the revelation of pathology that we saw in the dramatic monologue of 'Surrogate', in the sense of its method of narration as well as Hilary's viewpoint. In 'Buckets of Blood', although not in its successor 'A Mouthful of Cut Glass', Neil and Sheila are filtered through Hilary's consciousness, which offers the truth of perception if not of objective fact. While acknowledging the reverence Neil attracts from the other students, Hilary also sees her sister shrink to become 'brighter, funnier and smaller than her real self' in her efforts to encourage and attribute ideas to him (59). In 'A Mouthful of Cut Glass', Neil is perceived for the most part from Sheila's viewpoint, leaving him still opaque. We learn that he holds himself in reserve from his girlfriend, even making love 'with irony, holding himself back' (38), meaning that the absence of his viewpoint is a fitting one. Indeed, the only insight the narrator allows is a brief glimpse into his sexual subjectivity at the conclusion of 'A Mouthful of Cut Glass'.

The latter story is named, in the same way as 'Buckets of Blood', after its focaliser's memory of an all-important phrase. This time it is Sheila's horrified recall of an utterance heard by accident that provides the title. Hilary's 'cautious' response to Neil and his accent has its counterpart when Sheila meets Neil's parents. Once more, such a moment inherits the structure of its revelation from Katherine Mansfield's writing. In Mansfield's story 'Miss Brill' (1920), the eponymous protagonist's idealised view of a young couple who join her on a park bench as 'the hero and heroine' of her own inner drama, is shockingly disrupted by their overheard wish to be alone: 'Why does she come here at all – who wants her? Why doesn't she keep her silly old mug at home?', as the boy whispers to his girlfriend (553). In 'A Mouthful of Cut Glass', Sheila's and the reader's perception of reality is likewise abruptly disconcerted by overhearing the private words of Neil's mother, again those spoken by one half of a couple to another. The moment here has been prepared for in 'Buckets of Blood', where Hilary's 'vivid idea of how her mother must appear to strangers' focuses on the latter's chaotic and harried demeanour, by reason of which the signs of her class status are fragmented and overwhelmed by her domestic responsibilities. Mrs Culvert has a 'worn once-good coat she never had time to button up' and speaks in 'cut-glass enunciations ... of bits of sentences that never became any whole message' (43). In 'A Mouthful of Cut Glass', as if in ironic fulfilment of Hilary's fear of social humiliation, we see a 'stranger' form a 'vivid idea' of how Sheila appears, based on just such outward elements, and clashing with her own wish for 'intensity of engagement' (44) with the working-class authenticity embodied by Neil's family. Sheila's wish to 'offer up her real self at last' in an encounter with something 'dark and raw' is thwarted by the mundane reality of Neil's parents' home in a 'neat and respectable' estate, in place of the 'frowning Victorian concentration of population' that she had imagined (37). We learn that, despite Sheila's correction to Hilary, she considers Neil's accent in the same terms as those of her sister: his 'Birmingham accent, which she had thought so strong, was softened and compromised compared with the way his parents spoke' (40). But while Sheila makes no judgement here about Neil's parents, the reverse is not the case. She overhears Neil's mother, using almost the very term Hilary used of Mrs Culvert, demanding of her husband, 'How can I talk to her? ... With that accent like a mouthful of cut glass?' (47). Sheila sees aggression in the transferred epithet of the misquoted phrase: rather than being a description of a process of decorative faceting, it is as if the glass in this version of the phrase has been 'cut' into sharp pieces of 'broken crystal' that draw blood (48).

Neil's parallel failing when he visits Sheila's family home is more subtly class-related, despite starting out as once more concerned with accent. Although Sheila fears that her brothers, as 'horrible mimics', will be 'mentally rehearsing' the way Neil speaks, the latter cannot keep up with a different kind of linguistic challenge, that of a family game of charades. Like the holiday cottage, family games are both a narrative gambit and a class signifier. There is only a brief overt reference to charades in Mansfield's story 'The Swing of the Pendulum' (1911), but the protagonist Viola's notion of competing sides who take it in turn to 'act a word – just what she was doing now', reveals its importance as denoting a distant, carefree past of 'childish parties' and their replacement, in the present, by the alternations or 'swings' of emotional, financial and epistemological states (115). A similar overdetermination is apparent in Lorrie Moore's story 'Charades', in which the very process of acting out roles and words lays bare the real relations between family members. Such a parlour game is indicative of access to education and bourgeois leisure, even, in Melanie Dawson's words, a cultural space in which the middle-class could 'clarify, critique and question the[ir] everyday activities' (2005: 1). In 'A Mouthful of Cut Glass', the story's title takes on a wider symbolic meaning when it is applied to the painful humiliation undergone by Neil in his turn when he is drawn into playing at Sheila's family home, since the 'clarification' Dawson describes is not available to him. The focus during the game of charades here is on Neil but the discourse seems to be that of a middle-class onlooker. Earlier in the story we learn that he is 'very clever' and that his friends 'glanced quickly at him after they spoke, to see what he thought' (36). However, such an onlooker judges Neil bracingly during the game as 'hopeless', observes that 'he wasn't much better at guessing, either', and 'almost ruined everything' by his pointed muttering (54). This narrative voice sounds like the *skaz*, the written reproduction of oral utterance, of a family member, and the comment, 'poor Neil was out of his depth' (ibid.) sounds a note of communal judgement similar to that which characterises the frequent appearance of the epithet 'poor' in George Eliot's *Middlemarch* (1874). As with Hadley, the author Eliot herself is all too readily identified with this personified moment of the narrator's free indirect discourse. The charades themselves involve the construction of work-related words out of syllables given parodically gendered meanings, and it is implied that this adds to Neil's rejecting a theatricality which is at odds with Sheila's view of him as a repository of authenticity. The word 'Eucharist', central to Reverend Culvert's professional role, is fragmented into the enactment of a shepherd tending an 'ewe', followed by the Reverend himself acting out the last syllable dressed in a 'green silk dress' and carrying his wife's handbag on a 'drooping wrist' (54). The word 'seductress' that follows is performed in its entirety by Sheila, 'as Neil had never seen her': 'husky-voiced, rolling her hips, adjusting her stocking' (ibid.). Mrs Culvert is dressed as the 'shy boy', a surrogate for Neil, whose kiss Sheila demands.

Although an element is visible here of Dawson's notion of clarifying and critiquing 'everyday activities', it is one that paints a caricature of Neil and Sheila's relationship. While he enacts woodenly the role of the working-class shepherd in charge of the ewes, she takes on that of a worldly, heartless woman. Mrs Culvert's comforting remark to Neil, 'You'll get the hang of it next time' (55), is tellingly ambiguous, leaving unclear whether it is charades, sexual or class relations which she believes that he might perform better given a second chance. The conclusion to 'A Mouthful of Cut Glass' glances back to its precursor, 'Buckets of Blood'. This time the bucket in question holds 'rotting apples' (56) from the trees in the rectory garden, which Sheila and Hilary throw at the French windows of their father's study where Neil is listening to rock music. The moment is inspired by Hilary's assertion that he 'look[s] funny' (ibid.) sitting cross-legged, smoking and swaying his head in time with the music, and an 'atavistic' (Seymenliyska, n.p.) revenge taken on by Sheila for his failures in the parlour games of love and class.

Literary realism is not as definitionally associated with working-class representation as British realist cinema, although the central focus to be found in Hadley's stories on the bourgeois quotidian, either on its own account or in its relations to other class identities, is distinctive.[7] If the representation of lives other than those of the comfortable middle classes is unusual in *Sunstroke* and *Married Love*, then the detail of political struggle is similarly rare. Indeed, its presence often acts as a symbol of nostalgia for youthful passion in every sense. In 'The Enemy', the visit of Keith, her former brother-in-law of 'impeccable' miner's son pedigree and hard-left principle (79), inspires the formerly radical Caro to reflect that nowadays she considers that it is not patriarchy but biology that has determined women's lives (87). In another telling juxtaposition, 'In the Country' shows the protagonist Julie's husband Ed describing his mother as 'an old Maoist' at the very moment he helps himself to 'more of the potatoes roasted in olive oil' (127).[8] Yet insistence on the stories' class-related content, in the terms suggested by one of Hadley's interviewers, as 'a social tragedy that ironizes any and all choices one might make in life' (Interview with Mary Ann Kolton), obscures their other elements. These are an interest in particular states of mind, such as solitude or bereavement; in particular kinds of relationship, including (as Enright identifies) women's friendships, wrongly chosen marriages or illicit encounters, and those between mothers and their sons; and, most tellingly, reliance on a Bakhtinian polyphony to construct the social worlds of which we read. It is not only that polyphony allows for a chorus of voices, including that of the narrator, which debate, engage in dialogue, overhear, quote or filter each other. As well as this, the very subject of these stories is just such an interweaving of multiple utterances, the various and clashing views that characters have of each other and of the world, as well as individuals' internal voices that express uncertainty, contradiction and self-delusion.

Notes

1. Hadley's novels published before *Sunstroke and Other Stories* (London: Jonathan Cape 2007) are *Accidents in the Home* (London: Jonathan Cape, 2002), *Everything Will Be All Right* (London: Jonathan Cape, 2004), and *The Master Bedroom* (London: Jonathan Cape, 2007). *Married Love and Other Stories* (London: Jonathan Cape, 2012) followed her novel *The London Train* (London: Jonathan Cape, 2011). See also Hadley's university webpage, <https://applications.bathspa.ac.uk/staff-profiles/profile.asp?user=academic/hadt1> [Last accessed 10 August 1914.] Many thanks to James Bailey and Emma Young for their invaluable comments and suggestions in relation to an earlier draft of this chapter.
2. Liesl Schillinger describes Hadley's settings as those of 'upper middle-class British life' ('The Boy Next Door', *New York Times Sunday Book Review*, 5 August 2007), pointing perhaps to the contemporary fragmentation of the traditional tripartite class division – of working, middle and upper class – as identified in the 'Great British Class Survey'. According to this, Hadley's characters would for the most part fall into the category of 'established middle class', identifiable on the strength of wealth, cultural and social capital. See Mike Savage et al., 'A New Model of Social Class', *Sociology* 47 (2), pp. 219–50, April 2013.
3. See Gale, 'Stroking the silver'; Hadley's 'teaching specialisms' as listed on her university webpage (see n. 1) include Mansfield.
4. Hadley, 'She's the One', in *Married Love*. Such an identification is contrary to Gordon's, since he places Ally in the list of Hadley's characters with middle-class names in distinction to those with déclassé ones such as Pam and Shelley. It seems, rather, that the narrative as a whole must be considered in order to decipher such detail.
5. See David L. Jeffrey, *A Dictionary of Biblical Tradition in English Literature*, Grand Rapids: Eerdmans, 1992, p. 285; and the original context, Exodus 16: 3.
6. See Julia Kristeva, 'The Subject in Process', in *The Tel Quel Reader*, eds Patrick French and Roland-François Lack, New York: Routledge, 1998.
7. For a more detailed analysis of this subject, see David Forrest, 'The Films of Joanna Hogg: New British Realism and Class', *Studies in European Cinema* 11 (1) 2014, pp. 64–75.
8. In 'She's the One', Hilda's purchase of olive oil constitutes a signifier of both class and national difference, since she is an expatriate American buying what Ally considers to be 'food for the wrong climate' (174).

Works Cited

Anonymous (2010), *Kirkus Reviews*, review of *Sunstroke*, 24 June.
Bakhtin, Mikhail (1984), *Problems of Dostoevsky's Poetics*, ed. and trans. Caryl Emerson, Minneapolis: University of Minnesota Press.
Barrett, Michèle (1980), *Women's Oppression Today: Problems in Marxist-Feminist Analysis*, London: Verso.

Dawson, Melanie (2005), *Laboring to Play: Home Entertainment and the Spectacle of Middle-Class Cultural Life, 1850–1920*, Tuscaloosa: University of Alabama Press.
Enright, Anne (2007), Review of *Sunstroke*, *The Guardian*, 6 January.
Forrest, David (2014), 'The Films of Joanna Hogg: New British Realism and Class', *Studies in European Cinema*, 11:1, pp. 64–75.
Gale, Patrick (2007), 'Stroking the silver with polish – and pain', *The Independent*, 5 January.
Gordon, Edmund (2012), Review of *Married Love*, *The Observer*, 8 January.
Hadley, Tessa (2002), *Accidents in the Home*, London: Jonathan Cape.
Hadley, Tessa (2013), *Clever Girl*, London: Jonathan Cape.
Hadley, Tessa (2012), *Married Love and Other Stories*, London: Jonathan Cape.
Hadley, Tessa (2007), *Sunstroke and Other Stories*, London: Jonathan Cape.
Hadley, Tessa (2013), Interview with Mary Ann Kolton, *Los Angeles Times*, 8 May.
Hadley, Tessa (2010), Interview with Deborah Treisman, 'This Week in Fiction', <http://www.newyorker.com/online/blogs/books/2010/11/this-week-in-fiction-tessa-hadley.html> [Last accessed 6 June 2014.]
Jeffrey, David L. (1992), *A Dictionary of Biblical Tradition in English Literature*, Grand Rapids: Eerdmans.
Kristeva, Julia (1998), 'The Subject in Process', *The Tel Quel Reader* [1977], ed. Patrick French and Roland-François Lack, New York: Routledge, pp. 133–78.
Mansfield, Katherine (1937), *The Short Stories of Katherine Mansfield*, ed. J. Middleton Murry, New York: Knopf.
Minow-Pinkney, Makiko (1987), *Virginia Woolf and the Problem of the Subject: Feminine Writing in the Major Novels*, Brighton: Harvester.
Moore, Lorrie (1998), *Birds of America*, London: Faber.
Savage, Mike, et al. (2013), 'A New Model of Social Class', *Sociology*, 47:2, 219–50.
Schillinger, Liesl (2007), 'The Boy Next Door', *New York Times Sunday Book Review*, 5 August.
Seymenliyska, Elena (2012), Review of *Married Love*, *The Telegraph*, 8 February.

Chapter 11

Address, Temporality and Misdelivery: The Postal Effects of Ali Smith's Short Stories

Ben Davies

In 'Envois' (1980), Derrida's series of postcards in which he problematises the order and sequence of sending messages and the relationship between addresser and addressee, Derrida allows for his correspondence to be read in a number of ways. In the first line of the introductory post of 7 September 1979, he suggests 'you might read these *envois* as the preface to a book that I have not written' (1987: 3), and a little later he writes: 'you might consider them, if you really wish to, as the remainders of a recently destroyed correspondence' (ibid.). Furthermore, in a discussion of the letters of Plato and the scholarly debates surrounding them, he exclaims: 'as if one could not pretend to write fictive letters with multiple authors and addressees! and even oneself to write to oneself' (84). Throughout these postcards, then, Derrida reflects upon and complicates straightforward, one-to-one correspondence. Moreover, there is a sense in 'Envois' that Derrida himself is writing fictions, addressing himself – oneself to oneself – and thereby creating a complex type of 'one-to-one' correspondence. Consequently, we can, as Martin McQuillan writes in his essay 'Information Theory' (1999), read Derrida's 'Envois' as a type of 'short story' (140) or self-addressed fictions. In this essay, however, I want to address the inverse of this relationship between postcards and fiction, reading Ali Smith's short stories as narratives that create a series of postal effects. These postal effects are created, I shall argue, through the repeated use of the second-person pronoun throughout her collections and the way in which Smith's stories are highly self-reflexive, often focusing in particular upon the condensed, complicated, brief temporality of the short story.

Address

Throughout Smith's collections, many stories refer to and address a 'you'; indeed, this form of address can be seen as a characteristic of much of her shorter fiction. These 'yous', these 'second persons', are sometimes clearly identifiable as a character within the story, but there are also times when the addressee is left unidentified, ambiguous, enigmatic. The 'yous' the narrators address – characters or otherwise – are invoked for a number of different purposes and with differing effects. For example, in 'A Story of Love' (*Other Stories and Other Stories* [1999]), the you is needed to co-tell stories: the I and the you make up stories together, taking turns to tell different stories, and they also join together to tell a single story. These two approaches thereby show the way storytelling can – and often does – involve a literal dialogism between people. In 'The Theme is Power' (*Other Stories and Other Stories*), the you is needed as an addressee to whom the narrator can tell her story. As can be seen in these two stories, then, the 'you', the addressee, is seen as an essential part of the storytelling process: there is a reciprocal, if not symmetrical, relation between the 'I' telling the story and the 'you' listening, receiving, being addressed. The addressee participates, directly or otherwise, and is far from being merely a passive receiver.

The need for such a relation between teller and listener is made particularly evident in the story 'Cold Iron' (*Free Love and Other Stories* [1995]), as the narrator addresses an absent you in order to tell her narrative. She begins her narrative by asking: 'what can I tell you?' (77). This opening question asks about possibility, permission and, somewhat less obviously, the specific demands of the you being addressed: what does the *addressee* allow to be said? What does he or she wish to hear? Furthermore, the story itself is only able to be told – it emerges, comes about – through the address to the you, as the narrator interrupts her narrative throughout with mediations such as, 'I'm telling you' (78) and 'what was I telling you' (79). The addressee is therefore a fundamental part of the telling of this story, and is needed for the dialogical, dialectical relationship of telling and creating. Moreover, the narrator's constant reference to the storytelling process (through her invocation of the addressee) con-fuses the sequence of teller-delivery-receiver. Indeed, there is a sense that the narratee in some ways comes before the speaking of the narrator: the teller in 'Cold Iron' begins her story by asking the listener what she can tell her, and her constant mediations reinforce this sense of (re-)ordering. Therefore, the addressee comes *before* – or at least alongside or with – the telling. Such a reordering of narratorial sequence is also present at the beginning of 'Erosive' (*The Whole Story and Other Stories* [2003]), where the narrator asks: 'What do you need to know about me for this story? How old I am? how much I earn a year? what kind of car I drive?' (115). Here, needs become twistingly, self-reflexively, complex: the narrator asks the listener what is needed in order to begin; in short, she needs to know what the listener needs to know. Therefore, in both 'Cold Iron' and 'Erosive', the story is – even if only rhetorically – begun by the listener, and the narrators, like Derrida in 'Envois', create and put in motion a locutory-narratorial situation of which they could say: 'In advance *you* corrupt, *you* detour everything that I say' (Derrida 13; my emphasis). These narrators de-tour their stories via their addressees *in advance* and continue to do so throughout the storytelling act.

The importance of the addressee, the one apostrophised in these stories, is especially acute in 'The Theme is Power'. As with 'Cold Iron' and 'Erosive', this story also commences, is set in motion, with an address to an interlocutor: 'the thing is, I really need you with me in this story. But you're not home. You won't be home for hours yet' (121). In this beginning, the narrator sees co-presence as a prerequisite for narrative: the narrator requires the addressee be *with* her, there, *in* her presence, *in* the story. Despite the physical absence of this addressee, however, the narrator conjures her, imagining the 'you' there for the storytelling.[1] Throughout the story, the listener's non-presence is presented by parenthetical interjections, and the narrator fantastically creates the dialogue between her and her imagined other, breaking off from the telling to speak and respond to the other's imagined response: '(So it happened quite long ago? you say behind me.)' (ibid.). These imagined, created responses, the response of the you to the I and her story, enable the storytelling to take place, and the fantasy dialogue shapes and forms the narrative. Therefore, the narrator, like Derrida in his correspondence, comes 'to think as you' or via you; at least momentarily, she partly sees 'reality as you' (Derrida 40) and constructs her reality – both the story she tells and the 'reality' of the telling itself – with and by the absent-present you, even while acknowledging the fantastical nature of this scenario: '(I still don't really get the connection, you say.) Well, no. Okay. Actually, you don't say anything, you're not home yet' ('Theme', 135). Through this situation, therefore, the I creates the you, a process of creation Derrida similarly enacts in 'Envois' with his repeated phrase, 'I write you'. More than simply an Americanism for 'I write *to* you', Derrida writes *to* you but he also creates, writes, the you he addresses. Furthermore, he also reflects upon this writerly creativity, thinking '*En train* to write *you* (you? to you?)' (32). The narrator of 'Theme' is also aware of the process of creation she is undertaking, acknowledging 'you're not there. I knew that. There's no one here, just me, and my father breathing next door' (133). Therefore, where Derrida *writes* you, the narrator *tells* the you: 'I tell you' (124) is not simply the same as – but more than – I tell the story *to* you. Both writer and narrator create – write or tell – the other, and the addressee is made present through, in fact, their very absence. The needs of Derrida the postcard writer and the narrator of 'Theme' therefore manifest themselves through the creation of a complex 'interaction', and subject and object, addresser and addressee can be seen simultaneously as *one-and-the-same-but-different*.

Such complex correspondence and interaction also reveals the mutual importance of both participants in the narrative act. In 'The Second Person' (*The First Person and Other Stories* [2008]), a relationship narrative, the narrator begins: 'You're something else. You really are' (121). Declaratively, and somewhat accusingly, the speaker here tries to create and confirm the otherness of the you, the separation between the pair, the difference between 'I' and 'you'. However, the narrative itself is structured around and functions because of the reciprocity between the two, the interrelationship they have in storytelling. This relationship is at once carried out at the diegetic level – the two tell stories – and at the extradiegetic level, as the story of 'The Second Person' *is* a story of storytelling. Furthermore, the reciprocal relationship is substantiated by the closing words of the story – 'you're something else, you. You really are' (134) – as they mirror almost exactly the opening declaration but with addresser and addressee having switched places. A similar reciprocity is set up in 'Being Quick' (*The Whole Story and Other Stories*), as this narrative is structured into two halves told by both members of a couple in turn. Such perspectival and metaleptic shifts and mirroring create and emphasise the dialogic, reciprocal relationship between I and you: both members of the couple are 'I' and 'you', narrator and subject within the narrative. In these particular stories, then, there is an emphasis on correspondence, with each voice being allowed to respond, to speak for and by itself, something we never receive, or at least not directly, in Derrida's 'Envois'.[2] As a result, there is a sense in these fictions of mutual co-creation, with both narrators addressing and apostrophising the other.

The frequency of second-person address throughout Smith's short stories invites – provokes even – the reader to speculate upon the identity of these 'yous', and the question for the reader often becomes: who *is* this you? While some stories show the you to be an identifiable character, other stories leave the addressee's identity open and unanswered. Moreover, other stories, such as 'The Second Person', specifically address the question of the addressee's identity. The focus on, yet ambiguity of, the addressee throughout Smith's collections often leads to the reader being drawn into the narrative; the reader is another 'you', an other, and these stories create for the reader an uncertain positionality – he or she is at once addressed and not addressed, the you and not-you of the story. Consequently, the 'you', the second person pronoun, can seemingly refer to characters, correspondents and the reader simultaneously, a vertiginous effect Derrida identifies as part of the complexity of correspondence in his prefatory postcard of 7 September 1979:

> That the signers and the addressees are not always visibly and necessarily identical from one *envoi* to the other, that the signers are not invariably to be confused with the senders, nor the addressees with the receivers, that is with the readers (*you* for example), etc.—you will have the experience of all of this, and sometimes will feel it quite vividly, although confusedly. (5)

Within this reflection on the slippage between signers and senders and addressees and receivers, Derrida emphatically calls attention to the ambiguity and polyvalence of 'you': the *you* is both Derrida's supposed correspondent and the reader reading 'Envois' – me and/or you! As Derrida's thoughts imply, then, even when the 'you' is identified the use of the second person pronoun confusingly confuses addressee, receiver and reader in a strange moment of proximity and distance, identity and difference; the reader can imaginatively respond to the call of 'you', while at the same time realising that they have not done *x*, *y* or *z*, as the narrator claims. Within both Derrida's postcards and Smith's short stories, then, the difference and tension between the addressee and the receiver is played out, and consequently, the reader becomes another correspondent, addressee or interceptor. The question, often unanswerable, becomes: to whom exactly does the narrator address him or herself? For Derrida, this type of question is fundamental. Writing about the now famous postcard he discovers in the Bodleian Library in which Plato stands behind a writing Socrates, Derrida reflects: 'To whom do you think he is writing? For me it is always more important to know that than to know what is being written; moreover, I think it amounts to the same, to the other finally' (17).[3] In both Derrida's correspondence and in many of Smith's short stories, no definitive answer to such a question is given, and this unanswered and unanswerable question is an 'important' aspect of their respective texts: the 'you' is part of the 'what', and not being told who the 'you' is allows for the confusion of addressees, receivers, interceptors and readers to circulate endlessly.

The ambiguity and complexity of the 'you' in Smith's short stories is further complicated as the word 'you' in English is the same for both the second person singular and the second person plural: 'you' is at once single and discrete, multiple and collective. Correlatively, the reader, that vexed, ambiguous subject (implied, ideal, potential, and so on), is also at once singular (a specific reader) and multiple (all who *have read, are reading* and *will read* the text). This complexity is itself addressed in Smith's 'The First Person', when the 'I' says: 'you're not the first person full stop. But you're the one right now. I'm the one right now. We're the one right now. That's enough, yes?' (206). As well as leaving the identity of the 'you' open, the narrator indicates how the you is singular only at a particular moment, at the moment of address; for another you, the reader, this is the moment of reading. Similarly, and in a somewhat Barthesian formulation, the narrator points out that she, too, is 'the one' *right now*, at the moment of speaking, or for the reader, at the moment of narrating.[4] For both participants, then, their positionality is temporally inflected: at the moment of narrating and reading, there exists a certain specificity (which can, however, include multiple specific readers), but this lasts only for such moments of writing/narrating and reading, after and before which these specific participants and their relations do not exist.

As with the narratee, the position of the narrator in many of Smith's stories is also far from stable. While it may seem obvious that narratives within short story collections are not necessarily narrated, sent and signed by the same narrator, the frequent use of the homodiegetic voice for narrators who appear at once different and alike within and across Smith's collections problematises such easy conclusions. Often enigmatic, unidentified and anonymous, these different narratorial voices often take on similar tones and styles, and often have similar personal lives and relationships. As with the narratees, then, there exists a similar tension between singularity and multiplicity across many of Smith's narratives. Therefore, whereas Derrida confesses at the end of the preface to 'Envois' that 'we might be several' (6), for Smith's homodiegetically narrated short fictions we could say that the 'I *might* be several', with due emphasis given to possibility rather than actuality, to ambiguity rather than certainty. As a result of the often enigmatic and anonymous nature and multiplicity of narrators and addressees throughout Smith's collections, then, the reader is placed within a vertiginous play of correspondence and address, uncertainly addressed by multiple narrators who can appear both similar and different, at the same time.

'Length of time'

Throughout 'Envois', Derrida continually reflects upon the very cards upon which he is writing. In the post dated 6 June 1977, for example, he writes:

> First of all because of the support, doubtless, which is more rigid, the cardboard is firmer, it preserves, it resists manipulations; and then it limits and justifies, from the outside, by means of the borders, the indigence of the discourse, the insignificance of the anecdoque [sic]
> I have so much to tell you and it all will have to hold on snapshot post cards—and immediately be divided among them. Letters in small pieces, torn in advance, cut out, recut. So much to tell you, but all and nothing, more than all, less than nothing—to tell you is all, and a post card supports it well, it is to be but this naked support, to tell it to you, you only, naked. (21–2)

Here specifically, Derrida sets up a tension between the benefits and restraints of the postcard form, how it both supports and limits his writing. He notes that as postcards are rigid yet small, his addresses must be carried across multiple cards; his posts are divided and split, delimited *in advance of writing*. As a result of the physicality of which Derrida writes, the postcard reader is instinctively, yet perhaps not always consciously, aware of its spatial and structural restrictions. In a similar fashion – but through different means – the short story reader is also made aware of the 'support' and 'limits' of this particular narrative form. For the short story reader, this awareness is created not so much through physical features (even less so with e-readers) but through paratexts – titles, front and back covers, contents pages, and so forth. Consequently, the short story reader is aware of the support *and* the 'indigence of the discourse' put in place by the genre. The reader is aware that they are reading not a novel but a collection of stories, and, at least to an extent, of the demands that the short(er) narrative lengths imply. Compared to novels, short stories provide snapshot narratives, a relationship and difference similar to that between letters and postcards. In short story collections, the 'work' is divided up into separate (though sometimes interrelated narratives), short(er) stories that are cut out and possibly recut into different orders by the reader.

For readers of Smith's short stories, this awareness of form is made particularly acute. Firstly and most simply, four out of Smith's five collection titles to date end with 'and other stories', which immediately signals number, series and by simple perceptual-mathematics multiple stories of shorter length.[5] Moreover, many of Smith's short stories are highly self-reflexive, and thereby bring the form itself into focus. The most overtly self-reflexive story throughout Smith's collections is 'True

Short Story' (*The First Person and Other Stories*), which meditates upon the short story itself and its difference from the novel. At the beginning of this story, the narrator 'Ali' overhears a conversation between two adult men, in which the younger one describes the novel as 'a flabby old whore', who is 'serviceable, roomy, warm and familiar . . . but really a bit used up, really a bit too slack and loose' (4); in contrast, the younger man sees the short story as 'a nimble goddess, a slim nymph' (4). As a result of overhearing this discussion, 'Ali' pursues the question of this difference at (relative) length and the story itself becomes a story about how to define the short story. Towards the end of the narrative, 'Ali' provides a catalogue-list of definitions of the 'short story' by famous writers, and out of the thirteen listed four specifically refer to the short story's temporal qualities. These are: Nadine Gordimer ('short stories are absolutely about the present moment'); Elizabeth Bowen ('the short story has the advantage over the novel of a special kind of concentration, and that it creates narrative every time absolutely on its own terms'); William Carlos Williams (the short story 'is the only real form for describing the briefness, the brokenness and the simultaneous wholeness of people's lives'); and Cynthia Ozick ('a short story is more like the talismanic gift given to the protagonist of a fairy tale – something complete, powerful, whose power may not yet be understood, which can be held in the hands or tucked into the pocket and taken through the forest on the dark journey') (15–17). However much we agree with these writerly definitions of the short story or not, this list – and the story as a whole – foregrounds 'True Short Story's 'truth', its metafictional, metanarrative effects. Indeed, the reader is explicitly presented with the definitional problematics of the short story, which is defined and characterised by length, unlike the novel, the play or the poem. Moreover, 'True Short Story' brings together the important correlatives of length and time, a relationship emphasised at the beginning of the narrative by the almost Prufrockian way the narrator describes how one of the two men she listens to is 'keen to be a man in front of his father now that his father was opposite him for at least the length of time of a cup of coffee' (3).[6] As well as musing upon the status of the men's relationship, such a measurement emphasises the peculiar nature of time and the complex ways in which we have to try to understand, conceptualise and organise it.

The problematic of time features in many of Smith's short stories, as well as in a number of her novels (see, for instance, *There but for the* [2011]). Titles such as 'A Quick One', 'Being Quick', 'Present' and 'The History of History' all point to an interest in and concentration on time and temporality. As part of this focus on time – 'the crazy time'

(32) of 'unconditional, uncontextualised sex' (33) in 'A Quick One', for example – the stories are often structurally and temporally complex. To concentrate on just one example here, I want to turn to 'Erosive', a story that focuses on the narrator's falling in love. 'Erosive's narrative is structured into four sections: an untitled opening is followed (in terms of headings and narrative order) by 'middle', 'end', 'beginning', which thereby challenges the conventional conceptualisation of narrative and temporal sequence. The manipulation of narrative and temporal structures is evident from the beginning of 'Erosive', when the narrator says: 'Look at me now, here I am at the beginning, the middle and the end all at once, in love with someone I can't have' (115). In this beginning, the imperative calls the reader's attention to the present moment (which is always problematic, elusive and *never quite present*), and there is a suggestion even that this time is unique, that the narrator exists differently *now* than in the past or the future. Furthermore, the narrator places herself at the three conventional stages of narrative structure simultaneously, a convention 'Erosive' itself, however, abandons. Moreover, the narrator makes present now, beginning, middle and end at the same time and therefore gives them equal ontological status. Consequently, the narrator's declaration is more in keeping with the B series understanding of time, which does away with past, present and future in favour of before and after relations and sees all times as being ontologically equivalent.[7] This sense of temporal co-presence is enhanced in the text by the almost exclusive use of the present tense, and while the present tense does not necessarily indicate the present or the 'now', its continual use at least gives the same temporal quality to all the narrative sections, and to those events in the narrative we may wish to assign a past, present or future status to.[8] Therefore, whereas we might assume that the use of the present tense would be more in keeping with the A series conceptualisation of time (as this series ontologically privileges the present over the past and the future), in fact the adoption of the present tense throughout offers something of an untensed view of time. This sense of an untensed temporality is also created and substantiated by the narrative structure: by reordering the usual sequence of beginning-middle-end, any sense of linearity and straightforward movement from the past to the present and the future is undermined, or at least challenged. Moreover, there is little or no sense of the sections being linked in terms of past, present or future events. Rather, there is a lack of temporal specificity, and any movement of time is marked by before and after relations. Overall, then, the continual use of the present tense, and the temporal equivalence of each narrative section, forms a narrative in which time(s) seems to exist rather than pass.

The temporal complexity of 'Erosive' results, to some extent at least, from the discrepancy between story and discourse. This discrepancy between how we may expect the narrative's events to unfold and the order in which they are narrated is emphasised through various non-temporal markers. For instance, the narrator's garden tree is destroyed in 'end', the middle section, but is alive in the final section 'beginning'. Given the middle-end-beginning arrangement, however, 'Erosive's narrative structure is more than simply an inversion of the conventional beginning-middle-end sequence. Moreover, the disjuncture between story and discourse is further complicated by the way in which the last narrative section contains a complex ellipsis of days, weeks or months. The events elided here are narrated in the untitled opening section and in 'middle'. Therefore, this elision is a condensed, complex moment, which is both analeptic, as it takes the reader back to the events narrated in two previous sections, and also proleptic, as those same events come, diegetically speaking, after 'beginning'.

This elliptical moment can, moreover, be seen to stand in for 'Erosive' as a whole: like the gap in 'beginning', the text itself is a condensed temporal space or block, with past, present and future all being ontologically equivalent. Albeit in an accentuated way, 'Erosive's structure and the co-temporality of its sections can therefore be seen to point to the condensation and brevity of the short story form itself. In a more general fashion, the highly self-reflexive nature of many of Smith's stories also emphasises the shortness, condensation and brevity of this narrative form. In contrast to the novel, short stories are not drawn out and do not occupy us for long periods of time; rather, they are condensed and possibly fleeting and brief, often taking little longer to read than the length of time of a cup of coffee, as it were. As a result of metanarrative commentaries and temporal manipulation, a number of Smith's stories point to this difference of degree – if not of kind – between the novel and the short story, and where Peter Brooks argues in *Reading for the Plot* that 'the usual structure of desire in the novel . . . is oriented toward the end' (2000: 49), with the short story there is not so much a desire *for* the end but rather an awareness *of* the end, the end that will soon be upon the reader. Indeed, for both the reader of postcards and short stories, there is often an immediate awareness of a compact, condensed form, of beginning and end at once (as for the narrator at the opening in 'Erosive'), a sense of the end-to-come at the beginning. Smith's short stories do not, however, physically replicate the postcard format; they are not 'flash' or 'micro' fictions.[9] Rather, their self-reflexivity, temporal complexities, and sometimes even simply their titles, emphasise a condensed temporality and often point towards the soon-to-come end at the beginning. In short, they offer compact, brief forms – condensed narrative snapshots.

Misdeliveries

Together, the frequency of second-person address and the temporally self-reflexive nature of many of Smith's short stories create a series of postal effects: the address and invocation of 'you' points to an addressee, a receiver, an interceptor of these stories, and the recurring self-reflexivity points to a complex, condensed and brief temporal form. Significantly, however, these stories do not imitate the form and size of postcards but rather create their postal effects within and across the collections, acting like postal collections in circulation. Such postal effects are foreshadowed by the high number of Smith's stories that entail missed or misdirected messages: calls are cut off; phones go dead; unsigned letters tip off the tax man; anonymous cards are dispatched; and wrongly addressed parcels are delivered to unsuspecting receivers. There is, then, an overwhelming sense that these short stories are concerned with missed messages, non-reception and unintended destinations. They allegorise the postal effect the recurrence of address to the second person activates, the way the reader is the receiver or interceptor – if not the addressee – of the story. In short, these stories are (mis-)received deliveries.

Two stories in particular that narrativise the postal problematic of delivery and allegorise the postal effects of much of Smith's short fiction are 'Blank Card' (*Other Stories and Other Stories*) and 'Astute Fiery Luxurious' (*The First Person and Other Stories*). While 'Blank Card' is primarily concerned with the enigmatic nature of the sender, 'Astute Fiery Luxurious' centres on the contents of a misaddressed delivery. In 'Blank Card', the narrator receives a delivery of flowers, along with a blank, anonymous card. This unsigned, unaddressed, unwritten-upon card surprises and fascinates the narrator and her partner. It is the surprise that drives the narrative, with the question of the addresser's identity being the central enigma of the story, as is evident in the narrator's initial need to understand this delivery: 'I can't think of a single person they could be from. They could be from anybody. There's nobody they could be from. I don't know who they're from' (41). Surprised, and somewhat bewildered, the narrator works through her options, establishing a series of binary oppositions: anybody/nobody, total possibility/ impossibility, indistinct/distinct identity. The narrator cannot think who the sender might be, and she is ultimately unable to discover his or her identity. Moreover, such uncertainty concerning the sender mirrors the enigmatic nature of many of the narrators – or 'senders' – across Smith's collections.

As is evident early on in the narrative, then, 'Blank Card' focuses on the effects of delivery and reception. For the narrator, the delivery makes her become highly self-aware, and as she gets ready to go out for the evening, she considers how 'anybody could be standing out there able to see me, nearly naked. Maybe the person who had sent me the flowers could see me nearly naked' (43). Aware of the possibility of being seen, the narrator welcomes the potential attention, or at least the fantasy of being watched:

> I shrugged the towel off my shoulders, let my arms relax so that both the towels fell on to the bed and the floor. I watched myself in the mirror and it was as if there were a larger mirror all round me, or as if I were watching a film showing me every move I made, every touch and adjustment I gave to myself. I brushed my hair and it was as if I could see myself from outside myself, brushing my hair. (ibid.)

Having developed this sense of exposure, the narrator sets herself up as both subject and object of the gaze, and moving from a real to an imaginary mirror to cinematic reflection, she creates a form of *mise en abyme*. In a correlative fashion, the recurrent use of the second person throughout many of Smith's stories can create a similar effect upon the reader, who can become self-aware and self-reflexive, at once seemingly being called and 'seen' by an addresser. Moreover, both the narrator in 'Blank Card' and readers are receivers or interceptors of messages, if not addressees; for both the narrator in 'Blank Card' and the reader of Smith's short stories more generally, there is an element of unexpected interception and reception, and the misaddressed delivery creates and accentuates an effect of being exposed and of heightened self-awareness.

'Blank Card' can, then, be seen synecdochally (with the relationship between part and whole being particularly significant when discussing short story collections) in relation to the way in which all texts raise questions about addressers and addressees: texts always already present the problematic relationship between author and narrator – who tells? – and short story collections open up the additional question of the relation between one narrator and the next, as well as their relation to the narratee(s). In 'Blank Card', the narrator sees the card and torn envelope as 'evidence, though neither of us could say what of' (41), and similarly, texts are also 'evidence' of some form of relation between writer, narrator, language and reader. But what that relation is and how exactly it functions is not easy to say, as the history of literary theory attests! More specifically, the constant use of second-person address throughout Smith's short stories acutely emphasises the complex relationship between the narrator(s) and the reader(s), and the frequency of address to, and invocation of, the narratee can create a sense of personal communication; equally, this form of familiarity can also produce a feeling for the reader of being embroiled, watched, co-opted, coerced.[10] Moreover, as with the 'weird parcel' (169) in 'Astute Fiery Luxurious', which is not addressed to the narrator and her partner despite being delivered to their house, texts are at once addressed and not addressed to particular readers; while each individual reader can read the text in front of them, it is not sent to them specifically. Through this misdelivered parcel, which is later returned to the narrator and her partner after they try to dispatch of it in the post, 'Astute Fiery Luxurious' can be seen to allegorise the (a)destination of literature, the way in which each and every reading is only one stop on the literary postal route: all texts are 'a misdelivery' (169), 'reaching' a reader but never one particular reader. Furthermore, the narrator notes, the parcel 'looked as if it had been going around the postal system for years. But it was postmarked yesterday. I couldn't make out where from' (172). As with the package – and almost all of Smith's collections are 'packaged' with opening paratextual quotations – texts also possess peculiar temporalities, at once always old and new, postmarked yesterday but also marked *right now*, at and with every reading. With texts, it is also not easy (possibly impossible) to identify where they come from, or to whom they are sent, or when, or where, or why, and through their postal effects, Smith's short fictions circulate a brief, condensed (mis) delivery of such literary problematics.

Notes

1. Absent, spectral, haunting interlocutors and addressees occur frequently in Smith's work. See, for instance, the section 'for' in *There but for the* (2011), as well as *Artful* (2012).
2. *The Oxford English Dictionary* explains the changing importance of mutuality to the word 'correspondence' as follows: 'the etymology implies that the word was formed to express mutual response, the answering of things to each other; but before its adoption in English, it had been extended so as to express the action or relation of one side only, without however abandoning the mutual notion, which is distinct in the modern sense of epistolary correspondence' (June 2014).
3. The postcard picture upon which Derrida reflects so much in 'Envois' is a reproduction of the frontispiece of Matthew Paris's thirteenth-century *Prognostica Socratis basilei*.
4. In 'The Death of the Author' (1968), Barthes notoriously writes:

'linguistically, the author is never more than the instance writing, just as *I* is nothing other than the instance saying *I*: language knows a "subject", not a "person", and this subject, empty outside of the very enunciation which defines it, suffices to make language "hold together", suffices, that is to say, to exhaust it' (2001: 1467). Moreover, Barthes establishes a temporal difference between 'authors' who precede their work and the modern scriptor, who 'is born simultaneously with the text, is in no way equipped with a being preceding or exceeding the writing, is not the subject with the book as predicate; there is no other time than that of the enunciation and every text is eternally written *here* and *now*' (1468).

5. The only collection to break this pattern is *Shire* (2013), which was specially commissioned by Full Circle Editions.
6. In T. S. Eliot's 'The Love Song of J. Alfred Prufrock' (1915), Prufrock's sad, insignificant life is characterised by resignation and repetition, and it is encapsulated by the mundane, caffeine-inflected way he marks time:

> For I have known them all already, known them all –
> Have known the evenings, mornings, afternoons,
> I have measured out my life with coffee spoons. (1963, ll. 51–3)

7. In simple terms, philosophers distinguish two temporal series, A series and B series, which were first formulated by J. Ellis McTaggert in his 1908 article, 'The Unreality of Time' (*Mind*, 17:68, 457–74). In the A series, events are organised according to whether they occur in the past, the present or the future, whereas in the B series, they are organised according to *before* and *after* relations (for example, event *z* occurs *after* event *y*). In *About Time: Narrative, Fiction and the Philosophy of Time* (2007), Mark Currie provides an insightful analysis and problematisation of the A/B series distinction, with a specific focus on literature (17–18, 141–51). Most significantly for my purposes, Currie argues that reading narratives brings the tensed A series and untensed B series together: while reading a narrative, the reader's experience of the text comprises that which *is* being read right now (present), that which *has* been read (past), and that which will be read (future); yet the text itself can be seen as a block, with all of its times existing equally at once (147). While Currie is, I believe, correct to argue for this combination of the two series, as I contend above 'Erosive' goes out of its way at least to privilege the B series over the A series.
8. Two significant works that explore the complexity of tense and narrative time are Peter Brooks' *Reading for the Plot: Design and Intention in Narrative* (1984) and Mark Currie's *About Time*. In the former, Brooks proposes: 'the preterite tensed used classically in the novel is decoded by the reader as a kind of present' (2000: 22). This present 'is a curious present that we know to be past in relation to a future we know to be already in place, already in wait for us to reach it' (23). Currie also discusses this 'quasi-present' in his more recent study, stating: 'the present for a reader in a fictional narrative is not really the present at all but the past. It is somebody else's present related to us in the past tense. Though it seems like the present, because it is new to us, it is tensed as the past . . . we experience the past tense in the present' (2010: 5). Currie further complicates the

relationship between narrative and temporality when he argues that 'a fictional narrative encourages us to think of the past as present no more than it encourages us to think of the present as a future past' (5); it is largely the latter upon which he focuses in *About Time*. For a specific discussion of what Currie calls 'the divorce between tense and verb forms' (139), see the opening section of Chapter 8 of *About Time*, 'Tense Times'.
9. A number of stories in Lydia Davis's new collection, *Can't and Won't* (2014), for example, are short enough to fit on a standard postcard, with the story 'Bloomington' being comprised of a single sentence: 'Now that I have been here for a little while, I can say with confidence that I have never been here before' (8). For discussions of these types of short story, see, for example, the introductions to the edited collections *Sudden Fiction: American Short-Short Stories*, ed. Robert Shapard and James Thomas (1986) and *Flash Fiction: Very Short Stories*, ed. James Thomas, Denise Thomas and Tom Hazuka (1992). In the present volume, see Holly Howitt-Dring's chapter, 'Housewives and Half-Stories: A Question of Genre and Gender in Microfiction'.
10. For an insightful and comprehensive analysis of the ethical complexities of the second person in Smith's short stories, 'Envois' and other theoretical works, see Chapter 5, 'You', of Lisa McNally's *Reading Theories in Contemporary Fiction* (2013: 141–66).

Works Cited

Barthes, Roland (2001), 'The Death of the Author', *The Norton Anthology of Theory and Criticism*, ed. Vincent B. Leitch and trans. Stephen Heath, New York and London: W. W. Norton, pp. 1466–70.

Brooks, Peter (2000), *Reading for the Plot: Design and Intention in Narrative* [1984], Cambridge and London: Harvard University Press.

Currie, Mark (2007), *About Time: Narrative, Fiction and the Philosophy of Time*, Edinburgh: Edinburgh University Press.

Davis, Lydia (2014), *Can't and Won't*, New York: Farrar, Straus and Giroux.

Derrida, Jacques (1987), *The Post Card: From Socrates to Freud and Beyond*, trans. Alan Bass, Chicago and London: The University of Chicago Press.

Eliot, T. S. (1963), *Collected Poems, 1909–1962*, New York: Harcourt, Brace & World.

McNally, Lisa (2013), *Reading Theories in Contemporary Fiction*, London and New York: Bloomsbury.

McQuillan, Martin (1999), 'Information theory: From the Post Card to the Telephone Book and Beyond', *Continuum: Journal of Media & Cultural Studies*, 13:2, 139–51.

McTaggert, J. Ellis (1908), 'The Unreality of Time', *Mind*, 17:68, 457–74.

Shapard, Robert and James Thomas (eds) (1986), *Sudden Fiction: American Short-Short Stories*, Salt Lake City: Peregrine Smith Books.

Smith, Ali (2009), *The First Person and Other Stories* [2008], London: Penguin.

Smith, Ali (2005), *Free Love and Other Stories* [1995], London: Virago.

Smith, Ali (2004), *Other Stories and Other Stories* [1999], London: Penguin.
Smith, Ali (2004), *The Whole Story and Other Stories* [2003], London: Penguin.
Thomas, James, Denise Thomas and Tom Hazuka (eds) (1992), *Flash Fiction: Very Short Stories*, New York and London: Norton.

Chapter 12

Housewives and Half-Stories: A Question of Genre and Gender in Microfiction

Holly Howitt-Dring

I – Histories

Microfiction could be seen, to some degree, as the *enfant terrible* of short stories – the sometimes captivating but perhaps ill-bred offspring of a dalliance between the short story and poetry. To some, microfiction is just a glance at, or, at worst, a failed attempt at a short story; to others, it might be a botched poem written, perhaps accidentally, in prose (Howitt-Dring 2011: 57). However, microfiction should be seen as a genre in and of its own right, lying alongside the short story rather than living within it, rather like a novella and a novel. Microfiction could be described as, at its most reductive (which is in itself a rather pertinent adjective here), the shortest prose stories possible. They are tales in and of themselves, with no further wording, content or context needed than their final value on the page. They are written in prose, but often harness a moment of change, or of realisation, much like the epiphanic framework of a traditional short story, or, indeed, the turn in a poem. Microfiction encapsulates what Seán Ó'Faoláin describes as characteristics of the short story: both 'punch and poetry' (11). For the purposes of this chapter, I will discuss microfiction as its own genre, with its own generic patterns and, as Wellek and Warren usefully term, its own 'inner form' (cited in Dubrow 1982: 5). This inner form, or, in many cases what might be described as a particular tone, identifies microfictions from both within and without.

As its own complete genre, which shares some of the hallmarks of the short story and prose poem, while also retaining its own identity, microfiction is king (or queen) of its own nutshell, as will be explored. Similarly to the prose poem and short story, microfiction connects with a moment of epiphany, however big or small, and, using succinct, sometimes sensitive and sometimes sparse prose, tells a story in absolute miniature. This tonal idea of microfiction forms the lynchpin to my discussion, because it is within this inner form, and the idea of epiphany, that I will explore some of the most contemporary microfictions being written by British female writers: Jenn Ashworth, Tania Hershman, Sarah Hilary and Vanessa Gebbie, as well as my own work; I am discussing microfiction not just as a theorist, but as a practitioner, too. Could it be said that this inner form of a microfiction is a particularly fertile ground for contemporary British female writers? We will find out, both through exploration of other writers' works, and a close critical analysis of my own, and we will see that form and content – the brevity of a microfiction, and the flash of insight described – interlink, showing the completeness of the inner and outer form of a microfiction.

Before discussing these texts, it is also important to note the way I use the term 'microfiction'. For microfiction, rather like Juliet's rose, has many other names, which are usually more or less descriptive synonyms, though some are sweeter than others. Take postcard fiction, or smoke-long stories, for example, as some of the more creative terms for microfictions: stories which will fit on the back of a card, or take as long to read as it does to smoke a cigarette. Though you may have also heard the term flash fiction, using the term 'flash' to show the way microfictions reveal as a sudden flare, or drabbles, 69ers, 101s and other terms which designate a very particular word count within the form. Their popularity online has also bred new names for this tiny form, such as Twitlit and keitai fictions – written to fit Twitter feeds and text-message services. You might have also heard microfictions referred to more commonly as very short stories, sudden fictions, or short shorts. All, to me, are one and the same: prose narratives, usually shorter than 1,000 words – though this upper limit is sometimes disputed (Howitt-Dring 2011: 48). In general, these stories tend to be no shorter than six words, as epitomised by Hemingway's famous six-word short: 'For sale: baby shoes, never worn' (ibid.). Whatever the name, all these forms are, as I describe them, microfictions. For me, the word microfiction is an umbrella definition for all these other terms, and I will use it to discuss any story written in prose of under 1,000 words, especially, and usually, those with the same inner form, searching for some kind of epiphany, or expressing an idea of a turn, realisation or twist in the narrative as the pieces come to a close.

II – Half-Stories

If microfiction is a story at its most miniature, then it must be precise, yet manage to capture a single moment as a photograph or postcard might. It is a form which hinges on the writing being implicit, working the readers, encouraging them to form interpretations and understandings not obvious, perhaps, on a first reading. So much is encapsulated in such a small form, that readings are multiple, and interpretations are hugely variable. Microfiction is a way of distilling or compressing not just a story, but an event, emotion, identity, voice or time. It reminds me of making jam: hundreds of little fruits, like words, that have been squished down into one a tightly packed glass jar, conserving and preserving that moment forever, until the jar is opened. You can see the unidentified fruits' flesh pressed up against the unlabelled glass, and though you cannot quite see to the middle, you eat it anyway and you know immediately the fruit from the taste. Or it is like drinking espresso: one long sip of lots of tiny ground up beans – and shortly, you will be at the end. But that danger makes you keener to savour every last drop, and be thankful for its buzz half an hour later. Do you wish you had had a double espresso? No – that one was enough. Like the jam and the espresso, with a microfiction you cannot see to the bottom of the jar, the cup, the story, and you probably do not know what will happen at the end. Further, it could have been made or poured hundreds of different ways, but for that moment, as it exists on the page, it is whole and precise and compressed. Importantly, it is what you uncover under the framework that is unexpected – the sourness of the fruit that suddenly makes you doubt what you initially thought. The taste remains on the tongue afterwards, like a dream of a story, like the imprint of something much bigger. There is a constant tension in microfiction between what is said (written) and what is unsaid – the hugeness of an idea or story living in a tiny box.

The narrative compression means that microfictions can showcase women's writing in a way that perhaps other forms might not offer; or, rather, that microfiction is the perfect place for the distillation of an experience, voice or thought. The immediacy of the form, for both writer and reader, links to the experience of many female readers and writers, and the suddenness of meaning, of insight, is also a perfect pitch to explore women's experiences. Gendered writings and readings in this genre is a rich and rewarding study, shown as it is through the sparse, precise and minimalist focus of microfiction. In looking for stories to illustrate this point, I realised that many microfictions written by female writers told stories as a sudden flash of insight, sometimes using metaphorical ideas, but sometimes in a way more vested in reality, as in line with the idea of this inner form of epiphany that microfiction uses. I have closely analysed four key stories, identifying some of a multiple interpretations of offer, and the links to women's writing and experiences.

My first fantastical story with a huge yield of interpretation is 'Flight' (2012) by Vanessa Gebbie, in which a sea lion learns to fly.

> There was a female sealion learned to fly just the once, on the night of a storm, when the waves were higher than they'd ever been, the walls were breached and the rocks were strewn with things from the sea, living and dead and somewhere between. She flew to the cattle field beyond the strand and fell to earth by the standing stones where a heifer, at her first attempt, had given up trying to give early birth, lain down and died – but her bull calf had come, after all that.
>
> The next day, when the storm had blown itself out, the cowman came down to check that all was well, and found the new calf asleep against the body of the sealion – the rich milk on his muzzle smelling strangely of salt, and fish, and sea. (15)

A flying sea lion! The reader may think that this conceit is more than enough to create a story, with no further addition or attention to the narrative needed. But in fact, it is not the flight of the sea lion which becomes important as the story develops: it is the fact that the sea lion is female. The denouement of the tale implies that, after a calf is born to a dying cow, the sea lion nurses it: 'the rich milk on [the calf's] muzzle smelling strangely of salt, and fish, and sea'. If the sea lion could not fly, then she would not have seen the orphaned calf, but if she were not female, she could not nurse it; it is the latter fact which is important here. It is a story about maternal instincts, and not about the fantastical flight of a sea lion. Though the story is not literal or realistic in a true sense, a reader cannot doubt that the narrative, in which the sea lion is dropped into the cattle field to witness the mother dying and leaving her calf abandoned, is about motherhood, and not so much about fantasy. Here, the form of microfiction represents a gendered experience in which the reader becomes complicit in unpicking meaning(s).

From the outset, the language of 'Flight' gives some buried warnings of the inner idea here, such as 'breached' walls, alluding to the idea of a breech birth, and the standing stones perhaps an allusion to death, or even a cycle, again linking them to birth. Similarly, the storm at sea (insinuating uncontrollable tides) could be related to the idea of the moon, or a cycle, too. The idea of the moon, tides and cycles has obvious references to menstruation and female experience; these are reference points often used in women's poetry to identify women's experiences. The idea of a yearning to nurture is also a key theme of many other poems. The final paragraph of the story brought to my mind a strong connection with the poetry of Sylvia Plath, and in particular a line from 'Morning Song' (1965), in which the narrator describes the pull of breastfeeding a newborn: 'One cry, and I stumble from bed, cow heavy and floral / In my Victorian nightgown. / Your mouth opens, clean as a cat's' (11, ll.13–15). But of course, here we are dealing with prose. So it can be seen that microfiction slips between poetic image and the form of prose – again, the inner and outer form have a tension between them.

The fact that the sea lion took flight during a tempest is important because it marks a change in atmosphere, adds risk and excitement to the flight, and makes the plight of the calf more pitiful, but also, in a deeper implication, shows the cycle and rhythm of nature at its cruellest and most dangerous. There is also an interesting pattern of flow and rhyme in the story; look at the counterbalance of 'storm/walls' and 'sea/between', for instance. The language ties us into the story, almost as a poem might, engaging you immediately with the sea lion's story. The narrative seems to focus in upon itself, using repeated and rhythmical images – again, like a poem – and these overlapping images serve to condense and intensify meaning.

But is it the sea lion's story? For the sea lion herself is oddly passive throughout; her flight is not controlled by her own wishes, as far as the reader can see, and the lacuna between her fall and the nursing of the calf means that the question of how it happened after all is unanswered. Is this a metaphor for motherhood? It is, in many ways, a story in which, as the adage goes, 'nature will find a way'; again, the idea that the *mother* (Mother Nature) will provide. The story ends with a vision of the comforted calf, which, I note, is a bull calf, and the cow*man*'s surprise; the sea lion is no longer our narrative point of view, and, in fact, our focus is on the two male characters instead. And yet it is the female sea lion who is the answer, here, and not the cowman or the newborn calf: the patriarchal, institutionalised controls have failed, and the female protagonist is the solution. In this way, this story could be seen as an encapsulation of the maternal experience, and the control of nature over individualism; or about the power of maternal instinct, perhaps like Plath's poem. And the reader cannot forget about the fact that the sea lion falls – like Eve, her fantasy too is breached – as she enters into a new reality. The story is succinct and minimal, but the readings here are many times multiple, and the female experience of the sea lion, which could be metaphorical, is crucial to these readings.

Motherhood is not the only concept to be succinctly and yet intricately explored in microfictions written by women. Jenn Ashworth's story 'Shoes' (2013) describes a parental relationship through a series of childhood memories, in which the mother plays a key role:

> We lived in a big house in the countryside. This was years ago now though – back when we kids still had Rochdale accents and there were deer in the woods and garden.

> Dad was at work, mostly. There were traces of him. Every morning was a jigsaw. We tried to piece together where he had been in the short hours he had been home (after bedtime, and at getting up). A banana peel on the breakfast bar. Hairs from the shaving brush on the soap. That sort of thing. Mum used to clean the signs away before we could find them, and in that way it was like a race: trying to find his smell on the pillow before she beat the bed into tidiness.
>
> She was tidy. Used to make him leave his shoes on the porch, in case he tramped muck into her carpet. I saw Uncle Paul once, driving up in the van. He clocked Dad's shoes, gave me a wave, and reversed out again, without stopping to knock at the door. (56)

Here, the narrative voice is our informant. The story is not so much about the narrator, but about what the narrator has seen. Initially, the reader is looking for 'traces' of an absent father. The search is almost obsessive, and certainly thorough – and yet the mother 'beat[s]' these signs away from the children. At first, the reader is tricked into believing that this is just because the mother 'was tidy'. But can it only be that? Like Gebbie's story, here the readers realise that they are not being told everything, but, rather, are sitting above the story, looking down from a height, watching the characters run through the house like ants in an ant farm (rather like the sea lion in flight, looking down on the heifer and calf). The shoes, the reader might initially believe, are not allowed in the house simply because the mother was neat, and did not want mud on the carpets (the use of the phrase 'in case he tramped muck into her carpet' here could be read as a direct emulation of the mother's speech, with the possessive of 'her' exerting the mother's control over the house and all therein). But instead, the shoes act as a signal which Uncle Paul understands, causing him to drive away as they warn him off the doorstep.

Like the previous story, and the stories discussed later, this microfiction can and does contain multiple meanings. The reader could find many interpretations here: is Paul here for an adulterous purpose? Or perhaps because there is bad blood between him and Dad? Seen through the child's eyes, it seems that the mother is not only the matriarch, controlling all who enter and exit the house, but actually is in complete control of the relationships inside and out. Complicated familial relationships are distilled and shown as a flash. In the instant, the reader realises what a child may not. The mother is a secret protagonist here, and without her there would be no story. The narrator's power, which is generically seen to be considerable, especially when displayed in a first-person narrative, is disrupted by the real power and force of the mother.

Tania Hershman's 'Straight Up' (2010) is also reliant on a child's experience, told from a child's point of view, in which a father's dual life is exposed.

> My father was not a slouching man. Every night when he finished dinner, he pushed back his chair and sat up straight as a rod, the way he did when demonstrating posture to his class of teenage girls at our school. He drummed his fingers on the table, tap, tap, tap, and looked at me, my shoulders, my slumped neck, the way I was shovelling mashed potato into my mouth, and I felt the heat of his discontent. He jerked his head upwards, and this was the signal. I was to instantly drop my fork and, as if some invisible cord was sliding through my spine and out the top of my head, I was to ascend. My shoulders lifted, my neck unkinked, and I grew, and as I grew, so his face softened, his brow lost its furrows and the corners of his lips lifted. He would nod his head back and forth, saying nothing. This was how it was every night. This was how it was on a good day.
>
> I saw my father teach his class only once. I was supposed to be ill, supposed to be feverish and damply sweating into the over-washed sheets. But I was a faker and good at it. An accomplished liar by the age of ten, I knew the tricks, thermometer against light bulb, moans and groans. My mother, who couldn't miss a day at the factory, set me up with juice, water, a pile of comics and instructions to call if I vomited but otherwise to stay exactly where she left me.
>
> Of course, I didn't. I got dressed after I heard the front door slam, sidled downstairs and stood, breathing in the empty house, the sweet smell of freedom. What drew me to the school? It should have been the furthest thing from my mind. But I was pulled in that direction the moment I left the house.
>
> Like a spy, I slid along walls and around corners. When I got there, I crouched beside the window of the room I knew he was teaching in. Slowly, slowly, I straightened up until the window sill was at eye level and I peeked in.
>
> At first he didn't look like my father. The context was so strange; it was as if he was in front of one of those painted movie backdrops. He was pacing backwards and forwards by the blackboard upon which he had drawn a spine, with all its vertebrae, moving up into the neck and head. The girls were clearly not very excited about whatever he was telling them. I saw two of them passing notes, a few were chewing gum, none of them was sitting up straight. He didn't have them; they weren't eating out of the palm of his hand, not at all. They put up with him, as if he was a lost dog sniffing around their feet, but then, when the bell rang, they jumped up, grabbed their bags, streamed out of the door. And I saw my father standing by the blackboard, by his perfect drawing of a spine, standing up as straight as he could, and I could see in his face that he was hoping, straining, for some kind of reaction from them. But the girls didn't even see him. I was the only one. I was the only one who saw him standing there. (22–3)

Rather like in Gebbie's story, where the reader sees that the sea lion is female in the first line, it is interesting to note that here, posture is being taught to 'teenage *girls*'. It seems that gender is particularly relevant to the father's teachings; while he clearly believes good posture is important, he only seems to wish to bestow this knowledge onto his female students. It is not known for certain whether the narrator is female, too, but given the father's displeasure at his child's posture, it is not unreasonable to assume that she is. However, unlike her counterparts at school, she listens to her father's details and instructions about good posture, and, the reader assumes, 'eat[s] out of the palm of his hand', whereas his class of students do not – the bored class of gum-chewing girls are in direct contrast with our narrator, who reacts to her father's signals and displeasure at her posture and manners even when the directions and criticisms are unspoken. It seems that the father's child, if female, is suffering due to the regulations and expectation heaped on her by her father, but these expectations are unreal, and lead to a performance of femininity, rather than a truth of experience. But the school students are unwilling to perform in this way.

It is not just the narrator's role that is key here: it is the conflict she has seen in others' roles. The fact that when spied on he 'didn't look like my father' shows the narrator's confusion at her father's parental and paternal identity versus a professional one. The mother doesn't seem to have this kind of conflict in her roles: she is described as a shadow who 'over-washe[s]' the sheets and 'couldn't miss a day at the factory'. To me, both these ideas sum up a zealous and hard-working woman, which are not at conflict. But the father seems to hide behind a smokescreen of almost pompous importance at home; his real (in)credibility is exposed when he is at work. Here again, gender roles play a part in the interpretation of this tale: not only is the father exposed as non-credible, but he is also no longer a patriarch to be obeyed when he is seen to be unable to control his class. The reader can only guess what this event did to change the relationship between father and child; rather like Ashworth's story, the ending is not an end at all. The epiphany here is simply the start of something else.

Sarah Hilary's 'I Cannot Carry a Tune' (2010) uses a different tone to these previous pieces, but still has the inner form of a microfiction – a dawning moment of realisation, which is also a reveal to the reader, as well as encapsulating a full experience in miniature, residing in the outer form of a short block of text which makes a microfiction:

> I've taken to collecting sheet music. Anything and everything; it's a cheap hobby. Most of it I find in charity shops and at car boot sales. I've filled three boxes with famous scores and nursery rhymes, pop songs and violin solos.
> I'm tone deaf.
> It's one of the things you said you loved about me. I can't read music any

more than I can play it. It makes me sad. You always said it shouldn't, but it does.

I cannot carry a tune, no matter how I try. And I do try. Not operas, I wouldn't dare, now I haven't you to go with. Just little things, jingles on the television and radio, musak in supermarkets when I'm queuing to pay for a bag of oranges.

'Music can be orange,' you taught me, 'or blue or green. It has a scent and a colour. You don't need your ears; let it in through your other senses. See it. Taste it.'

Your tune was the colour of pomegranates, with the same quick bright flavour, surrendered one note at a time. It is in my fingertips. It fills my palms and dances under my skin. I carry you with me everywhere and it makes me lighter, and it makes me less.

So I sit with my boxes of sheet music and I search for you there, the sound and smell and taste of you. I think—if I could piece together enough sheets, the right sheets, I could make a whole.

Your curves are in the clefs, and in the empty eyes of notes. I've searched and I have found you there. (Hilary 2010: 30)

The synaesthesia of the music, shown as colours and tastes, alleviates the sadness of being 'tone deaf', and fulfils something, but ultimately the search 'makes me lighter, and it makes me less' – it cannot fulfil as it could, and makes the reader suppose ideas of starvation. The isolation and feeling of incompleteness is realised through what some might say is an incomplete form. However, in fact, the form and content are closely matched and the 'inner form' of epiphany is apparent, too. There is also a sense that the direct address of the second person engages in an intimate way, almost as if the writing is addressed to the reader as an overheard thought-process. The gender roles are blurred in this piece, as neither narrator nor 'you' are gendered throughout the story, but there is certainly a sense of isolation and want which shows the more poetic side of microfiction, a side which I often use in my own writings.

The idea of loss in this story does not become fully realised until the final two paragraphs; this structure is similar to the previous two pieces, where a slow reveal is brought into focus as the story ends. There is a warning of the revelation in the statement 'now I haven't you to go with', but the revelation of loneliness and loss only becomes complete (ironically) with the idea of 'I could make you whole' and 'I have found you there'. It is also one of the few pieces explored here that contains dialogue, although it is interesting to note that the narrator is 'taught' or told, and does not actively respond in speech; instead, the response is through action.

The physical nature of this story, and the tension between the ideas of being tone-deaf but needing to hear to play or sing a tune, show some similarity to Gebbie's story, where the physical solves a problem as the sea lion nurses the calf. But here the tension is solved in a different way, because the disparity between 'carry[ing] a tune' and tone-deafness lead to a startling revelation: that the lover is music in and of her/himself. The music becomes physical and concrete within or even to the structure of the lover, where it can be 'read', even when the lover is perhaps no longer with the protagonist. But the genders here are unclear, and the 'readings' the narrator finds are not explained to the reader; again, the reader has to make assumptions about loss and how the lover is re-found or reformed in sheet music, until some 'wholeness' can be found. But the 'empty eyes of the notes' make me suspicious that this completeness can ever be found. This reflects a common technique in microfiction, where the ending is unexpected and oblique.

The four pieces discussed here are different in shape, length, tone and structure, but all show the possibility of distillation within the form of microfiction, discussing relationships shown in different guises and from different perspectives. All four female writers have chosen to create these stories in miniature to tell minimal tales, focusing on a central idea of epiphany, realisation or turn to explore the bigger ideas only hinted at in the pieces. Each story can be read in multiple ways, from analysing gender and gender roles inside, to considering structure and the search for epiphany in microfiction – the 'inner form' of the genre. But all are complete stories, in and of themselves, which are creating precise, distilled moments which show flashes of something else.

III – Housewives

The idea of 'housewives' mentioned in the title of this chapter actually comes from the title of the first microfiction I ever read: 'Housewife' (1996), written by Amy Hempel. This is the story in its entirety:

> She would always sleep with her husband and another man in the course of the same day, and then for the rest of the day, for whatever was left to her of that day, she would exploit by incanting, '*French* film, *French* film.' (100; original italics)

Hempel uses the idea of the 'housewife' as a tongue-in-cheek, shorthand reference to a stereotyped image of a married and presumably adulterous woman, inciting excitement by 'incanting "*French* film"'. In many ways, Hempel's use of a specific female narrative angle is something seen in other microfictions written by women, such as those pieces previously explored above. But Hempel was my personal starting point to microfiction, and it was this story that was the start of what was to become my main writing and reading focus for many years. The story, I felt, showed me that microfiction offered an opportunity to show my own experiences in a precise, focused way. In my own writing, I sometimes use semi-fictionalised accounts of personal experiences, although in many other cases, the work, as the 'fiction' moniker decrees, is made up. But most of my microfictions seem to come from the same voice, or, as Dubrow noted in the earlier quote, use the same 'tone' or inner form.

Female narrators, narratives and points of view are crucial in many of my stories, not least because they come from this well of personal experiences. While the accounts are not autobiographies, they are certainly reflections of female identities, gender roles and patriarchal issues I have witnessed within contemporary culture, and wanted to explore as distilled ideas through the form. Several of my pieces describe ideas of violence within relationships, such as the running 'Dinner Time' sequence in my collection *Dinner Time and Other Stories* (2008). The first illustrates a relationship which is fantasised yet somehow pinned onto reality.

> Every night at eight forty-five precisely, he would say 'Dinner time' and flatten her bones into the sofa, even though the used cutlery lying on the table proved that he had already eaten.
> Tonight, she had bathed in garlic as preparation.
> 'My clove,' he muttered as he bit her collarbone. 'What do you say?'
> 'Eat me bite me eat me bite me eat me.'
> Her monotone tickled as he tasted earwax. He turned her over and bit a hollow of skin at the cusp of her spine, until she cried salty tears, the tip of her tongue tasting yesterday's brine. He crawled away and lay by the fire till he slept with his head in the brown dog's belly.
> In the kitchen, she ticked the paper box marked 'Tuesday' sellotaped to the man-sized fridge. She picked at her scabs till they wept pinpricks of blood. Collarbone to knuckle to ankle. She joined the blood with a naked fingertip and knew that just one more day would do it. The dog barked. She folded herself into the dishwasher. (60)

The details here are mostly grim; the female is somehow passive within this piece, yet she 'bathed in garlic' and 'folded herself into the dishwasher' seemingly freely. But there is an obvious itinerary that is being followed within this narrative world ('at eight forty-five precisely'; 'she ticked the paper box marked "Tuesday"', the remembered incantation she speaks). Here, I wished to show the creation of a fantasy which was so staged as to follow a running order, in which a narrative or a world is on the edge of implosion. What is the 'she' here planning if 'just one more day would do it'? Is there an escape? And how is it that the relationship has come to a stage where her male lover is almost consuming her? These metaphorical devices are used to create a sense of control and domination in the relationship, with a hint of freedom and rule-breaking towards the end of the piece. As the sequence of five stories develops, the reader follows the female's escape to freedom without a man's control.

My story 'Water' (2008) has a similar tonal quality to Hilary's piece discussed above, but, like the 'Dinner Time' sequence, uses fantasy to locate a narrative.

> There was that time – do you remember it? – where the government said that we must share baths because the sea was evaporating, so we did, you and I, and you soaped my toes and I flannelled your back (most of the loofahs were dead by then) and we thought we were making a difference. Then we were told to drink our bath water as water was precious, and we did. You used that tall glass and I used the blue whisky one. It seemed somehow tastier then, like it looked on those adverts, in that blue glass. Finally we were told that we must only use water if it were to boil one or the other for supper, water being scarce. So I put you in that big pot that we used to put coal in when it still existed and I boiled you dry. After I'd ladled you out of the water, I washed my hair in your stock. (Howitt 2008: 32)

Here, the reader is again presented with an unstable world, one which is unsustainable and in which the complicit narrator creates her own loss. I wanted to use the idea of distillation here to create a packed paragraph which, while it could be read as fantasy, could also be read as a metaphor, as Gebbie's piece above. This is a metaphor for consumption, ownership and control, which are similar themes to the 'Dinner Time' series of writings.

Some of my other stories also use these ideas, but in a more diffuse or sometimes realistic way. 'Flesh and Blood' (2008) describes in obvious tones the paranoia of a difficult relationship.

> She smiles at the note he left for her, in the centre of the sticky kitchen table. *Don't be late. I'll phone you.* The note is written in his hard, cursive text; there are no kisses. She fondles her scarf in the hall mirror. It is blue, like her eyes – a present. There is no one else to admire her reflection, cut neatly into the spotted glass, as if always meant to be framed by it. She poufs her hair and smudges her lipstick with a trembling, bent finger. There is a mark on her neck she has hidden with a fold of fabric. It's too adolescent, she thinks. It's my secret. She has forgotten to tell him where she's going – he has, unusually, forgotten to ask. She pouts at her own reflection – her last chance at owning this face, at this time, and feels the heavy thaw of cool panic, snaking inside like a dead man's tongue, still feeling a final spasm of fear. The stars are bright tonight. Shutting the door behind her, she sends him a message, detailing where she will be and until what time, sending it from the phone he bought her. Crossing her arms as she exits the street, she bites back a small amount of excitement, feels it on the necks of frozen grass. (Howitt 2008: 33)

Perhaps a more obvious, literal story than those previously discussed, it still makes clear gender roles and expectations – and given the sparsity of the story, and the tightness of the genre itself, it again demonstrates how experience can be distilled into such a small form to make bigger meanings and connections. The epiphany, rather like in Hilary's piece, is the start of something else – something the reader does not (yet) see.

My writings are not, of course, fixed by or upon gender or gender roles, but it does strike me that many of my stories work with these experiences, showing a snapshot of female identity and even femininity at the point of writing. Of course, the critic might interpret these stories wholly differently from the way I have presented them – in fact, it could be argued that I should not be discussing my own work at all as a critic – but it seems that the links between my own works and the previous writings explored in part II show that female, British microfiction writers are exploring similar territory, tones and form within their writings.

IV – Wholeness

My writings do not necessarily express views, ideas or themes which can, or should, only be associated with women's writing, nor, of course, would I argue that the idea of writing about motherhood, relationships, control, domination and loss is an exclusively female domain. But the microfictions explored in this chapter are all testament to the idea that this short form is rich in meaning, and that microfictions are alive and being written by contemporary female writers. The form seems the perfect place to create a flash of meaning or grow an epiphany; it is also clear that female writers are using the form with creativity and in many differing ways. This engagement with a genre which is still nascent, though teetering on huge popularity, is to me remarkable given that the term 'microfiction' itself was only used formally in print some twenty years ago (Howitt-Dring 2011: 51).

Popular for longer in America, it seems that British writers are using the form more readily, and the female writers discussed in this chapter already renowned for their writings in the form. Half-stories seems to be a derisive title for something so rich and dense in meaning; I am willing to bet that in the next twenty years, microfiction can only become more popular, with many more writing and reading it. From the (fictional?) housewife who first got me exploring microfiction to the many real women now writing it, the form appears to be growing from the *enfant terrible* of the short story to become instead a composed literary sibling in its own right. These are not mistakes, or aberrations of short stories:

these are complete, tiny narratives that function alone, and are not reliant on further words or contexts. Let us not forget that jam: do not ever try to eat the whole jar in one sitting; you only need a spoonful.

Works Cited

Ashworth, Jenn (2013), 'Shoes', *Scraps*, ed. Calum Kerr and Holly Howitt, Southampton: Gumbo Press, p. 56.
Dubrow, Heather (1982), *Genre*, London: Methuen.
Gebbie, Vanessa (2012), 'Flight', *Jawbreakers*, ed. Calum Kerr and Valerie O'Riordan, Southampton: National Flash-Fiction Day, p. 15.
Hempel, Amy (1996), 'Hostess', *Micro Fiction: An Anthology of Really Short Stories*, ed. Jerome H. Stern, London and New York: W. W. Norton, p. 100.
Hempel, Amy (1996), 'Housewife', *Micro Fiction: An Anthology of Really Short Stories*, ed. Jerome H. Stern, London and New York: W. W. Norton, p. 101.
Hershman, Tania (2010), 'Straight Up', *Exposure*, ed. Holly Howitt and Jan Fortune-Wood, Blaenau Ffestiniog: Cinnamon Press, pp. 22–3.
Hilary, Sarah (2010), 'I Cannot Carry a Tune,' *Exposure*, p. 30.
Howitt, Holly (2008), *Dinner Time and Other Stories*, Blaenau Ffestiniog: Cinnamon Press, p. 60.
Howitt-Dring, Holly (2011), 'Making Micro Meanings: Reading and Writing Microfiction', *Short Fiction in Theory and Practice*, 1:1, 47–58.
Plath, Sylvia (1965), *Ariel*, London: Faber and Faber.
Ó'Faoláin, Seán (1972), *The Short Story*, Cork: Mercier.
Wellek, René and Austin Warren (1963), *Theory of Literature* (3rd edn), Harmondsworth: Penguin.

Chapter 13

Postscript: British Women's Short Story Writing
Clare Hanson

The essays in this collection open up a rich field of study, revealing the closeness of British women writers' relationship to the short story and illuminating the range and vitality of their work in the genre. Engaging with texts from the late nineteenth century to the twenty-first, the contributors uncover a distinctive literary tradition which has been obscured for a number of reasons. One is the general critical neglect of the short story in Britain, which is bound up with the wider publishing context. The initial flowering of the form was linked with the expansion of the UK periodicals market, but as this market became more differentiated a gap opened up between the 'literary' short story (which was often published in financially insecure little magazines) and commercial stories (which brought financial rewards but critical disdain). The literary short story was exiled to the far fringes of literary production, a situation that persists to the present day. Very few writers have specialised in the genre (among British women writers Katherine Mansfield and Helen Simpson stand out as exceptions) and though many British novelists have also been prolific short story writers, the form is under-represented on school and university syllabuses. As a result, there have been few critical studies of the British short story and none which has focused on the intersection of gender and genre. It is especially surprising that the part played by British women writers has been neglected, given the publication of several critical anthologies of women's short stories over the last two decades, notably Elaine Showalter's *Daughters of Decadence* (1993) and Hermione Lee's *The Secret Self: A Century of Short Stories by Women* (1985).

This volume is an important corrective, charting the specific part played by women in the evolution of the form. In contrast with previous studies which have emphasised the link between the short story and modernism, these essays tease out the connections between gender, genre and the broader contexts of modernity. The short story proved an apt form for mapping the opportunities associated with the opening up of education and employment for women in the late nineteenth century, a period which also brought increased social and geographical mobility. Women writers explored the transformative potential of these transitions while taking a more sceptical approach to other changes, exploiting the story's Gothic heritage, for example, to dramatise tensions between 'progress' in the shape of advances in science and technology and the persistence of the past (often represented by spectral hauntings). The short story was also used to map the new modalities of gender and sexuality associated with the energies of the Suffrage movement and to map the sensorium of modernity from a gendered perspective. The concept of the sensorium has dominated many accounts of the changes brought by modernity, with a recurring emphasis on the febrile complexity of modern life. Elizabeth Bowen makes this point in her well-known essay on the short story, when she argues that modern consciousness entails a rapid succession of discrete impressions and that 'the new literature' must therefore be 'an affair of reflexes, of immediate susceptibility, of associations not examined by reason' (38). This emphasis on the immediate and the experiential prompts finely grained explorations of gendered embodiment from many women short story writers. George Egerton, for example, explores ambiguously entwined currents of sexual desire and revulsion in her stories of the 'new woman' of the 1890s, while Katherine Mansfield registers the tensions generated by same-sex desire in the context of companionate marriage and Jean Rhys charts the exploitation and commodification of female sexuality in the interwar metropolis. And as the contributors to this volume demonstrate, the politics of gender and sexuality have remained central to women's short story writing from Egerton's *Keynotes* (1893) to Jackie Kay's *Reality, Reality* (2012).

The collection also draws attention to the recurring theme of war in British women's short stories. The unexpected affinity between war and the short story is noted by Bowen, who argues in the postscript to her collection *The Demon Lover* (1945) that it was the appropriate genre for expressing the hallucinatory, dreamlike experiences of wartime. Her focus is on the impact of the Blitz, which she experienced as both fearful and liberating, commenting that she 'hardly knew where I stopped and somebody else began. The violent destruction of solid things, the explosion of the illusion that prestige, power and permanence attach to bulk and weight, left all of us, equally, heady and disembodied' (95). Her fiction depicts wartime experience as outside time and beyond social constraints, opening up currents of feeling and fantasy which usually run underground, often to terrifying effect (as in the title story 'The

Demon Lover'). In this respect, her short stories explore the refraction of violence in the individual consciousness, creating a psychological archive of the Blitz. The disorientations and disjunctions of World War II are also registered in the post-war short fiction of Muriel Spark (for example in 'The Pawnbroker's Wife' [1953] and 'The Portobello Road' [1958]) and Doris Lessing ('The Habit of Loving' [1957] and 'The Eye of God in Paradise' [1957]). However, the link between the short story and war can also be traced back to the World War I, as evidenced by Katherine Mansfield's exploration of the complexities of bereavement and survivor guilt in such stories as 'The Garden Party' (1922), 'The Fly' (1922) and 'Six Years After' (1923).

Further themes which come to the fore in this collection are those of the uncanny, the spectral and the spiritual. While acknowledging the short story's proximity to the traditional ghost story and the Gothic tale, the contributors explore the specifically modern and gendered aspects of memory and the unconscious as they are articulated by writers ranging from Edith Nesbit to Angela Carter. In so doing, they reveal the existence of a body of work which engages with experience at the limits of consciousness and which registers the pressure of inchoate and repressed feeling. Subject position and narrative voice are unstable, the boundaries between subjects are breached and the memories of the protagonists merge into each other in short stories by, among others, Dorothy Edwards, Stevie Smith, Muriel Spark and Angela Carter. The mutability of subjectivity is another recurring motif, as in Dorothy Richardson's 'Tryst' (1941), Bowen's 'The Happy Autumn Fields' (1944) and Ali Smith's 'Writ' (2006), stories which map the ambiguous interplay between past and present incarnations of the self. In addition, the borders between the past and the present are crossed in hauntings which may signal a fear of repetition (particularly in connection with family relationships) but may equally express a sense of cultural loss, calling in question the narrative of progress associated with enlightened modernity. Such spectral presences also breach the boundaries between life and death and open up the theme of mortality and the afterlife which, as Ali Smith has noted, has always been central to the short story form.[1]

Turning to more concrete issues, a number of contributors comment on the relationship between short fiction and the evolving phases of feminism. The short story was adopted by a number of 'new woman' writers in the 1890s and was subsequently mobilised by writers such as Evelyn Sharp to explore the political and ethical questions raised by the Suffrage campaign.[2] With the rise of second-wave feminism, the short story again emerged as a key site where issues of female power, sexuality and autonomy were debated, as for example in the short story collection *Tales I Tell My Mother* (1978), written by a feminist writing collective which included Michèle Roberts, Sara Maitland and Zoë Fairbairns. Angela Carter's collections *The Bloody Chamber* (1979) and *Black Venus* (1985) were also hugely influential during this period, with their reshaping of patriarchal narratives, foregrounding of female sexual desire and recalibration of the power dynamic of heterosexual relationships. In the third millennium, the intersectional interests of third-wave feminism are mirrored in Helen Simpson's short stories, which anatomise the politics of parenthood from multiple points of view, while Jackie Kay's short fiction is attentive to the multiple modalities of age, class, sexuality and race as they shape the consciousness of her (female) protagonists. While these writers are fully in tune with the interests of third- and fourth-wave feminism, their success builds on the platform created by feminist publishers and writers' groups during the lean years of the late twentieth century when, as Ailsa Cox shows, the short story was perceived as an endangered species. Throughout the 1980s and 1990s the form was supported by small presses, while feminist publishers like Virago, The Women's Press and Pandora played a key role in publishing the work of Mansfield, Bowen, Rhys, Grace Paley and Alice Munro and establishing a women's short story writing canon. If writers' groups (often in community settings) were crucial for women short story writers in hard times, the impact of the recent dramatic expansion of creative writing courses in UK universities appears to be a positive one for all practitioners. The fact that the short story is widely taught on these courses may be linked with its current popularity, together with the existence of high-profile literary prizes such as the BBC National Short Story Award and the Sunday Times EFG Short Story Award.

 The short story seems always to be on the brink of extinction or on the cusp of a revival but whatever its vicissitudes, it is unlikely that it will ever rival the novel in popularity. As Tzvetan Todorov has pointed out, the brevity of the form means that the reader is always self-consciously aware of its fictional status, denied the pleasures of identification which are associated with the novel (143). Moreover, the formal properties of the short story (disjunction, inconclusiveness and obliquity) encourage an engagement with forms of experience which may be at odds with dominant cultural narratives. As many critics have noted, short stories are often concerned with the perspectives of those who are marginalised or possess an understanding which is in some sense uncomfortable or disturbing. Helen Simpson makes this point when she argues (echoing Todorov) that the short story form is particularly good for uncomfortable or edgy subjects because it doesn't allow you to sink down or lose yourself. When you read a novel, it feels natural to hand yourself over and suspend your critical faculties – you're lulled and dulled as (on the whole) less is demanded of you. Whereas reading a short story you have to stay alert; it's more of a performance. (xxv)

She goes on to explain that the form is 'ideal for an awkward subject like climate change' which is at the centre of her most recent collection *In-Flight Entertainment* (2010). Whereas in the twentieth century such 'awkward' subjects were often connected with gender and race, in the twenty-first century they are frequently associated with the complex, unpredictable and apparently unmanageable effects of globalisation. Writers like Smith and Simpson are prominent among those who are broaching such uncomfortable issues, in a genre in which as Simpson says, 'you can just skip all the gossipy stuff and go for the jugular' (xxvii).

Notes

1. In an interview with Noah Charney, Smith notes of life, death and the afterlife that 'the short story form is pretty much always concerned with all three' ('How I Write', n.p.).
2. Evelyn Sharp's collection *Rebel Women* was published by the radical publisher A. C. Fifield in 1910.

Works Cited

Bowen, Elizabeth (1983), 'The Happy Autumn Fields' [1944], *The Collected Stories of Elizabeth Bowen*, introduced by Angus Wilson, Harmondsworth: Penguin, pp. 755–71.
Bowen, Elizabeth (1950), 'Introduction to *The Faber Book of Modern Short Stories*', *Collected Impressions*, London: Longman, Green & Co Ltd, pp. 38–46.
Bowen, Elizabeth (1986), '"Postscript" to *The Demon Lover*', *The Mulberry Tree: Writings of Elizabeth Bowen*, ed. Hermione Lee, London: Virago, pp. 94–9.
Carter, Angela (1985), *Black Venus*, London: Chatto & Windus.
Carter, Angela (1979), *The Bloody Chamber*, London: Gollancz.
Egerton, George (1893), *Keynotes*, London: John Lane.
Kay, Jackie (2012), *Reality, Reality*, London: Picador.
Lee, Hermione (1985), *The Secret Self: A Century of Short Stories by Women*, London: Orion.
Lessing, Doris (2008), 'The Eye of God in Paradise' [1957], *Stories*, London: Everyman's Library, pp. 103–62.

Lessing, Doris (2008), 'The Habit of Loving' [1957], *Stories*, London: Everyman's Library, pp. 3–37.
Mansfield, Katherine (2002), 'The Fly' [1922], *Selected Stories*, Oxford: Oxford University Press, pp. 357–61.
Mansfield, Katherine (2002), 'The Garden Party' [1922], *Selected Stories*, Oxford: Oxford University Press, pp. 336–49.
Mansfield, Katherine (2006), 'Six Years After' [1923], *Collected Short Stories*, Ware: Wordsworth Classics, pp. 380–2.
Richardson, Dorothy (1989), 'Tryst' [1941], *Journey to Paradise: Short Stories and Autobiographical Sketches*, ed. Trudi Tate, London: Virago, pp. 56–60.
Sharp, Evelyn (1910), *Rebel Women*, London: A. C. Fifield.
Showalter, Elaine (1993), *Daughters of Decadence: Women Writers of the Fin-de-Siècle*, London: Virago.
Simpson, Helen (2012), 'Introduction', *A Bunch of Fives: Selected Short Stories*, London: Vintage, pp. xix–xxviii.
Simpson, Helen (2010), *In-Flight Entertainment*, London: Jonathan Cape.
Smith, Ali (2008), 'Writ' [2006], *The First Person and Other Stories*, London: Penguin, pp. 151–65.
Smith, Ali (2014), 'How I Write' (Interview with Noah Charney) <http://www.thedailybeast.com/articles/2013/01/23/ali-smith-how-i-write.html [Last accessed 30 September 2014.]
Spark, Muriel (2011), 'The Pawnbroker's Wife' [1953] *The Complete Short Stories*, Edinburgh: Canongate, pp. 132–47.
Spark, Muriel (2011), 'The Portobello Road' [1958] *The Complete Short Stories*, Edinburgh: Canongate, pp. 495–524.
Tales I Tell my Mother: A Collection of Feminist Short Stories (1978), ed. Fairbairns, Zoë, Sara Maitland, Valerie Miner, Michèle Roberts and Michelene Wandor, London: Journeyman Press.
Todorov, Tzvetan (1977), *The Poetics of Prose*, Oxford: Basil Blackwell.

Contributor Biographies

James Bailey is a PhD candidate at the University of Sheffield. His thesis examines the treatment of time and free will in the fiction of Muriel Spark. His work has been published in *Holocaust Studies* and *Contemporary Women's Writing*.

Rebecca Bowler is Research Assistant on the Dorothy Richardson letters publication project at Keele University. She gained her PhD, on Dorothy Richardson and visual culture, from the University of Sheffield in 2013. She is co-founder of the May Sinclair Society and has published work on Dorothy Richardson and Katherine Mansfield.

Ailsa Cox is Reader in English and Writing at Edge Hill University. Her books include *Alice Munro* (Northcote House), *Writing Short Stories* (Routledge) and *The Real Louise and Other Stories* (Headland Press). She has also published essays and chapters on short story writers including Alice Munro, Nancy Lee and Elizabeth Bowen. She is the editor of the peer-reviewed journal *Short Fiction in Theory and Practice* (Intellect Press).

Ben Davies is Lecturer in English at the University of Portsmouth. His research focuses on contemporary fiction and theory, specifically conceptualisations of sex, time and space. He is the co-editor of *Sex, Gender and Time in Fiction and Culture* (Palgrave 2011).

Maura Dunst recently completed her PhD at Cardiff University, where she wrote her dissertation on music in New Woman fiction. Her research interests include Victorian literature, New Woman fiction, Britain in the 1890s, women's writing, Elizabeth Gaskell, George Egerton, and music in literature. She has a forthcoming article in *Interdisciplinary Literary Studies* on the cathedral chime in Sarah Grand's *The Heavenly Twins* and is preparing her doctoral research for publication as a monograph. She is currently an Instructor of English at the University of Wisconsin-Stout.

Clare Hanson is a Professor at the University of Southampton. She was formerly the co-editor of the journal *Contemporary Women's Writing* and has published an edited collection, scholarly monograph and numerous articles on the short story. Her primary research interest is in the relationship between literature and science. This has led to two monographs, *A Cultural History of Pregnancy* (2004) and most recently *Eugenics, Literature and Culture in Post-war Britain* (2012). Current research focuses on the cultural implications of post-genomic science.

Holly Howitt-Dring is a writer and Senior Lecturer at the University of Portsmouth, where she leads the MA in Creative Writing. She writes in a range of forms but her creative work is mostly short fiction, poetry and novels. Her novella, *The Schoolboy*, was published in 2009, and her collection of microfictions, *Dinner Time and Other Stories*, published in 2008, both with Cinnamon Press. She was also the co-editor of an anthology of microfictions and prose poems, *Exposure* (2010) with Cinnamon, and has worked as a judge and editor of several microfiction competitions and collections since. She also writes academic articles for journals such as *Short Fiction in Theory and Practice* and *Flash* magazine, and is currently working on a collection of poetry and a novel.

Emma Liggins is Senior Lecturer in English Literature at Manchester Metropolitan University. She has published *Odd Women? Spinsters, Lesbians and Widows in British Women's Fiction, 1850s–1930s* (Manchester University Press 2014), (with Andrew Maunder and Ruth Robbins) *The British Short Story* (Palgrave 2011) and *George Gissing, the Working Woman and Urban Culture* (Ashgate 2006). She also has a forthcoming article on Vernon Lee's supernatural short stories in *Gothic Studies* (2014), and has introduced new editions of the ghost stories of Rhoda Broughton and Charlotte Riddell for Victorian Secrets.

Adam Piette is Professor of Modern Literature at the University of Sheffield, and is the author of *Remembering and the Sound of Words: Mallarmé, Proust, Joyce, Beckett* (1996), *Imagination at War: British Fiction, 1939–1945* (1995), and *The Literary Cold War, 1945 to Vietnam* (2009).

Michelle Ryan-Sautour is *Maître de Conférences* (Associate Professor) at the Université d'Angers, France where she is director of the short story section of the CRILA research group and Associate Editor of *Journal of the Short Story in English*. She is also co-founder of the European Network for Short Fiction Research (ENSFR) with Ailsa Cox (Edge Hill University). Her research focus is the short stories of Angela Carter, Rikki Ducornet and Ali Smith, with a special emphasis on authorship, reading pragmatics, game theory and gender. Her work has been published in *Marvels and Tales, Journal of the Short Story in English, Etudes Britanniques Contemporines*, and in edited collections such as *Angela Carter: New Critical Readings* (Continuum Press 2012) and *Identity and Form in Contemporary Literature* (Routledge 2013).

Sue Vice is Professor of English Literature at the University of Sheffield. Her recent publications include *Shoah* (2011) and the co-edited volume, with Jenni Adams, *Representing Perpetrators in Holocaust Literature and Film* (2012). Her most recent publication is *Textual Deceptions* (2014), a study of false memoirs and literary hoaxes.

Emma Young recently submitted her PhD thesis at the University of Lincoln. This work examined the relationship between contemporary women writers, feminist politics and the short story genre. Previously, Emma has published journal articles on the contemporary author Emma Donoghue. Emma is a Learning Development Tutor at Bishop Grosseteste University Lincoln and a member of the Contemporary Women's Writing Association Executive Committee.

Index

ageing, 38, 135–9
anthologies (for short stories), 9, 34–5, 118, 193
Ardis, Ann, 18
Ashworth, Jenn, 'Shoes', 183–4
Asquith, Cynthia, 34–5
awards (for short stories), 4, 125, 196

Bakhtin, Mikhail, 12, 105, 148, 160
Baldwin, Dean, 3–4, 117
Barthes, Roland, 168, 175–6n
Bates, H. E., 6
Black and White, 37, 40, 53
Bowen, Elizabeth, 5, 11, 34, 35, 36, 37, 50, 57, 170, 196
  'Attractive Modern Homes', 36, 37
  'Coming Home', 36
  'The Demon Lover', 77–9, 194
  The Faber Book of Modern Short Stories, 8, 66–7, 67–9, 123, 194
  'The Happy Autumn Fields', 195
  'The Last Night in the Old Home', 36
  'Mysterious Kôr', 72–6, 77
  'The New House', 36
  'The Shadowy Third', 47
  'The Short Story', 67–9
  'Sunday Afternoon', 69–72, 75
Bradbury, Malcolm, 6, 114
Braddon, Mary Elizabeth
  'Good Lady Ducayne', 38
  'The Shadow in the Corner', 40
Brooks, Peter, 172, 176n

Butler, Judith, 105
Byatt, A. S., 8, 118
  'Medusa's Ankles', 117

Caird, Mona, 17, 18, 29n
Carter, Angela, 8, 11–12, 96–7, 105–6, 117, 118, 196
  'Alice in Prague *or* The Curious Room', 100
  'Black Venus', 99
  'The Bloody Chamber', 46
  'The Cabinet of Edgar Allan Poe', 99
  'Elegy for a Freelance', 102–3
  'The Fall River Axe Murders', 97, 99–100
  'Flesh and the Mirror', 98, 115
  'In Pantoland', 100
  'Lizzie's Tiger', 99–100
  'The Loves of Lady Purple', 100
  'The Merchant of Shadows', 106–7
  Nights at the Circus, 100–1
  'Our Lady of the Massacre', 99
  'Overture and Incidental Music for *A Midsummer's Night's Dream*', 100
  'Penetrating to the Heart of the Forest', 100
  'Peter and the Wolf', 100
  'Reflections', 102, 103–4
  'The Smile of Winter', 98
  'A Souvenir of Japan', 98
Chekhov, Anton, 6, 67, 75–6
Commonword (writing group), 120–2
Cosmopolitan, 9, 117, 144

Cox, Ailsa, 3, 196
  'Into the Sun', 123
Craig, Cairns, 5
creative writing, 5, 120, 123, 126, 148, 196
Currie, Mark, 176–7n

Dane, Clemence, 'Spinster's Rest', 35
D'Arcy, Ella, 7, 29n
  'The Villa Lucienne', 46
Defoe, Daniel, *Moll Flanders*, 99
Derrida, Jacques, 'Envois', 163, 165–6, 167, 168, 169, 175n
devolution, 14
Dostoevsky, Fyodor, 105
doubles, 91–2, 97–8

Eagleton, Mary, 10
Egerton, George, 7, 13, 15–20, 28–9, 194
  'The Elusive Melody', 10, 27
  'Her Share', 25
  'Pan', 10, 25–7
  'A Psychological Moment at Three Periods', 23–5
  'The Star-Worshipper', 27–8
  'Under Northern Sky', 10, 20–3, 25
Eliot, George, *Middlemarch*, 159
Eliot, T. S., 42
  'The Love Song of J. Alfred Prufrock', 176n
  'Rhapsody on a Windy Night', 137

fascism, 71–2
Federation of Worker Writers and Community Publishers (FWWCP), 120–1
feminism, 1, 8–9, 12, 18, 44, 60, 76, 78–9, 96, 105–6, 108n, 118–19, 121–2, 133–46, 152, 195–6
feminist and women-only publishers, 118–19
fin-de-siècle, the, 15–18, 42
flash fiction, 180, 181
Ford, Ford Madox, 50
Freud, Sigmund, 32, 35, 92
Futurism, 72, 76

Galloway, Janice, 114, 125
  'Blood', 127–8
  'Scenes from a Life', 129–30
  'Tea and Biscuits', 127–8
Gebbie, Vanessa, 'Flight', 182–3, 184, 185, 187, 190
Genette, Gérard, 82, 85
ghost story, the, 11, 27–8, 32–48, 77–9, 81–94, 195
Gordimer, Nadine, 2, 10, 170
Gothic, 32–8, 42–7, 67, 77–8, 87, 98, 194, 195
Grand, Sarah, 15, 17, 18, 29n
  'The Undefinable: A Fantasia', 134
Granta, 4, 118

Hadley, Tessa, 12, 148
  'Because the Night', 154
  'Buckets of Blood', 156–60
  'The Enemy', 160
  'Exchanges', 152–3
  'Friendly Fire', 153, 155
  'In the Country', 160
  'Mother's Son', 153–4
  'A Mouthful of Cut Glass', 156–60
  'Phosphorescence', 151
  'Sunstroke', 150–1
  'Surrogate', 156
  'The Trojan Prince', 149–50
Haggard, Rider, *She*, 73–4
Hakim, Catherine, 140
Hanson, Clare, 2, 8, 115
Hawthorne, Nathaniel, 1
Head, Dominic, 2, 34, 62, 64
Hemingway, Ernest, 16, 190
Hempel, Amy, 'Housewife', 188–9
Hershman, Tania, 180
  'Straight Up', 184–6
Hilary, Sarah, 180
  'I Cannot Carry a Tune', 186–8
Hochschild, Arlie, 140–1, 143
Howitt, Holly, 5
  'Dinner Time', 189–90
  'Flesh and Blood', 190–1
  'Water', 190
Hunter, Adrian, 7, 115

James, Henry, 16, 70–2, 75
  'The Chaperon', 70
  'The Jolly Corner', 77
  The Turn of the Screw, 77
Journal of the Short Story in English, 115
Jouve, Vincent, 101–4, 106, 108, 110n
Joyce, James, 6, 18, 28–9

Kant, Immanuel, 57
Kay, Jackie, 4, 117, 194, 196
  'Grace and Rose', 6
Kennedy, A. L., 114, 124–5, 129, 130
  'As God Made Us', 6
  'Night Geometry', 125–7
Kristeva, Julia, 122, 157

Lee, Hermione, 9, 10, 193
Lee, Vernon, 36
Lessing, Doris
  'The Eye of God in Paradise', 195
  'The Habit of Loving', 195

McCrory, Moy, 'The Vision', 119
McGovern, Jimmy, 121–2
McHale, Brian, 85
McRobbie, Angela, 139, 145
McTaggert, J. Ellis, 171, 176n
Mansfield, Katherine, 5, 6, 8, 11, 50, 53–4, 61–2, 64n, 161n, 193, 194, 196
  The Aloe, 54, 61
  'At the Bay', 55, 62
  'The Fly', 195
  'The Garden Party', 149, 195
  'Je ne Parle Pas Français', 53
  'Miss Brill', 157
  'Prelude', 54–5, 62–3
  'Six Years After', 195
  'The Swing of the Pendulum', 158
Maunder, Andrew, 3, 4
Maupassant, Guy de, 67, 75–6
May, Charles E., 2, 3, 96, 101, 116
metafiction, 34, 40, 42, 47, 88, 102, 107, 170
metalepsis, 82–5, 166

microfiction, 5, 12, 13, 117n, 179–92
modernism, 2–3, 7–8, 11, 13, 18, 29, 32–47, 50–64, 66–7, 67–9, 69–72, 75–6, 76–9, 150, 193–4
Moore, Lorrie, 'Charades', 159
motherhood, 12, 135, 140–1, 143–5, 151–2, 182–4
Mslexia, 4, 9
Munro, Alice, 'Who Do You Think You Are?', 120
music, 10, 13, 15–30

Nesbit, E., 8, 11, 33, 37, 48n, 195
  'From the Dead', 46
  'The Haunted House', 38
  'The House of Silence', 36
  'The Mystery of the Semi-Detached', 41
  'No 17', 38
  'The Pavilion', 38
  'The Shadow', 40–1
  'The Three Drugs', 38–9
  'The Violet Car', 11, 39–40, 42
new traditionalism, 139
New Woman writer, the, 7–8, 15–30, 134, 156n, 194, 195

O'Connor, Frank, 2, 6, 107

Panurge, 115, 118
patriarchy, 11, 45–6, 70, 72, 78, 88–93, 106, 134, 136, 140, 186, 196
Picard, Michel, 101
Plath, Sylvia, 'Morning Song', 182–3
Poe, Edgar Allen, 1
postmodernism, 85, 96, 98, 100, 108n, 115, 116–17, 133
prose poetry, 179–80

Rich, Adrienne, 9
Richardson, Dorothy, 8, 11, 50–2, 58, 63n, 64n
  My Six Months Solitude, 58
  Pilgrimage, 51–2, 58–60, 62–3
  Pointed Roofs, 58
  'Seen From Paradise', 58–60

'A Sussex Auction', 52
'Tryst', 195
Roberts, Michèle, 9, 12, 133, 134–5, 145–6, 196
  'Fluency', 135–6
  'Just One More Saturday Night', 137–9
Rohrberger, Mary, 2, 98, 109n
Romanticism, 67–9, 72–4, 75–6, 76–7

Sackville-West, Vita, 79n
'Save Our Short Story' (campaign), 4, 114, 117
Scarborough, Dorothy, 35, 41, 44–5
self-reflexive fiction, 5, 70–1, 84–5, 139, 145–6, 163, 165, 169–70, 172–3, 173–4
sexual violence, 26–7, 86, 103–4
Sheba, 118–19
Showalter, Elaine, 7, 9, 18, 134, 193
Simpson, Helen, 12, 117, 133, 135, 144–6, 193, 196, 197
  'The Bed', 117
  'Burns and Bankers', 143–5
  'Hey Yeah Right Get a Life', 139–42
Sinclair, May, 8, 11, 33, 42–3, 44–5, 52–3, 60, 61, 62–3, 64n
  The Creators, 56
  The Dark Night, 56
  A Defence of Idealism, 56–8
  'The Finding of the Absolute', 57–8, 63
  'The Flaw in the Crystal', 43–5, 56–7
  'The Intercessor', 42
  The Life and Death of Harriett Frean, 62
  Mary Oliver: A Life, 62
  'The Nature of the Evidence', 45–6
  'A Study from Life', 53
  The Three Sisters, 56
  'The Villa Désirée', 35, 46–7
  'Where Their Fire is not Quenched', 42–3
Smith, Ali, 12, 163, 195, 197
  'Astute Fiery Luxurious', 173, 175
  'Being Quick', 166, 170
  'Blank Card', 173–4
  'Cold Iron', 164–5
  'Erosive', 164–5, 171–2, 176n
  'The First Person', 168
  'The History of History', 170
  'Present', 170
  'A Quick One', 170–1
  'Scottish Love Songs', 6
  'The Second Person', 166–7
  'A Story of Love', 164
  'The Theme is Power', 164, 165
  'True Short Story', 170
  'Writ', 195
Spark, Muriel, 11, 195
  'Authors' Ghosts', 82–3
  'Bang-Bang You're Dead', 90–2, 93n, 94n
  The Comforters, 84–5
  The Driver's Seat, 90
  'The Girl I Left Behind Me', 88–90, 92
  'Harper and Wilton', 83–5, 93
  The Hothouse by the East River, 94n
  'The House of the Famous Poet', 81
  'The Leaf-Sweeper', 81, 94n
  The Mandelbaum Gate, 94n
  Not to Disturb, 94n
  'The Pawnbroker's Wife', 195
  'The Pearly Shadow', 81
  'The Portobello Road', 85–8, 93, 195
  'The Seraph and the Zambesi', 81
  'The Twins', 81
Stand, 123
Storia, 118
'Story' (campaign), 4
Surrealism, 73–6

Taylor, Debbie, 4
technology, 11, 33, 35–7, 44, 47, 76–7
  motor vehicle technology, 37–40, 78–9
temporality, 12, 42–3, 66–7, 76–9, 105, 134, 163–77
Todd, Richard, 115–16
Todorov, Tzvetan, 196–7
trauma, 10, 15–29, 32, 42–3, 126–7

uncanny, the, 11, 13, 32–8, 41–7, 55, 73, 77–8, 84, 92, 195

Victorian era, the, 7, 17–19, 32, 35–6, 39–40, 47, 70, 75
Virago, 118, 196
Voices, 121–2

Weldon, Fay 8, 114, 117
Woman's Journal, 117

Woolf, Virginia, 7–8, 35, 60, 78, 157
  'A Haunted House', 32
  Mrs Dalloway, 78
  'A Room of One's Own', 60, 78, 79n
World War I, 8, 35–6, 195
World War II, 8, 11, 66–79, 194–5
writing groups, 5, 120–2

Yellow Book, The, 7, 9, 37, 46